The Four Fields
of Leadership

The Four Fields
of Leadership

How People and Organizations
Can Thrive in a
Hyperconnected World

Tom Goodell

ROWMAN & LITTLEFIELD
Lanham • Boulder • New York • London

Published by Rowman & Littlefield
An imprint of The Rowman & Littlefield Publishing Group, Inc.
4501 Forbes Boulevard, Suite 200, Lanham, Maryland 20706
www.rowman.com

6 Tinworth Street, London SE11 5AL, United Kingdom

British Library Cataloguing in Publication Information Available

Library of Congress Cataloging-in-Publication Data

Names: Goodell, Tom, 1952- author.
Title: The four fields of leadership : how people and organizations can thrive in a hyperconnected world / Tom Goodell.
Description: Lanham : Rowman & Littlefield, [2020] | Includes bibliographical
references and index. | Summary: "In a world that is changing faster and with more
complexity than at any other time in history, Tom Goodell explores how to make sense
of it all, and how individuals and organizations can thrive in a world this complex. He
taps into hot business management trends of mindfulness, simplicity science, and agile
leadership along the way"—Provided by publisher.
Identifiers: LCCN 2019056371 (print) | LCCN 2019056372 (ebook) | ISBN
9781538117262 (cloth) | ISBN 9781538117279 (epub)
Subjects: LCSH: Leadership. | Success in business.
Classification: LCC HD57.7 .G6647 2020 (print) | LCC HD57.7 (ebook) | DDC
658.4/092—dc23
LC record available at https://lccn.loc.gov/2019056371
LC ebook record available at https://lccn.loc.gov/2019056372

For Barbara, Sarah, and Julia,
whose patience and love knew no bounds
throughout this project.
It would never have been conceived,
much less completed, without them.

Yesterday I was clever, so I wanted to change the world. Today I am wise, so I am changing myself.

—Rumi

Contents

Acknowledgments

This book is the product of more than thirty years' experience working with leaders, managers, and individual contributors in organizations of all types and sizes, throughout the United States and overseas. The problems and opportunities they have asked me to help with have varied widely, but they all come down to the question of how to get people to cooperate and take collective action in ways that best serve the mission of the organization. I am indebted to their trust and willingness to experiment and let me learn with them.

I began journaling my thoughts for this book around 2000 and began writing in earnest in 2012. Needless to say the work evolved enormously over those years, but certain themes have remained: the full power of the human spirit only emerges when people bring their whole selves to everything they do; our whole selves involve our bodies, our emotions, and our intellects; leadership emerges from the relationships among members of a group, it is not an attribute of a single person; we are more connected than we imagine, and it is from mastery of the connections that true leadership emerges. These principles are true for all human organizations, including families, neighborhoods, churches, governments, and businesses.

Any book that attempts the breadth and depth of *The Four Fields of Leadership* owes a great debt to many thinkers and writers whose work precedes it. I cannot begin to list all of the writers and thinkers who have influenced my thinking, but the principle ones include Gregory Bateson, whose writings first revealed to me the deep power of seeing systems instead of parts; Margaret Wheatley, whose writings have so deeply incorporated the human spirit into a systems view of human organizations; Peter Senge, whose writings have taught us the meaning and power of learning organizations; Daniel Goleman, who introduced to the world the importance and power of emotional intelligence; and Antonio Damasio, whose work has revealed so much about the brain that is relevant to human performance.

While I am the named author of this book, it has truly emerged from the support and efforts of many people over a great span of time. I can't possibly do justice to all of them, but a few who must be mentioned include those who have served as my teachers, mentors, and coaches. In the order in which they appeared in my life: my parents, who taught me from an early age to be curious about the world and never assume that knowledge is fixed; Dainin Katagiri Roshi and Shohaku Okumura Roshi, who introduced me to the wisdom and practice of Zen; Larry Freeborg, who opened doors, guided me in the early development of my business, and encouraged me to never stop learning; Julio Olalla, who taught me the power of ontological coaching, freeing me from so many limiting beliefs along the way; Staci Haines, who showed me how to let go of those parts of my past that held me back; and Richard Heckler, who taught me the power of the somatic self and introduced me to the wisdom of the body.

My good friend Carly Evans encouraged me to write and keep writing, and enriched my thinking through her deep questions and insights.

I must also acknowledge those who were directly involved in the writing and production of this book: Pat Francisco, my writing coach, without whose patience, wisdom, guidance, and support, this book would never have come into being; Sarah Howard, who was indefatigable in reading and rereading the manuscript, catching everything from typos to conceptual inconsistencies; Dave Hanson, who prepared all the graphics for the book; Masayo Ozawa, who came up with the cover design; my assistant Michelle Schelp who freed up so much valuable time for me to focus on writing, and helped with the final manuscript preparation; those who read sections of the book and provided invaluable feedback, including Greg, Caroline, and Dan Goodell, Erin Heitkamp, Dan Grizzle, and Kraig Keck; Arielle Eckstut at the Book Doctors, who guided me through a critical phase of preparing the proposal and thinking through the organization of the content; Herb Schafner at Big Fish Media, who immediately "got" the message of the book, helped me shape it, and guided me to Rowman & Littlefield; and Suzanne Staszak-Silva, my editor at Rowman & Littlefield, whose patience and support to stay true to my voice was invaluable.

My close friend, thinking partner, collaborator, and fellow traveler on this journey of many years, Richard McDonald, has been a constant source of support and inspiration.

And finally I must thank my wife Barbara Babbitt and our daughters Sarah and Julia, who supported me through seven years of thinking, writing, rewriting, endlessly disappearing into my home office, and endlessly disappearing into my portable office while on vacations. More than anyone, they made this book possible.

Introduction

Wild Possibilities in the Age of Connection

> In times of change, learners inherit the earth, while the learned find them-
> selves beautifully equipped to deal with a world that no longer exists.
>
> —Eric Hoffer

In the year 1609, Galileo Galilei, one of the most brilliant scientists and in-
ventors of all time, was sentenced to life imprisonment. His crime: declaring
the Earth circles the sun rather than the other way around. This was heresy
and could not be tolerated. He would spend the last eight years of his life
confined to his home under house arrest, but his ideas and methods would
forever change how we think about ourselves and our place in the universe.

In the year 2000, a forty-year-old upstart named Reed Hastings walked
into the executive offices of Blockbuster Video to meet with John Antioco,
Blockbuster's CEO. Blockbuster dominated the world of video rentals; they
were approaching nine thousand stores and sixty thousand employees nationwide. A few years earlier, Hastings had started his own video rental business.
You'd order your video online, and within a couple of days it would arrive in
the mail. He called his business Netflix.

Hastings had an offer for Antioco: they would form a partnership, with
Blockbuster managing brick-and-mortar rentals and Netflix managing online
rentals. Hastings was "just about laughed out of their office" (Sandoval,
2010). Perhaps Antioco believed he knew how the world worked: people
rented movies in stores, not on the internet. They didn't want to wait a couple
of days for them to arrive. And when customers didn't return movies on time,
they paid late fees, which were a substantial part of Blockbuster's revenue. (In
2000, Blockbuster made $800 million on late fees [Rossen, 2016].) Hastings

let people keep their videos as long as they liked with no late fees. Antioco didn't buy this new approach.

I remember that time well. My daughters were in grade school during those heady years for Blockbuster. There was a store just four blocks from my home, and walking down the street to pick up movies was a pleasant ritual for us. But the late fees drove me crazy. Though we had the best intentions, we often missed the deadline, sometimes by as much as a week. And every time I saw the charge of two dollars or five dollars or more, I felt resentful. Of course, my resentment wasn't logical. After all, I'd freely signed the rental agreement that clearly laid out the fee structure. But emotions and logic are separate responses, and every time I got dinged by Blockbuster, I felt they had taken advantage of me. I had no loyalty to Blockbuster, so when Netflix showed up, I was one of the first to jump ship. Ten years later, in 2010, Netflix had 20 million subscribers and $2.16 billion in revenues (Fritz, 2011). That was the year Blockbuster filed for bankruptcy.

Galileo ushered in the Age of Reason, a new way of thinking that transformed our understanding of the world. The entrepreneurs of the twenty-first century are also ushering in a new way of thinking. They are bringing us into the Age of Connection and showing us how to thrive in a hyperconnected world.

The past thirty years have seen more transformation in the world of business than occurred in the previous two centuries. The very nature of business seems to have changed. It is more complex, more connected, more dynamic, less stable, and far less certain than ever before. And we all know the rate of these changes is accelerating. Hyperconnectivity has transformed everything.

Until recently, people lived mostly local lives and were content to assume that the larger world would sort itself out. They had time to gradually absorb and adapt to new ways of thinking as the world slowly evolved. Today, we experience dramatic changes in technology, healthcare, politics, and marketplaces every day. The old world was based on logical analysis and the laws of physics. The new world is based on relationships and hyperconnected communication. The business and leadership principles of the Age of Reason are insufficient in the Age of Connection.

Every two years since 2004, IBM has published a massive survey of thousands of CEOs and other C-Suite executives from organizations around the world. In each survey, they explore the executives' thinking about the most pressing challenges and opportunities their companies face. The results are telling. In the first three surveys, CEOs identified coping with change as their most pressing problem. In 2006, two-thirds of the CEOs interviewed said their organizations were facing substantial or very substantial change. In

2008, that number had increased to 80 percent, and CEOs overall rated their *ability* to manage the change 22 percent lower than their *need* to manage it—nearly triple the "change gap" they identified in 2006. Ad J. Scheepbower, CEO of KPN Telecom, the largest provider of telecom and IT services in the Netherlands, said, "We have seen more change in the last ten years than in the previous 90" ("IBM 2008 CEO Study," 2008).

Then in 2010, the focus of the IBM survey abruptly changed. In his introduction to the study, Samuel Palmisano, CEO of IBM, said, "We occupy a world that is connected on multiple dimensions, and at a deep level—a global system of systems . . . events, threats, and opportunities aren't just coming at us faster or with less predictability; they are converging and influencing each other to create entirely unique situations." In the "Executive Summary," the authors state, "Our conversations identified a new primary challenge: complexity. CEOs told us they operate in a world that is substantially more volatile, uncertain, and complex. . . . Today's complexity is only expected to rise, and more than half of CEOs doubt their ability to manage it. Seventy-nine percent of CEOs anticipate even greater complexity ahead" ("Capitalizing on Complexity Insights from the Global Chief Executive Officer Study," 2010).

The 2012, 2014, and 2016 studies emphasized hyperconnectivity and the threat of disruptive innovation. Collectively, this series of studies reveals the challenges of twenty-first-century business: rapidly increasing complexity, deep reliance on massive networks of connections, ever-stronger relationships with individuals and organizations, and the necessity for companies to constantly transform as technology evolves and markets change and morph. Hyperconnectivity creates fluid networks of customers, vendors, competitors, and partners. Vast networks of communication loops—all those organizations and individuals sending messages back and forth—adds up to extreme complexity and a high potential for chaos.

While these insights revealed emerging challenges and opportunities in the world of business, they were neither new nor surprising to mathematicians and scientists who have been studying complexity and chaos for over a century. Understanding the discoveries of these scientists and mathematicians can help leaders navigate complexity and leverage its rich opportunities without falling into chaos. This book will incorporate the insights of science and mathematics, as well as wisdom from spiritual traditions and practical guidance from leadership and management studies, into a roadmap for managing complexity and leading in a hyperconnected world.

Business always trails science in its thinking. That is as it should be. Science does the hard, time-consuming work of pure research and deep thought, pursuing insight and knowledge for its own sake. When science reveals new insights and new ways of thinking, business puts them to use. Scientists,

engineers, mathematicians, business leaders, and even mystics have all applied themselves to the deep and difficult questions of how to make our
complex world work. Their knowledge, wisdom, and insights are available to
all of us. Collectively, these insights point the way not only to making sense
of the world we have created but also to thriving in it. It is time to pull all of
that wisdom together.

Fundamentally, the new opportunities and challenges of a hyperconnected
world include:

Global Marketplace
- The gig economy, which is the direct result of hyperconnectivity, in which
  large numbers of people work as free agents and can quickly change where,
  how, and for whom they work.
- The globalization of workforces, customers, vendors, partners, regulatory
  agencies, and competitors for organizations of all sizes.

Information and Technology
- The internet and telecommunication connect everyone to everyone.
- The production of oceans of data that contain valuable information yet cannot possibly be comprehended, much less analyzed and leveraged, by any
  one or even small groups of individuals.
- The emergence of artificial intelligence and its application to problems that
  were once considered solvable only by humans.

Social Transformation:
- The workforce is becoming vastly more diverse, with women, people of
  color, ethnic groups, and LGBTQ+ people bringing their unique sensitivi-
  ties and perspective to leadership and teams.
- Greater autonomy and participation in decision making being demanded by
  the millennial generation.
- Heightened levels of stress at all levels of organizations, negatively im-
  pacting all dimensions of performance, including employee engagement,
  loyalty, health, creativity, and ability to collaborate.
- Greater need for employee engagement, cross-functional collaboration,
  and teamwork.
- Greater requirement for communication skills and strong interpersonal
  relationships as essential capabilities at all levels of organizations.
- More knowledge-based and fewer mechanical skill sets required than in
  the past.

These transformations are challenging leaders everywhere. They threaten the worldview and self-identity of those who are comfortable with the old ways, stripping away much of what they have been taught about how to lead while offering no clear alternatives. Nonetheless, these transformations point the way forward, and leaders must strive to understand them and integrate them into the form and function of their organizations. Businesses that evolve will thrive in a hyperconnected world. The rest will go the way of the dinosaurs.

We will never have the kind of control or certainty that we once believed possible. Our hyperconnected world can be seen as an untamed land rich with wild possibilities. We should not even attempt to tame this land because taming a wild thing kills its spirit. We should, however, learn to live in harmony with the wild possibilities that emerge from hyperconnectivity and complexity. We must learn not to control them but to influence and be influenced by them, learning, growing, and evolving together.

In this book, I provide a new definition of leadership, and I define new principles for leading and thriving in a hyperconnected world. It is an exciting journey, but it is not for the faint of heart.

The questions you might be asking are: where do we start, when do we start, and how do we do it? The answer to the first question is: right here, with yourself. The answer to the second question is: right now. Reading this book will help to answer the third question; it is a first step into the land of wild possibilities.

Section I

LEADERSHIP (RE)DEFINED

Chapter One

Leadership Isn't What It Used to Be

Leadership isn't what it used to be—or at least what we believed it was. It used to be that one could lead with a degree of certainty about what the future held. Major changes happened over years or decades, and they could often be anticipated. The world was relatively orderly; the number of relationships in which you engaged was manageable. Leaders today are asked to lead in a world vastly more complex, dynamic, and hyperconnected than at any time in history, yet most leadership tools and guidance that are presented to them are designed for the simpler and more orderly world of the past.

The challenges of leadership today are not because of *leaders*. There are plenty of good, committed people leading organizations, and plenty more are willing to step up. They want to do good work and lead well. But the old definition of leadership—being in charge, setting direction, telling people what to do—no longer serves. The job of the leader is no longer to tell people what to do but to cultivate in them the capability to do the right thing at the right time, whatever the circumstances. Without a clear, shared understanding of how to accomplish that in a hyperconnected world, leaders are left adrift, not knowing how to serve either those they lead or the organizations for which they work.

In our hyperconnected world, human workers must be much more than mechanics carrying out repetitive tasks; they must be creative, collaborative, and inspired. Work must be meaningful. The old leadership models don't cultivate that. The problem with leadership lies not in leaders; it is more fundamental than that. The problem lies in our *understanding* of leadership—what it is, how to develop it, and what it means to lead.

A new definition of leadership is emerging, and it is radically different. It shows up in business literature in terms like "Connected Leadership," "Purposeful Leadership," "Self-Awareness," "Collaborative Leadership,"

"Transformational Leadership," "Agility," "Authentic Leadership," "Servant Leadership," "Selfless Leadership," "Emotional Intelligence," "Learning Organizations," "Contextual Leadership," and many more.

A few decades ago, only a few of these terms had been coined. And it seems that every week new ideas are added to this list. The business sections of bookstores are packed with books about them. But because they emerge from so many traditions and disciplines, each book speaks its own language, building a Tower of Babel with no way to connect the dots among them and no way to create a coherent understanding of leadership. And each of these approaches represents only a piece of the puzzle. They are like the proverbial blind people, each touching one part of the elephant, arguing about whose understanding of the elephant is the right one. Mostly, all are right, but what's needed is not more descriptions of the pieces but a clear-sighted picture of the whole. That is what I offer in this book: a simple, concise definition of leadership that accommodates all of the terms and concepts in the Tower of Babel. And with that definition, I will show you how to cultivate leadership that's perfectly suited to the complex, dynamic, and hyperconnected world we have created.

To begin, let's take a look at how confusion can be resolved into understanding through *unifying principles*.

UNIFYING PRINCIPLES

Major breakthroughs in science happen when seemingly disparate phenomena are discovered to be deeply related. Such a discovery is usually presaged by confusion—scientists sense that certain phenomena are somehow related, yet the phenomena appear distinct and the nature of the relationship cannot be discerned. At some point, someone sees through the haze to something fundamental from which the observed phenomena arise, the connection is made, and coherence replaces confusion. The discovery that electrical and magnetic phenomena are just different aspects of electromagnetism is an example. Einstein's famous equation $E=mc^2$ showed that energy and mass, which had been believed to be distinct and noninterchangeable, are different aspects of the fundamental fabric of the universe. They can, in fact, be interchanged. The discovery of DNA unified our understanding of all living organisms on this planet.

Such discoveries are unifying principles. The electromagnetic field, Einstein's equation, and DNA all profoundly simplified our understanding of the world. The discovery of unifying principles reveals powerful new possibilities. Understanding the relationship between electricity and magnetism made the electric motor possible, Einstein's equation made it possible to release and utilize nuclear energy, and the discovery of DNA made genetic engineering possible.

The study of leadership is in a state similar to these scientific disciplines before their unifying principles were discovered. There is much confusion today about the nature of leadership—the Tower of Babel. There are dozens upon dozens of definitions of leadership, with collections of attributes like "leadership style," "leadership qualities," and "leadership skills." There is overlap among some, but many seem as different from one another as electricity seems from magnetism.

Consider the notion of "leadership style." It's a hodgepodge of notions from all kinds of disciplines, all of which seem somehow related to how different leaders lead. A list of just some of the leadership styles I found doing a quick internet search included:

- Democratic
- Autocratic
- Laissez-faire
- Strategic
- Transformational
- Transactional
- Bureaucratic
- Despotic
- Command and control
- Consensus
- Coach
- Visionary
- Servant
- Pilot
- Pacesetter

It is intuitively obvious that all of these definitions and attributes fall under the rubric of leadership, yet the connections among them are not clear. Without understanding the common root that ties all of these elements together, they create more confusion than clarity. This confusion is a necessary step on our way to understanding leadership, but it's time to find a definition of leadership that unifies all these attributes and brings coherence to them—a unifying principle.

Let me start with a premise: **leadership is a dynamic condition that arises from the interactions of individuals**. This premise immediately reveals one of the problems with much of our leadership literature. The

Chapter One

literature is largely based on the premise that leadership is, in fact, an attribute of an individual.

The perspective I offer is that leadership only arises through the interactions of individuals. It cannot be understood as an attribute of an individual any more than a beehive can be understood as an attribute of a bee. Thus, leadership is fundamentally an *emergent* phenomenon. The term *emergent* is used to describe properties and behaviors of a system that occur at the level of the whole system and cannot be predicted or understood by understanding the parts alone. Emergence has been discovered in virtually every field of research, from physics and biochemistry to sociology, organizational development, and leadership. Emergence gives truth to the saying that the whole is greater than the sum of the parts. A few examples of emergence include:

- Army ants assemble themselves into bridges that span chasms they could not otherwise cross. No matter how much you know about ant neurobiology, biochemistry, and physiology and about the physics of bridges, you cannot explain how they accomplish this (Graham et al., 2017).
- When disasters strike, human communities spontaneously form to help those in need. There is no organizational structure or design, yet these can be highly efficient and effective; they have come to be viewed as a critical component of disaster recovery, especially in the immediate aftermath of a disaster. Sociologists refer to such groups as emergent response groups (Sebastian and Bui, 2009), thus explicitly acknowledging their emergent nature.
- Some of the most successful software and web services have been created through distributed, emergent development (Schrape, 2019). For example, Linux is a widely used operating system that was created by developers around the world in the open-source software movement. Wikipedia was created and is maintained by a diverse, leaderless, and constantly changing community of individuals around the world who choose to donate their time. Open-source software and wikis are both emergent phenomena.

I explore emergence in depth in interlude 3. What is important to understand right now is that emergence stands in contrast to the traditional process view of the world. The process view, fundamental to the Age of Reason, is based on the belief that you can understand a whole system by taking it apart and studying the parts, and all you need to design a system is to design the parts and put them together in a logical, orderly arrangement. That is the view that has informed business and leadership development for centuries, but it is no longer serving us. Let's see how the notion of emergence might help resolve the confusion.

The most fundamental characteristic of all emergent phenomena in living systems is that they arise from cooperation and collective action. This is their essence. I propose it is also the essence of leadership, that the common root of everything we call "leadership" is the same as the common root of emergent phenomena: the need to cooperate and take collective action. I propose we define leadership as **the means by which two or more individuals develop the ability to cooperate and take collective action**. With this definition, *any* means that give rise to cooperation and collective action is leadership. The army ants, human emergent response groups, and open-source software development all exhibit leadership, though it looks quite different from our traditional view that locates leadership exclusively inside a leader. The definition I propose does not exclude all the excellent work that has been done to understand and develop leadership in our organizations. Rather, it is a unifying principle that brings together and makes sense of all that has been developed and written about leadership and shows how leadership can arise in the presence or absence of an individual leader.

THE SPECTRUM OF LEADERSHIP

This definition suggests that leadership manifests along what I call the Spectrum of Leadership. At the opposite ends of the spectrum are *emergent leadership* and *intentional leadership*. I use the word *intentional* because leadership at the right end of the spectrum requires consciousness, a view of the future, the ability to make choices, and intention. In human systems, it may be that neither extreme exists in pure form, but there are certainly circumstances under which we approach the extremes.

Emergent   Intentional
Leadership   Leadership

Figure 1.1. The Spectrum of Leadership

This definition emphasizes that the essential characteristic of leadership, its fundamental purpose, is to enable cooperation and collective action. Thus, leadership is implicit in all emergent phenomena and explicit in intentional leadership. We tend to assume that consciousness and an intentional future are essential elements of leadership. But if the essence of leadership is to establish cooperation and collective action, consciousness and an intentional future are not necessary for leadership to arise.

The earliest manifestations of cooperation and collective action appeared in simple bacteria (Igoshin, 2013) and were based entirely on hardwired rules coded in genes. These were the first, primitive forms of leadership, and they were strictly emergent. But when more complex organisms developed, consciousness emerged, a sense of self developed, and social relationships arose. With a sense of self comes the ability to form a vision of the future, have specific desires for what that future looks like, and have opinions about how to get there. And the minute two conscious individuals encounter one another, conflict can arise because different individuals have different desires and opinions. Conflict can be healthy because it enables differing points of view to be expressed. But left to itself, conflict can be destructive to cooperation and collective action. With conflict comes the need to resolve it in a way that maintains cooperation and collective action.

All of this creates enormously greater complexity in social interactions than is experienced by bacteria and insects. New leadership capabilities were needed to address the new level of complexity. As the social capabilities of organisms became richer and more complex, leadership also became more complex. One way of resolving conflict while maintaining social cooperation and collective action is to enable one or a few individuals to have outsize influence over the group—to have leaders and followers. That was the path nature took. A new set of behaviors was layered over the primitive behaviors, and intentional leadership began to develop. Intentional leadership is a more specialized and evolved form of leadership than emergent leadership; it appeared quite late in the evolution of leadership. Intentional leadership confers enormous advantages to social organisms, but it also brings with it a new set of challenges.

Leaders today must move fluidly along the spectrum. In some circumstances, optimal leadership is more intentional, in others more emergent. Different contexts call for landing in different places on the spectrum. A carefully planned dinner party is at the intentional end. A potluck is nearer the emergent end. Both result in a dinner party.

THE FOUR FIELDS OF LEADERSHIP

The notion of *fields* is fundamental to much of modern science. As we all learned in grade school, magnets can repel or attract one another and draw metal objects to themselves. This was deeply puzzling to scientists: how can two things that are physically separated affect one another? Isaac Newton, born just one year after Galileo died, struggled with the same question with respect to gravity: how could two objects, like the Earth and the moon, affect each other without any apparent connection? Scientists described these phenomena as "forces" exerted by objects, but that begged the question of how such a force could pass through empty space.

We're all familiar with electricity, magnetism, and gravity, so it's easy to take them for granted. But when you study them closely, they quickly become confusing. If I kick a ball that is lying on the sidewalk, it will fly away—the result of the force of my foot encountering the ball. But if the ball is sitting a few feet away and I kick at it without touching it, it won't move. That was the conundrum in which scientists found themselves. Electricity, magnetism, and gravity all influence objects at a distance from where the electricity, magnetism, or gravity originates. How could that be?

Michael Faraday was born to a blacksmith in 1791. He had minimal early education—just the basics of reading, writing, and arithmetic. At around the age of twelve, he was apprenticed to a bookbinder. This gave him the opportunity to read the science books that came through the shop. When he was nineteen, still working for the bookbinder, a kind customer gave him two tickets to attend a series of lectures being given in London by Sir Humphry Davy, a brilliant professor of chemistry at the Royal Institution of London. Faraday attended the lectures, and his life was changed. He wrote up extensive notes on the lectures and sent them to Davy, expressing his interest in becoming a scientist. Davy hired him as a laboratory assistant, and his career was launched (MacDonald, 1964). He would become one of the most important scientists of the nineteenth century.

Faraday studied electromagnetic phenomena extensively and was the first scientist to develop the notion of a "field." The term first appears in his notebooks in 1849. He suggested that electromagnetic objects have fields that arise around them. Fields extend infinitely in all directions, but their strength diminishes rapidly as you move away from their source. We cannot see them directly any more than we can see the wind. But just as waves on the water or branches swaying on a tree reveal the presence of the wind, we can detect the presence of fields. The interactions of these fields explains how objects that are not visibly connected can influence one another. James Clerk Maxwell, a contemporary of Faraday's, built on his work to develop the mathematics that describe the behavior of fields. The work of Faraday and Maxwell stands today as fundamental to much of our understanding of the physical universe.

As scientists examined the basic building blocks of the universe in ever-greater detail, the field concept became ever more important. In the first half of the twentieth century, it was used to explain gravity and the interactions of subatomic particles. Today, some scientists believe the universe consists only of energetic fields (Hobson, 2013). A physical object is just the center of a field, the point where the energy is most concentrated. Like so much of modern science, the view of the universe as being made of nothing but fields is profoundly counterintuitive. But it actually explains many phenomena that are otherwise confusing, even paradoxical, and it has been supported over and over by experiments.

You can think of a field as the spread of influence that emanates out from an object. Of course, that influence is strongest at its source. Like a ripple in a pond emanating out from where a stone is dropped, a field influences everything it encounters. The further you are from the source, the less influence it has, but to some degree, the influence extends forever. This gives truth to the ancient wisdom that ultimately all things are connected, and every action, no matter how insignificant and local it may seem, has ripple effects that go far beyond what is easily noticed.

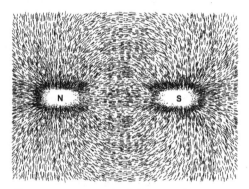

Figure 1.2.   Magnetic Field Around the North and South Poles of a Magnet

What does all of this have to do with leadership and business? Living organisms—and human beings in particular—also have fields of influence. The fields of physics are mediated by strange phenomena with names like gluons, quarks, and leptons. The fields of human beings are mediated through our sense organs—sight, sound, smell, taste, and touch.

Have you ever been in a room full of people and noticed when one or two start laughing, others join in? Noticed when someone smiles at you, you may smile back without even thinking about it? That is the interaction of human fields. When you laugh, you change your field and the fields of those around you. Your emotional state changes your field and the fields of those around you. Everyone has had the experience of walking into a room of people and immediately knowing the mood of the people. It may be worried, festive, angry, frightened, or thoughtful. This is the field of the gathering showing itself, emerging from the interacting fields of the individuals in the room.

Just as scientists could not make sense out of two distant objects interacting over empty space, our view of leadership as residing in an individual person creates a quandary. Leadership only emerges in the context of multiple people, so it cannot be an attribute of a single person. The *field view of leadership* resolves this paradox. When leadership is seen as arising from the interacting fields of multiple individuals, there is no disconnect between how we think about leadership and our observed experience of it. There is no "empty space" between people being led and the source of leadership. It is all around them in the interactions of their fields. Leaders play a specific and vital role in giving rise to this field, but everyone participates. In a meeting, the role of the leader is to shape the field as a whole so the meeting is successful.

You can find examples of a field view of leadership throughout nature. Flocks of birds fly with remarkable collaboration and efficiency. Yet what we think of as leadership in our organizations is often partially or entirely absent in flocks. Flocks of starlings appear to fly without any bird in a leadership role. In others, the role of leader rotates among the birds, with even those lowest on the pecking order sometimes leading. From a field perspective, leadership emerges from the flock as a whole, regardless of whether or not there is an identifiable leader.

Traditional approaches to leadership development fail to address the collective nature of leadership and instead address it solely as an attribute of the leader. For example, they may focus on developing listening skills, self-awareness, or emotional intelligence in the leader. But in a hyperconnected world, they overlook a vital truth: everyone contributes to the collective nature of leadership. Thus, the skills necessary for leaders must be cultivated in everyone.

Viewing leadership as a field is a powerful concept. And it can be overwhelming. Physicists know that while the universe can be conceived as a single vast energetic field, it is useful to recognize that there are subfields that collectively give rise to the universal field. It appears that a small number of fields are all that is needed to understand the physics of the entire universe. The subfields in physics include the electromagnetic and gravitational fields.

In the same way, it is vital to understand the following four subfields of leadership. From the collective interactions of these four fields, leadership emerges. The four subfields are:

- The Field of the Self
- The Interpersonal Field
- The Field of Teams
- The Enterprise Field

These four fields form embedded circles.

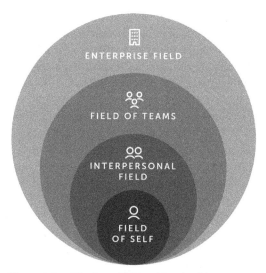

Figure 1.3.   The Four Fields of Leadership

The Field of the Self is the product of how you show up and conduct yourself in your life. It is the foundation of the other three fields. The Interpersonal Field is the product of two people interacting with one another in an interpersonal relationship. The Field of Teams is the product of individuals and interpersonal relationships coming together to form teams. And the Enterprise Field is the product of individuals, relationships, and teams collectively coming together to form entire organizations.

These are the Four Fields of Leadership. Leadership development must therefore address all of them, and leaders must cultivate all of them.

From this perspective, leadership effectiveness is determined by the extent to which everyone, not just leaders, masters all four fields. Leadership in a simple, hierarchical world may function reasonably well with a leader commanding others to carry out tasks and people who follow orders. For effective leadership to emerge in a complex world, everyone must be creative, inspired, accountable for making decisions, and able to interact effectively with one another in all four fields. An individual leader cannot mandate that to happen, though they can inspire it and create a context from which it will emerge.

The Field Leadership model also provides a useful way of understanding the function of culture in an enterprise. In fact, the function of culture is the same as the function of leadership: to foster cooperation and collective action. In the same way that leadership emerges from the interactions of the Four Fields, so does culture. To develop effective leadership, you must also develop effective culture, and vice versa. The same disciplines and practices that build leadership also build culture. In this book, I often refer to *leadership culture* to reflect the deep relationship between the two. And I refer to a philosophy of leadership based on the four fields as Field Leadership.

Throughout this book, I suggest practices and exercises with which you can develop your Field Leadership skills. I also suggest that you keep a "field journal" in which to record your thoughts, reflections, and experiences as you go.

THE SPECTRUM OF LEADERSHIP AND THE FOUR FIELDS

What is commonly referred to as "leadership" in business literature is what I am calling intentional leadership. It is embodied in one or a few individuals that cultivate an intention for where the group will go, what they will do, and how they will do it. Breakdowns in cooperation and collective action are common in human organizations and they are costly. It is the leader's job to prevent them when possible and resolve them quickly when they occur. Keeping the emotional engagement of all the followers while resolving differences of opinion can be challenging. Integrating differing opinions and desires, resolving conflict, and maintaining healthy cooperation and collective action were not as significant in the old command-and-control approach to leadership. But it is one of the major challenges for leaders in a hyperconnected world, where complexity overwhelms the ability of a leader to take a command-and-control approach. That is where the disciplines of the four fields become essential tools in the leader's toolbox.

Establishing shared purpose, establishing behavioral rules, and cultivating the ability of people to function effectively in the four fields: these are the capabilities required of leaders in a hyperconnected world. *How* these are established and maintained is a function of where leadership falls on the spectrum. At the emergent end, you might have just a few simple rules and tremendous autonomy for individuals to decide how they will follow those rules. An example is open-source software, in which the behavior of participants is similar to that of insects or birds: the simple rules that are followed dominate the overall field, and leadership is relatively obscured. Attempts to assert intentional leadership are discouraged, so to the extent it happens, it is subtle and may not even be conscious. Nonetheless, it is there to a degree: certain individuals will have greater influence than others.

For most human endeavors, this is too far to the left on the Spectrum of Leadership. It relies too heavily on just the Field of the Self, trusts what will emerge will be desirable, and does not permit sufficient intentionality and cultivation of the other three fields. Individual creativity can thrive in this environment, but collective reflection, intentionality, and planning are severely inhibited.

At the other extreme is command and control, potentially going all the way to despotism. This destroys the rich potential of the community by starving it of the insights and talents of its members. It suppresses the greatest capabilities of human beings: complex relationships, creativity, passion, experimentation, learning, discovery—all of the elements required for an organization to thrive in a hyperconnected world. Field Leadership requires a balance and the ability to move up and down the Spectrum of Leadership in various circumstances.

The Four Fields of Leadership are present along the entire Spectrum of Leadership. They are hidden and implicit at the emergent end, just as leadership itself is hidden and implicit at that end. But they are functioning even in primitive bacteria. Bacteria sense the world, differentiate between food and nonfood, and move toward nutrients. That is the Field of the Self in its infancy. In time, those bacteria developed the ability to sense one another and respond to one another's signals; the Interpersonal Field emerged. And as the interactions among the bacterial cells became more complex, they formed teams and enterprises. Primitive, simple, and thoroughly unconscious though they were, the four fields were there not long after the beginning of life.

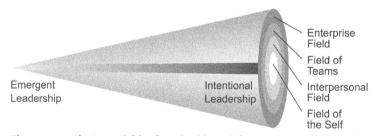

Figure 1.4.   The Four Fields of Leadership and the Spectrum of Leadership

They have also remained largely hidden and implicit at the intentional end of the spectrum because we have not previously named them as fields. But they have been poking their heads up in the literature for some time. Since the late twentieth century, leadership literature has hinted at them more and more. Books like *Servant Leadership*, *Emotional Intelligence*, and *The Seven Habits of Highly Successful People* were tremendous bestsellers. These books continue to be in print some thirty years after their publication because they reveal vital aspects of leadership and culture that had not previously been identified. But they also helped build the Tower of Babel, showing us seemingly disparate phenomena that all relate to leadership.

The breakdowns organizations face today in leadership, culture, and human effectiveness stem from a lack of awareness and skill in moving along the Spectrum of Leadership and in applying the disciplines of the four fields. Leaders can no longer afford to leave these distinctions hidden and implicit. They must understand them and learn to leverage them. As we go from emergent to intentional leadership, the Spectrum of Leadership and the disciplines of the four fields must also become intentional.

Before diving into the four fields, we need to take a look at the scientific foundations of complexity and the challenges of understanding a hyperconnected world.

Chapter Two

Strange Things

How is it that we have arrived at this place, where hyperconnectivity and complexity have turned our traditional ways of thinking upside down and left leaders adrift? The answer goes back to the time of Galileo. This chapter lays out the conceptual foundations for the Spectrum of Leadership and the four fields. It will serve us well throughout the book.

Before Galileo's time, our senses and emotions overwhelmed our intellect, leading us to believe in magic and unknowable forces. Bad weather, illness, and misfortune were believed to be caused by curses, witches, gods, or magicians. Life appeared mysterious and beyond comprehension or control. Galileo was a voice for combining careful observation with rigorous analysis and for choosing reason over magical thinking. He and his contemporaries set the stage for the period known as the Age of Reason, during which scientists and mathematicians threw off the shackles of mythology. They developed rigorous methods of observing the world and analyzing data, prying open nature's secrets and learning to leverage the power hidden within. Looking through microscopes, they could see that what looked like one thing—a drop of water, a leaf—was actually many things. The drop of water contained many, many microorganisms. The leaf was constructed of many parts. We became aware of organisms and heavenly structures we had never dreamed of. And we learned how to use those insights to control and manipulate the world, sparking a long period of explosive discovery and invention. Business as a dominant force in shaping the human race and the planet was also beginning its rise. The first corporation—the British East India Company—was formed on December 31, 1600, just thirty-three years before Galileo would be charged with heresy.

The clear, logical thinking Galileo and his contemporaries promoted mitigated the interference of our emotions, physical sensations, intuition, and magical beliefs, enabling us to focus on using just our intellect. Ever since, we have seen the world as mechanical, following strict, logical laws that could be understood with reason alone. Logical thinking is the method par excellence for solving mechanical problems because mechanical problems are entirely rational, yielding to careful observation and analysis. Emotions can distract us from the pure thought that is so effective for solving mechanical problems.

With the power of our intellect unleashed, the world no longer seemed magical and beyond comprehension, governed by the whims of magicians and gods. We became convinced it was purely mechanistic, governed by the laws of physics and logic. The success of mechanical thinking made life seem comprehensible and controllable. The behavior and output of mechanical systems are perfectly predictable: if everything can be understood through mechanical thinking, then when we have enough data and can analyze it sufficiently, everything will be predictable and controllable.

Galileo and the founder of Netflix, Reed Hastings, bookend an era of astonishing progress, an era filled with vast possibilities that transformed the human race. In less than four hundred years, the human population went from about 500 million to approximately 7.5 billion. We developed the ability to peer into, understand, and manipulate matter and energy on the tiniest of scales and to observe the cosmos on the grandest of scales. We connected virtually every human being on the planet with radios, televisions, telephones, and now the internet, and we developed an extraordinary ability to understand and influence our own bodies, our health, and our minds. We discovered and learned to manipulate the fundamental molecules of life, and we are building machines that outperform us in many domains. We may even be on the verge of creating machines that outperform us in our intellectual, intuitive, and creative capacities. We have come to dominate the physical world, and we can make everything work according to the laws of logic—or so we would like to believe.

Since Galileo's time, the problems people wanted to solve, and on which businesses made their money, have typically dealt with taking things apart, moving things around, and putting things together. Those are mechanical problems. Agriculture, manufacturing, information technology, telecommunications, transportation, healthcare—virtually everything we have done for the past four hundred years has been done through the lens of mechanical thinking. During this period, the world was awash in opportunities for people who could solve mechanical problems. Doing so yielded untold riches.

The Age of Reason could also be called the Age of Certainty and Control, for the driving impulse was to eliminate uncertainty and to control the world through the power of our intellect. We became convinced that by breaking the world down into its parts and understanding the interactions among the parts, we could predict with perfect precision how events would unfold.

Throughout the Age of Reason, the mechanical view of the world must have been extremely seductive, even irresistible. Emotions could cause suffering, conflict, and wasted time and effort. Worse yet, they could lead to irrationality and magical thinking. If we indulged in such things, chaos could rear its ugly head, and we could lose the sense of certainty and control we had worked so hard to establish. So we struck a deal. There was a wild side to nature and to humanity that we chose to ignore. We suppressed our emotions and our spirituality, and scientists and mathematicians restricted their methods to only those fitting with the mechanical model of the world. While we couldn't deny the existence of the wild side, it was off limits to scientific study. We split the world in two and believed that by making that trade, we could rule the world with reason alone.

But ignoring something doesn't mean it's not there. As we pursued mechanical thinking to ever-greater extremes, strange things began to happen. Nature's wild side reared its head, revealing itself in unexpected and baffling ways that I explore later in this book. To understand nature more deeply and to address the opportunities and challenges we had created, we had to expand our thinking and discover new and richer mental models. We could no longer think of everything as a machine.

And that takes us full circle, back to what we so intentionally ignored during the Age of Reason—our emotions, spirit, and the wild, unpredictable side of life. We have entered a new age, an age of chaos and possibility—the Age of Connection—in which our wild side is as essential to leadership and the design of our organizations as is reason and logic. In the age of connection, the full spectrum of leadership must be leveraged for organizations to thrive. Emergent leadership accesses our whole selves—our minds, bodies, and spirits—releasing extreme creativity and wild possibilities, which are necessary and inevitable in a hyperconnected world.

The limitations of mechanical thinking started catching up with scientists and mathematicians in the mid-1800s. While business was reaping the benefits of mechanical thinking and transforming the world, mathematicians and scientists were gaining profound insights into nature's deeper secrets. This did not go smoothly. Some of the most brilliant scientists and mathematicians clung to the belief that eventually all problems would yield to mechanical thinking; they just needed to improve the accuracy or skill with which they wielded it. In 1814, the great mathematician and scientist Pierre Laplace wrote:

> Given for one instant an intelligence which could comprehend all the forces by which nature is animated and the respective situation of the beings who compose it—an intelligence sufficiently vast to submit these data to analysis—it would embrace in the same formula the movements of the greatest bodies of the

universe and those of the lightest atom; for it, nothing would be uncertain and the future, as the past, would be present to its eyes. (LaPlace, 1902)

This was the ultimate statement of confidence in mechanical thinking and in the possibility of certainty. But while science had given birth to the certainty of mechanical thinking, science would also be its executioner. The death knell was sounded by four seismic discoveries in science and mathematics. They were among the first indicators that the world is fundamentally uncertain and complex and that mechanical thinking is insufficient for understanding how the world works. These insights are reverberating today throughout the world of business.

An important distinction explains the limitations of mechanical thinking and reveals the potential in transcending it. This distinction has only become apparent in relatively recent years. It is the distinction between phenomena that are *complicated* versus phenomena that are *complex*. Complicated phenomena can be understood by breaking them down into their parts, understanding the logic of each part, then building up a view of the whole from that understanding. This approach is termed *reductionism* because it reduces things to their parts in order to understand the whole. There may be many parts, and they may interact in many ways, but it can all be understood as a machine that follows the laws of physics and logic. Complicated phenomena yield their secrets to mechanical thinking. Virtually all of humanity's success up through the late twentieth century came by applying mechanical thinking to complicated problems.

Complex phenomena, on the other hand, cannot be understood by mechanical thinking. Every attempt to do so meets with frustration and confusion because complex systems as a whole behave in ways that cannot be understood or predicted from an understanding of their parts. In the past, when scientists and mathematicians were running up against this limitation, they assumed the problem was that they didn't yet have sufficient understanding of the parts. We now know that is not the case; no amount of knowledge of the parts will enable us to understand or predict the behavior of a complex whole. And our hyperconnected world is exceedingly complex. Uncertainty is built in.

The unspoken holy grail of business—to have sufficient knowledge to anticipate all significant changes and always come out a winner—can never be attained. In fact, we can't even get close. The loss of the principle of certainty undermines the premise that the world can be fully comprehended. And the science of complexity tells us we need a fundamentally different approach to understanding and leading our organizations because they are not only complicated, they are also complex.

What were the four discoveries that led scientists and mathematicians to give up on certainty? What are the limits of mechanical thinking, and why are they important to business? To answer those questions, we have to explore briefly these discoveries in the more recent history of science and mathematics. These discoveries are often glossed over in business books because they get a bit technical, but I think that does a disservice to business readers. Without a basic understanding of key scientific and mathematical discoveries and insights of the past century and a half, you cannot make sense of the current state of the business world. If you can't make sense of it, you will struggle to lead in it.

EVERYTHING IS RELATIVE

In 1905, Albert Einstein published his famous paper on relativity, in which he made the astonishing claims—now supported by many experiments—that objects in motion become physically shorter and move through time at a different rate than objects standing still. These are profoundly counterintuitive claims. Compared to how we experience the world, it sounds crazy. With the work of Einstein, our grasp on reality—the correspondence between how we think the world is versus how the world actually is—was threatened, just as it had been by Galileo.

When Laplace articulated his view that with sufficient data it would be possible to fully comprehend all aspects of reality, including the past and the future, he assumed "reality" would be the same for all observers. Einstein showed us reality is not the same for all observers. The world is relative: what is real for one person might not be real for another. If that is the case, then certainty is a lost cause.

Einstein's work may seem abstract, hard to understand, and even harder to connect to business. But consider the basic notion here: what is real for one person may not be real for another. One of the few constants in today's business world is the steady increase in customer expectations. Amazon, Netflix, and Google, among others, have all driven this change. But assessing those expectations—obtaining the appropriate feedback from customers and interpreting it accurately—is a challenge. Different realities show up all the time in sales conversations. Customers have one set of expectations—one "reality" about what they need—and salespeople have a different reality. The sales conversation is one of resolving the differences and together crafting a reality that works for both parties. Reality is not fixed; we create it.

UNCERTAINTY IS BUILT IN

The second event occurred in 1927. It was called, appropriately, the Uncertainty Principle.

(Copyright 1927, by the *New York Times* Company. By Wireless to the *New York Times*)

LEEDS, England, Sept. 1.—Of thirty addresses delivered today before the various sections of the British Association for the Advancement of Science, one of the most important was that of a young German, Dr. W. Heisenberg. Fully 200 mathematical physicists listened to his brief exposition of a conception which will make it necessary to modify belief in what we are pleased to call "common sense" and "reality." (Kaemppfert, 1927)

The Uncertainty Principle comes from physics and shows that it is impossible to fully know all aspects of the state of a physical object. For example, the more accurately you know an object's position in space at a particular point in time, the less accurately you can know its momentum. And the more accurately you know its momentum, the less accurately you can know its position. These effects are not apparent at the scale most of us observe—people and cars and baseballs—but when scientists developed the tools to study things at very small scales, the effects became apparent. Heisenberg proved that even if Laplace was right, that with complete knowledge we could perfectly predict the future, it is not possible to acquire complete knowledge. Another nail had been pounded into the coffin of certainty.

Realizing you can never have complete information about anything is humbling, especially when you lead an organization and have to make decisions on which people's livelihoods depend. We live today in an ocean of information, and for decades we believed that the promise of that ocean of information was to finally give us all the data we would need to make perfect decisions. Heisenberg showed us that no matter how much data we have, it will never be sufficient to deliver a complete picture of reality. Every decision involves some guesswork. The most rigorous application of knowledge, data, and reason would never lead to perfect predictability.

AMBIGUITY AND PARADOX ARE INEVITABLE

The third event in the demise of certainty occurred in 1931.

More than any other field of human endeavor, mathematics has been the standard bearer for certainty. It is also the ultimate form of mechanical reasoning. It is based on pure logic and leaves no room for ambiguity or paradox. At least that's what mathematicians believed at the dawn of the twentieth century.

Mathematicians labored long to demonstrate that mathematics could meet two criteria: there is no ambiguity, and paradox never arises. This was the holy grail of the Age of Reason, the ultimate expression of a perfectly ordered world. Alfred North Whitehead and Bertrand Russell were leading mathematical philosophers of the late nineteenth and early twentieth centuries. They labored for over ten years to produce their monumental work, *Principia Mathematica*, a three-volume treatise intended to prove mathematics is free of ambiguity and paradox.

The final volume was published in 1913. The work has such depth and rigor that proving one plus one equals two takes over 360 pages ("Russell and Whitehead," 2016). Imagine their surprise when, in 1931, an unknown twenty-five-year-old Austrian mathematician named Kurt Gödel not only proved them wrong but also proved that what they were attempting was impossible. He proved, using the tools of mathematics, that within any system of mathematical thinking, it is possible to make ambiguous statements—statements that cannot be proven true or false—and it is also possible to make paradoxical statements. These fundamental limitations in the nature of mathematics can never be overcome. Gödel demonstrated that even in mathematics, we cannot find certainty.

Gödel's theorems were a major blow to anyone seeking proof that science and mathematics could lead to certainty. And if mathematics can be uncertain, think about how much less certain we can be about a statement like, "This project is going well." Ambiguity and paradox are inevitable conditions of life.

In other areas, equally strange things were happening. Mathematicians were creating formulas that violated fundamental beliefs about the very nature of mathematics. They were, for the first time, seriously exploring chaos and complexity. The products of their work were seemingly impossible structures that made no sense in the usual ways of thinking about mathematics. For example, the Swedish mathematician Helge von Koch wrote a formula for creating a circle that could enclose an arbitrarily small area, yet have a circumference that was infinitely long. (Don't try to picture this in your head; you can't.)

Other mathematicians termed these creations "monsters" and claimed that their creators' intent was to destroy the foundations of mathematics. That left them with a quandary: they were insisting on sticking to the age-old tradition of mechanical thinking, but if you tackle complex problems with mechanical thinking, the problems become increasingly difficult and solutions never appear. The more they tried, the more confused and frustrated they became. The only way forward was to brave chaos and plunge into complexity. The modern sciences of fractal geometry, cellular automata, and complexity theory all emerged from this work. These sciences are essential in myriad applications, including the design of computer chips, materials science, and understanding the nature of heart attacks. And, as it turns out, developing an effective model of leadership in a hyperconnected world.

THE BUTTERFLY EFFECT

The fourth event in the end of certainty was the discovery that complexity is ubiquitous and profoundly shapes every aspect of our lives and our organizations. You live in the midst of more complexity and closer to chaos than you could ever know. But we have also discovered that complexity and chaos can be studied, understood, and managed, though not with mechanical thinking. The recognition of complexity's importance came about over a long period of time, through the work of many mathematicians and scientists. Let's see how they came to understand it.

In the early 1800s, scientists and mathematicians believed they could model and predict any phenomena using the same kind of mathematics used to predict the motion of the planets and the force of falling objects. Biologists had been trying to use these methods to predict how animal and human populations would vary in size over time, but they continually met with failure. In 1838, a Belgian mathematician named Pierre Verhulst had taken issue with this approach. He saw the problem was too complex for traditional mathematics, so he tried something new. He created a mathematical function he called the logistic function. This function was far more effective at predicting changes in populations than anything anyone had previously achieved. (In 1840, he used it to make a prediction of what the population of the United States would be one hundred years later, in 1940. His prediction was off by less than 1 percent ["Logistic Growth, Part 1," 2016].)

The logistic function (today, it is also known as the *Verhulst* function) remained obscure for over eighty years until 1920, when the biologist Raymond Pearl began to experiment with it (Kingsland, 1982). He publicized its utility widely. Over the ensuing decades, an increasing number of mathematicians and scientists studied this type of function, discovering that it applied to a vast range of natural phenomena.

What was unique about the logistic function was that it employed feedback. More traditional types of functions are straightforward—you put in a value, and the function produces a new value. For example, if the function is f(x) = x + 2, the function adds 2 to whatever goes in. If you put in a value of 3, then f(x) produces 5. Each time you put in a value, it produces a new value and then it's done. There are two things that are unique about a feedback function: it takes whatever it produces and feeds it back into itself, and it runs forever. These two characteristics are what make feedback functions powerful, threatening, and full of possibility. I explain feedback and its relevance to business and leadership in a hyperconnected world in more detail in interlude 1.

Verhulst was studying the behavior of a population. That is very different from studying the behavior of an individual. It ignores all the specifics of biology and biochemistry that occur at the level of the individual and instead focuses on the population as an entity unto itself. This is precisely the way we think about businesses. Senior executives, boards of directors, the stock market, regulators, customers, and other constituents all focus primarily on the behavior and performance of the entire enterprise, and not so much on the behavior of individuals. What Verhulst learned about the behavior of animal populations—that it is complex and follows patterns dictated by feedback—has immediate relevance to anyone concerned with the performance of a business.

One hundred and twenty-two years after Verhulst, in 1960, a young mathematical meteorologist at MIT named Edward Lorenz was attempting to model something quite different from animal populations. He was creating computer simulations of the weather. He wanted to come up with a way to forecast the weather with greater accuracy than had ever been possible. He ended up doing the opposite—proving there are severe limits to how well we will ever be able to predict the weather. As you will see, in the twenty-first century, his work is also helping us understand leadership and organizational design in a complex, hyperconnected world.

Lorenz was curious about why the weather varies so dramatically even though the large-scale patterns that determine the weather—the Earth's movement around the sun, the four seasons, global wind patterns, ocean currents, and more—were consistent year after year. Just as Verhulst knew that animal populations could not be understood using mechanical reasoning, Lorenz knew the weather could not be modeled using traditional mathematical functions. So, like Verhulst, he used feedback functions.

Because his computer was quite primitive and slow relative to today's computers, it took a long time to run one of his simulations. One day, he saw an interesting weather pattern develop near the end of one of his runs, and he wanted to run it again for a longer period of time. Rather than start all over, he looked at the printout and chose the numbers the program had generated shortly before the interesting pattern began. He used those as the starting point for the program and ran it again. However, the printout he used had truncated the numbers slightly, from six decimal places to three. For example, one of the original numbers was 0.506127, but on the printout it showed as 0.506, which is what he entered for the rerun. It was a minuscule difference, less than three hundredths of a percent.

Lorenz went to get a cup of coffee and came back about an hour later. To his surprise, the weather patterns that were coming out were different from the first run. At first they were similar, with only a slight divergence, but the longer the simulation ran, the more the patterns changed from the original run. By the time the computer had simulated two months of weather, the pattern of the second run bore no resemblance whatsoever to the pattern of the first.

Initially, Lorenz thought something was wrong with his computer, but as he studied the output, he discovered the truncation. He realized his computer was working properly and was revealing something quite unexpected and profound. Changing the starting numbers by a minuscule amount had a huge effect later in the model. He referred to this phenomenon as "sensitive dependence on initial conditions." By this he meant that for some systems, very tiny changes in the starting conditions result in wildly different outcomes. He later coined the now well-known phrase "the butterfly effect," proposing that a butterfly flapping its wings in South America could cause a hurricane in Texas.

This was a defining moment in the science of meteorology. In fact, it was a defining moment in the study of all complex systems. It proved there are severe limitations to how accurately we will ever be able to predict the behavior of complex systems. Feedback allows a very small change to feed back into the system, where it gets amplified slightly each time around. After numerous cycles, the change can become enormous. The butterfly effect graph uses the Verhulst function and Lorenz's original and truncated values to show this.

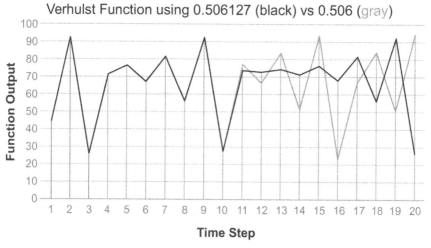

Figure 2.1. The Butterfly Effect

The function generates a nearly identical pattern for both starting numbers up to time step 11. But after that, they begin to diverge. If you look at the left side of the chart up to time step 11, you can see the patterns appear to be identical. But from time step 12 on, they are quite different. The actual data behind these graphs shows that after the first iteration of the function, the difference between the two is less than three hundredths of a percent; after the twentieth iteration, the difference is over 252 percent.

Lorenz published his results in 1963 in what is considered one of the most important scientific papers of the twentieth century (Lorenz, 1963). His discovery went largely unnoticed for some time; in the next ten years, it was referenced in only three scientific papers outside the field of meteorology. But in subsequent years, the implications of his discovery were recognized in virtually all fields of science. In James Gleick's wildly popular 1987 book *Chaos: Making a New Science*, the importance of Lorenz's work and the creativity of his thinking reached a vast audience of general readers. Lorenz became something of a cult hero, invited to speak at conferences far and wide. By October 2016, his original article had been cited in over sixteen thousand papers by scientists working in all disciplines all over the world (Siegfried, 2013).

Predicting the behavior of animal populations, the weather, and human organizations seem like very different kinds of problems, and in many ways they are. But they share a common foundation: all are complex and driven by feedback. Feedback determines which behaviors are—and are not—possible. Understanding feedback is the key to unlocking the potential of complexity.

For business to unlock that potential, business leaders must catch up with science. Long ago, business leaders wholeheartedly embraced the mechanical thinking of the Age of Reason. The business version of mechanical thinking is process thinking. Process thinking views a business as a collection of parts interacting through logical sequences of events. Just as scientists picked apart the physical universe, businesses have picked apart their processes, analyzing them down to the finest detail, striving to control them completely. For centuries, organizations have refined the ability to design and execute processes for everything from the management of materials to the management of ideas and people. There is a vast industry of process improvement methodologies, including TQM, Six Sigma, Kaizen, flowcharting, BPM, and numerous other methods. All of these are well suited to tackling the complicated problems faced by larger and larger businesses and global value chains. They have produced tremendous value for businesses, creating efficiencies and minimizing costs across all industries. But process thinking ignores the complexity of human beings and their relationships with one another, and those are the roots of the challenges and opportunities of a hyperconnected world.

Consider Blockbuster and Netflix. Antioco's decision to reject Hastings's offer probably didn't seem like a big deal. Blockbuster was booming and the future looked certain. Netflix was a struggling startup; rejecting Hastings's offer was just one of many business decisions Antioco must have made every day. But it took Blockbuster into one set of feedback loops and Netflix into another. Those feedback loops led to the demise of Blockbuster and to Netflix becoming a global force in the world of entertainment media delivery—a great example of the butterfly effect.

Interlude One

Leadership Lives in Communication Loops

Communication loops are feedback loops that arise in living systems. Communication loops go round and round, back and forth, evolving and changing as people interact. They are dynamic and alive and are much more than the sum of their parts. Communication loops make human relationships possible. They are the source of creativity and innovation. Understanding their behavior is essential for understanding the four fields and how leadership emerges from them in a hyperconnected world.

To understand how communication loops work, we should briefly revisit the logistic function of population biologist Pierre Verhulst. Studying a mathematical feedback loop is useful because in the pure realm of mathematics, we can see more clearly the essence of how communication loops work. We can then use that insight to understand how communication loops shape behavior in the four fields and determine where you are on the Spectrum of Leadership. And when we understand that, we can see how leaders can choose their position on the spectrum and cultivate the four fields so that the people and organizations they lead can thrive. But I'm getting ahead of myself.

Verhulst's logistic function is a deceptively simple example of a feedback function. Anyone with a basic understanding of algebra can see at a glance how it works. The logistic function takes an initial value, multiplies it by one number and subtracts it from another, and feeds the result back into itself to start over again with the new value.

Consider a conversation you might have with another person. We'll call her Michelle. Suppose you start the conversation with the question, "How do I get to the grocery store?"

Michelle replies, "You go straight down this street and turn north on Main Street. You go two blocks, and the grocery store will be on your left."

You say to Michelle, "Do I turn right or left on Main Street?"

Michelle replies, "You turn right on Main Street."

And the conversation is over. This is a communication loop. The starting point of the conversation was your request for directions to the grocery store. Michelle took the question, did something with it, then fed the result back to you. You did something with her reply and then fed the result back to her. Feedback functions work the same way: you start them with some kind of input, and they operate on it and then feed the result back as the next input.

But understanding how feedback functions work and how they behave over time are two very different things. Depending on the starting values that go into a feedback function, it can exhibit behavior ranging from the mundane to the vastly complex and chaotic.

Think of how differently the conversation with Michelle might have gone if the initial conditions were different. Let's say she is your daughter, home from college, and you say to her, "How could you have run up such a big credit card bill? And why aren't your grades better?" This conversation would likely be quite a bit more complex, potentially going through many phases. Feedback functions can do that too. Their behavioral complexity can be daunting. But mathematical research has revealed a surprising property of feedback functions: all of the behaviors in which feedback-driven systems can engage fall into just five categories (Radzicki and Taylor, 1997). They are:

- Grow
- Reach steady state and stay there
- Oscillate, shifting back and forth among a set of values
- Explode in chaos, becoming utterly unpredictable in what they will do in the next moment
- Die

These are the possible behaviors that can arise from any communication loop, and thus they are the behaviors that can arise in all of the four fields.

The five behaviors are broad categories, and each has subsets. For example, there are many types of oscillation patterns. And one feedback loop may exhibit more than one behavior. But all the behavior of feedback-driven systems ultimately comes down to some combination of these five possibilities. That can be reassuring: because complexity arises from feedback, it is not as daunting as it might seem. Let's look at some examples of communication loops.

- A CEO opens her remarks to the all-employee meeting with an announcement of a large sale the company has just closed. Enthusiastic applause breaks out. She laughs and thanks the audience, then launches into a short unplanned history of the company and the important role the employees play in its success. The mood of the audience goes even higher, and she becomes more animated.

- As her dog charges across the field, a young woman releases a Frisbee with a powerful flip of her arm. The dog's head arches back as he leaps into the air, catches the Frisbee, lands, and returns to the young woman, who looks at the dog and exclaims, "Let's do it again, Beau!" sending the dog back down the field, and the cycle repeats.
- A student works hard at his homework and receives a good grade. He slacks off, not working so hard, and his grades go down. Then he starts studying hard again, and his grades go up. He becomes complacent, and his grades go down. This pattern continues throughout the year.
- A manager gives an employee harsh criticism. The employee becomes defensive and makes a disparaging remark back to the manager. The manager gets angry, and the conversation escalates into a full-scale argument. This pattern repeats over time, and eventually the employee resigns.

These seemingly disparate events are all examples of communication loops. The CEO and her audience are in a communication loop of growing enthusiasm. The young woman responds to her dog's exuberance with her laughter and by throwing the Frisbee again, which keeps the dog in the game. The dog's behavior keeps the young woman engaged in the game. This is a stable communication loop. The student is in an oscillation: when his grades go down, he is motivated to work harder; when his hard work pays off and his grades go up, he loses his motivation, causing them to go down again. The manager's anger at the employee pushes the employee into anger, which causes the manager's anger to increase. This is a rising feedback loop that escalates into chaos, with both of them shouting at each other. The pattern repeats until the employee resigns and the relationship ends, at which point the communication loop dies.

In each of these examples, the interacting parties influence each other through their responses and communication loops, following the hidden but well-defined behaviors I described earlier. The breadth of these examples demonstrates the pervasive role communication loops play in all human systems. It is no wonder that a vast industry has grown around communication training. Communication loops cause some things to go well, some to go terribly, and some to just chug along at an unremarkable pace. Understanding and effectively managing communication loops is one of the most under-realized opportunities available to leaders today. It is essential for managing behavior in the four fields.

I coached Carlos, a team leader, and Amina, his boss, over a period of several months. Consider the following conversation I observed when I first started working with them:

Carlos (nervous, speaking rapidly): "We need to talk about the product development project. It's running seriously behind schedule."

Amina (angry tone): "What the hell happened?"

Carlos (more nervous, defensive): "I've done everything I can, but some of the team members don't pull their weight."

Amina (even angrier): "I put you in charge of this project, and I expect it to be managed well. Don't come to me blaming other people."

Carlos (fear and anger dominating his voice): "I told you from the start this team wasn't working out. You ignored everything I said."

Amina (frustrated, angry, defensive): "First you blame the team, now you're blaming me. When are you going to take accountability for your job?"

And so it went.

This is a classic example of a communication loop gone bad. It's a loop of anger and defensiveness that could keep growing. The forces shaping the conversation are not well managed. Let's look at how this communication loop operates.

Carlos's initial statement triggers an angry response from Amina. Amina doesn't manage her response; she allows her emotions to drive it, mostly unconsciously. Carlos feels threatened by her anger. His intention had been to immediately get into a problem-solving conversation about the team, but now he responds with defensiveness—and also without much awareness. His defensiveness is driven by unchecked emotion. This cycle continues, each time around reinforcing and escalating their emotional states. Carlos and Amina's Fields of the Self are creating a toxic communication loop and thus a toxic Interpersonal Field. To rectify this dynamic, they both have to develop better self-management. Until they are each managing their Field of the Self, there is no hope of working on their Interpersonal Field. In Section 2, I provide practical strategies for managing the Field of the Self. Section 3 explores methods for developing effective interpersonal relationships.

Consider just a few of the ways communication loops are important. They are foundational to:

• Learning: it is the mechanism through which you are able to explore the world, discover what works and what doesn't, and build new neural pathways that give you new options in how you respond to events.

- Conversation: it is impossible to converse effectively with another person if you cannot sense how they are responding to your words and actions. Conversation always has the possibility of ambiguity and misinterpretation. These cannot be corrected without communication loops. Communication loops enable you to test the accuracy of your listening and to confirm that you are being accurately heard.
- Cooperation and collective action among individuals, teams, departments, and organizations: every interaction that takes place in the living world is based on communication loops. We are all embedded in multiple layers of communication loops, many of which we are often entirely unaware. Communication loops make cooperation and collective action possible.
- Trust: it is our response to one another's requests, needs, and concerns that trigger trust. In other words, trust arises from the communication loops we have with one another.
- High performance: high performance arises through a constellation of communication loops acting in concert, synchronizing and supporting one another. Constant adjustments are required to keep them in harmony.
- Poor performance: just as communication loops can create all of the desirable effects listed here, they can equally create undesirable effects. Gossip is a communication loop that engenders cynicism. Mockery is a communication loop that engenders shame and resentment. Dishonesty is a communication loop that engenders mistrust.

In short, communication loops are the means through which order emerges in human organizations. "Communication training," "team building," "leadership development," and "relationship skills" are really just various approaches to managing communication loops. That's good news because it tells us all of the various phenomena that affect organizational performance and all of the complexity present in organizations can be understood in simple terms.

The scientists and mathematicians of the nineteenth and twentieth centuries resolved confusing, paradoxical observations by discovering simple underlying patterns like feedback functions and fields. In the same way, understanding communication loops, the Spectrum of Leadership, and the Four Fields of Leadership can resolve the complexity that sometimes seems paradoxical, confusing, and incomprehensible in organizational performance.

All too often, we think of "giving feedback" as meaning a one-way communication: "This is what I think . . ." You don't actually "give feedback." Rather, you enter into a communication loop with another person. To be effective, you must be aware of how their behavior influences your inner state and how your behavior influences theirs. That means being aware of your physical, emotional, and cognitive responses to the other person's words and actions. Only then will you accurately understand them and they understand you. The question for leaders is: what will be the nature of the communication loops that occur in the organization you lead? Will they give rise to trust, accountability, high performance, and value creation? Or will they lead to mistrust, blame, poor performance, and waste?

Human beings have internal communication loops as well as those that arise between people. There is a constant inner dialogue among your body, your emotions, and your thoughts. This can be deeply habituated, unconscious, and uncontrolled or can be made conscious and managed with intention. That regulation happens in the Field of the Self. I explore it in section 2.

In simple organisms like bacteria and insects, communication loops are dictated entirely in the programming of their DNA. The rules dictating their behavior are hardwired. They have no choice and little or no learning is possible.

Human beings and organizations have the capacity to learn. Many of our communication loops are hardwired, as they are in insects, but many are not. They change naturally over the course of our lives in response to experience. Often they change unconsciously and not always in ways that serve us. But they can also be changed intentionally. We can unlearn old habits—even ones that have become buried in our unconscious—and we can learn new ones.

Habits are communication loops. When it's a habit that is local to you, it emerges from internal communication loops in your body, emotions, and thoughts—the Field of the Self. When it is a habit in a relationship, it arises from the communication loop between the two individuals in the Interpersonal Field. Habits also appear in the Field of Teams and in the Enterprise Field.

Habituated reactions and behaviors are largely, often entirely, unconscious. That is both a strength and a weakness. It is a strength because it frees us to focus on the things that are important to us. Habituated behavior happens automatically—it takes virtually no conscious effort to open an email or click on the reply button. The habits are formed, the internal communication loops between your intention and your muscles are in place, and it happens without thought. This is highly efficient. Your conscious mind can focus on writing your reply. But there is also a downside to habituation. We are complex creatures driven by complex emotions that are sometimes at cross-purposes to our values and the things we want to achieve with our lives. Our complex and sometimes primitive emotional reactions to one another can habituate us to behaviors that actually prevent us from getting what we want. That's what was happening with Carlos and Amina. Neither of them desired or sought out conflict. Neither of them got up in the morning, looked in the mirror, and said, "I think I'll go pick a fight with Amina/Carlos today."

The power of altering habituated communication loops that give rise to suboptimal behavior is evident when you interrupt or change one of these loops, thus altering a recurring pattern. You then have the opportunity to establish a new pattern through a new communication loop that gives rise to optimal behavior. You replace an old habit with a new one.

For example, consider a person who is always late for meetings. You could address the behavior at the specific meeting level—you could call them fifteen minutes before the meeting and tell them it's vital they be there on time. You may succeed in getting them to that meeting on time. But these "instance" solutions are exhausting, always requiring effort to get the person to the meeting on time. On the other hand, if you can help that person discover the internal communication loops—the physical predispositions, the emotions, the beliefs—that make them late all the time, and help them find ways to break those loops, you can stop worrying about them being late because they stop being late.

Human beings and human organizations are extremely complex networks of communication loops. Each of the four fields has its own particular communication loops that determine its behavior, so each has its own unique challenges for leaders. By understanding and working with communication loops in the four fields, leaders can guide their people to develop habits that optimize the performance of the whole system, freeing the leader from worrying about the details.

Let's explore the Field of the Self, where it all starts.

Section II

THE FIELD OF THE SELF

Chapter Three

The Disciplines of the Self

Everything starts in the Field of the Self. The origins of leadership are here, where the behavior of individuals and how they relate to one another is rooted. As a leader, your Field of the Self determines how you will behave and the presence you will create with others. And for those you lead, their Fields of the Self determine how they will respond to your behavior and follow—or not—your direction. The Field of the Self is thus the foundation of how people will cooperate and take collective action. Field Leaders must cultivate the Field of the Self in themselves and establish the conditions for others to do so as well.

The Field of the Self is as rich and varied as your inner life. It fluctuates from moment to moment with the flow of your physical sensations, emotions, and thoughts. It is what establishes your influence on others. The Field of the Self is your inner state emanating out beyond the boundaries of your body. In leadership literature, it is often referred to as your *presence*. Some would call it your spirit. In the Interpersonal and Team fields, your Field of the Self— your presence—determines how you influence others.

Developing presence may sound like a simple challenge—stand tall, speak with authority, exhibit confidence and clarity, and so on. But that is an intellectual approach focused on controlling the mechanics of your behavior. It is not authentic and others will see through the façade. The art of cultivating an authentic leadership presence begins with the authentic inner state of a leader.

Presence is a tricky word, one that's in vogue in leadership training but is difficult to define. In this book, the word *presence* is synonymous with the Field of the Self. Recall that a magnet's field extends out in space and determines the influence of the magnet on objects that enter its field. In the same way, your Field of the Self extends out from you and determines the influence you have on those who come into your field. That is why leadership begins in the Field of the Self and why it is so important for leaders to do the hard work of developing it.

There's a lot wrapped up in these concepts, and there are benefits far beyond your role as a leader. As you cultivate your Field of the Self, you may find that you become a better spouse, parent, and friend. You may find your life imbued with more meaning and a greater sense of purpose. Your emotional life may become deeper and richer. You may worry less and take more joy in the present moment. Your physical health may improve. And while not all of these transformations are directly related to leadership, they all impact positively on your presence as a leader.

An executive client of mine, we'll call him Joseph, went to work straight out of college in the IT group of a small light manufacturing company. He was bright, technically skilled, outgoing, and gregarious. When others saw problems, he saw opportunities. As the company grew, so did Joseph's career.

I met Joseph when he was in his mid-forties. Married with three children, he was a devout Christian. His faith was his guidepost for how he lived. By that time, the company had grown to fifteen thousand employees with plants in North America, South America, Europe, and Asia. It was generating over $2 billion a year in revenue and growing rapidly. Joseph had risen to the level of CTO. He was proud of his success, but he also felt he was capable of more, though he wasn't sure what "more" was.

Joseph had advanced through the ranks with the combination of a sharp mind and a demanding personality. Those who worked for him respected him and were loyal to him. He built team camaraderie by hosting team gatherings at his house and buying tickets for his team to attend sporting events. He was generous with others and a great conversationalist. He let people know he liked them and respected them. But Joseph also had a dark side.

Joseph liked to say he did not suffer fools. He was known to dress people down in front of their peers when he was not happy with their performance, and one-on-one meetings with him could be agonizing. So while people respected him and were loyal to him, they were also afraid of him. His direct reports often kept bad news from him. They avoided bringing their direct reports to meetings with him out of concern they would witness, or even be the target of, his abusive behavior. Which, to Joseph's credit, was why he asked me for help. He knew his actions were not creating the leadership presence that would best serve those he led and the company for which he worked.

The inner state of human beings is extraordinarily complex, with millions of communication loops interacting continuously. Nonetheless, throughout my career I have seen it effectively managed with a simple model. Think of your inner state as being composed of three "minds":

- The physical mind (your body)
- The emotional mind (your emotions)
- The analytical mind (your intellect)

Your body—the physical mind—is your interface with the world. It is where you sense what is happening around you, and it enables you to take action. The emotional mind is the place of rapid assessment, where you initially interpret what you have sensed and where meaning and intention first arise. The analytical mind is the powerhouse of analysis and reasoning, where you can scrutinize more carefully what you have sensed and adjust your interpretation of it, study logical relationships, and predict logical outcomes. To establish the most effective leadership presence, you must be skillful in all three minds.

Managing your inner state means managing these three minds and the *core communication loop* that connects them.

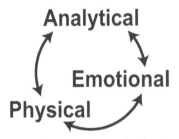

Figure 3.1. The Core Communication Loop

Your core communication loop consists of the continuous dialogue that connects the three minds. Your body influences your intellect and emotions, your emotions influence your body and your intellect, and your intellect influences your body and your emotions. Your body might trigger an emotion that triggers a thought that reinforces or diminishes a physical sensation—or initiates an entirely different physical sensation. Within this "three-part" loop, any two minds may also have a loop. Your intellect and your body may go back and forth, or your body and emotions, or your emotions and your intellect. These loops may exhibit any of the behaviors I identified in section 1—they may die off, they may escalate, they may oscillate, they may go into chaos. All of these loops collectively are what I refer to as your "core communication loop." All other communication loops in the four fields emerge from it.

The model of the three minds and the core communication loop is simple, so it may seem simple to manage them, but learning to do so is a lifelong journey. The three minds interact in complex and often unconscious ways. For example, imagine you are approaching an intersection in your car. You have the right of way; the cross street has a stop sign. Someone runs the stop sign, appearing out of nowhere in front of you. Your foot will be on the brake before your analytical mind has any idea what's going on. As your body reacts, adrenaline and cortisol flood into your bloodstream and emotions surge—fear and anger, among others. When you stop in time and the other car speeds away, relief mixes in with the fear and anger. And at some point, thoughts and words spill out, your intellect awakened. Perhaps you shout out what an idiot that driver was. You immediately think of what might have happened to you, and what the other driver deserves to have happen. And there, in a nutshell, you see how the three minds of body, emotion, and intellect create your inner state, and your core communication loop drives your thoughts and behavior.

This is a dramatic example, but it plays out in small scenarios all day long. Your body senses the world, stimulates emotions, and responds with actions. Eventually, consciousness catches up. We are exquisitely designed to respond to dangerous situations with tremendous speed and efficiency. That's because for most of human history, the world has been a dangerous place, with life-threatening encounters sometimes happening multiple times a day. But many of us no longer live in that world, and our design hijacks us. Joseph never intended to intimidate or shame the people who worked for him, but it happened over and over again. When he felt let down, he also felt threatened, and he lashed out. Have you ever said something to another person, or sent an email, only to regret it afterward? Of course you have; it's part of being human. The same design that saved your life in the car can hijack your behavior in interpersonal relationships. And therein lies the conundrum: how do you allow these remarkable capabilities to serve you in the places they do and keep them from hijacking you in the places they don't? How do you tame the beast within without killing it? That is what mastery in the Field of the Self is about.

WHOLE THINKING

In section 1, I used the term *mechanical thinking* to describe the logical thought that dominated the Age of Reason. The business version of mechanical thinking is process thinking. Mechanical, or process, thinking attempts to work exclusively in the analytical mind, using the intellect alone and shutting out any interference from the physical and emotional minds. I have enormous regard for the scientists, mathematicians, and philosophers who focused their lives on mastering the analytical mind. They devoted themselves to articulating profoundly elegant logical explanations, models, and insights about how the world works, and they created enormous value for humanity. But their approach ignores much of what it is to be human.

In more recent times, the term *critical thinking* has become popular in the business and leadership literature. It is written about extensively and is widely recognized as an essential leadership trait (Baldoni, 2010). But it is also a confusing and poorly defined term. The word *critical* has negative connotations, and it is strongly oriented toward mechanical thinking. As such, it fails to tap some of our greatest capabilities for addressing the challenges and opportunities of living and leading in a complex, hyperconnected world. For that, we need our whole selves.

In this section, I will explore the notion of thought more deeply, particularly as it relates to leadership. To do that, I introduce another kind of thought: *whole thought*. Whole thought involves your whole self; it engages all three minds. Whole thinking includes accurately perceiving all relevant aspects of a situation, including the complex relationships and communication loops that arise in all four fields, accurately interpreting what you have perceived, and making the best possible choices based on your interpretation. Whole thinking is adaptive, enabling you to adjust your interpretations to different situations. Whole thinking includes mechanical thinking, but it involves much more as well. Because whole thinking involves thinking with all three minds, it requires being aware of all three minds.

MENTAL MODELS

To understand the Field of the Self, you need to understand the notion of mental models. Though not a difficult concept, leaders often overlook its importance because it can seem abstract and irrelevant to their day-to-day challenges. Nonetheless, mental models have a profound effect on your ability to lead effectively, particularly in a hyperconnected world.

A mental model is the construct you hold in your mind of the world in which you operate. You are able to drive to work because you hold in your mind a mental model of the route to work. You have a mental model of how your email software works, so you know where to click to open an email. But mental models have far more depth than just images of the physical world. When you are driving to work, your mental model includes the level of urgency that you arrive quickly and what will happen if you are late. That will influence how you drive. Most of your mental models are entirely unconscious. Scientists have studied these unconscious mental models and learned much about how mental models in general work, how they serve you, and how they might undermine you. Optical illusions are a great way to quickly get a sense of them.

Consider parallel lines. Your brain knows that when two lines are parallel and you look down their length, they appear to converge. If you've ever looked down the length of train tracks or up the sides of tall buildings, you know what I'm talking about. It takes a lot of brainpower to figure out that lines that appear to converge are actually parallel. Brainpower is a precious resource, so rather than expend that brainpower every time you encounter parallel lines, your brain has a shortcut. When it perceives two lines converging as they recede from you, it assumes they're parallel. Conversely, when it sees two lines that are not converging, it assumes they diverge. There's no processing necessary for this because it's built into the brain's model of the world. This assumption is not just an idea or belief. It's hardwired into your brain. The image created in your mind is a result of this hardwiring.

You can see what I'm talking about in figures 3.2 and 3.3.

Figure 3.2.   **Figure 3.3.**

Look at figure 3.2. The railroad tracks appear to converge as they get farther away. Your brain interprets this to mean that they are parallel—and it's right. When you look at this image, you have no confusion about whether or not the tracks get narrower as you walk down them. You know they don't, and you don't need to think about it.

Figure 3.2 and figure 3.3 appear to be shot from somewhat different angles. The tracks in figure 3.2 appear angled more to the left than in figure 3.3. Compare the left-hand track in figure 3.2 with the left-hand track in figure 3.3. If I asked you if those two tracks were parallel, you would say obviously not. In figure 3.3, the left-hand track appears to be angled much more to the right—not at all parallel to the left-hand track in figure 3.2. These two corresponding lines obviously diverge.

In fact, these are the same image. If you copy them and lay one on top of the other, you will see that they are identical. The image formed in your brain of diverging lines is an illusion, but no matter how much you know that intellectually, you can't change how it looks. You will always see them this way when they are arranged side by side. Your brain forms its images of the two copies using its hardwired model of how parallel lines occur in the real world. Because parallel lines in the real world appear to converge, and the tracks in figure 3.2 don't appear to converge with the corresponding tracks in figure 3.3, the shortcut your brain uses says that they must diverge. Your brain therefore forms a mental model in which they do.

This is just one example of the hardwired models that are deeply embedded in your brain. As you can see, the interpretations your brain makes based on those models do not always correspond to reality. But these shortcuts, while not perfect, enable your brain to dramatically speed up processing and make fast decisions so you can successfully navigate the world. Your brain takes in billions of bits of information every second. Anything it can do to speed up processing gives you a survival advantage. From an evolutionary perspective, it's a good tradeoff. These deeply hardwired models developed over hundreds of millions of years. They are extremely effective for navigating the real world—we have to go to considerable length to create artificial conditions that reveal them. We wouldn't have survived as a species if they didn't work so well.

I refer to these models as hardwired because they are built in and you can't change them. But there are other models that are not so hardwired. These are models you create through your experiences as you live and grow. They are based on much less experience and on much less data than the hardwired models. They didn't have hundreds of millions of years to experiment and perfect themselves; they've only had the short span of your lifetime. And they didn't have billions of generations of brains to work out the kinks and perfect them. They just have your brain. Consequently, these models contain significant distortions, missing pieces, and inaccuracies. Fortunately, they are also malleable. They can be changed. I refer to them as softwired models.

These softwired models are models of the specifics of your life—the people you know, your relationships with them, your job, the things you own, where you live, all the specifics of all of your experiences. They are unique to you. And they can affect you just as profoundly and unconsciously as the hardwired models. It seems that once a model is formed, your brain uses it in much the same way as any other model—as a shortcut to bypass costly information processing and jump to a quick conclusion. It doesn't matter whether the model is hardwired or softwired.

Joseph's mental model of people who disappointed him was that they were irresponsible, or lazy, or didn't care enough to do good work. Even when there was good evidence to the contrary—that things had gone awry because of circumstances beyond their control—he interpreted their behavior based on his habitual mental model.

Many softwired mental models are a direct reflection of your inner state. Because these softwired models are malleable, you can change them as new information comes in—if you are willing to invest the time and effort. Changing mental models is not easy. It takes time, patience, and humility. All of those were in short supply for Joseph. But the ability to change your mental models is an essential capability for leading in a hyperconnected world, and Joseph was willing to learn.

The softwired models your brain creates through experience often live more in your physical and emotional minds than in your analytical mind. Many of them are embedded deep in your being and are accessible only through practices of introspection and self-awareness. Logical analysis often doesn't make a dent in them when you cling to them emotionally. It may be hard to admit that your view of the world is inaccurate or incomplete, but the cost of clinging to these mental models can be enormous. Certainly if you want to lead, you cannot indulge yourself in such avoidance. It is up to you to clear up any distortions and fill in the missing pieces so that your mental models are as complete and accurate as they need to be for you to arrive at the best decisions.

Softwired mental models often reveal themselves in words—"He's not to be trusted," "She's competent"—but that's just the tip of the iceberg, emerging from the emotions and sensations constantly coursing through you. The tip of an iceberg goes wherever the mass hidden beneath the water goes. In the same way, your thoughts are inclined to go wherever your emotions and physical sensations take them. However, unlike an iceberg, you have the remarkable ability to become conscious of your mental models and of the preintellect emotions, sensations, and beliefs that form them. Because of that, you can change them. You can have agency over your inner state and thus your life. As you uncover these hidden forces and make them visible, you can see how they influence your decisions and affect your behavior. As your awareness of these models and their inner sources grows, you develop the ability to choose whether and how they affect you. This takes courage, integrity, and humility. You must observe and take accountability for your emotional attachment to these models, and you must be willing to give up that attachment when you know, in your heart, it doesn't serve those you lead. This is hard work, and leading in a hyperconnected world will require it of you every day. But the more you practice, the easier it gets.

THE THREE DISCIPLINES IN THE FIELD OF THE SELF

The three disciplines in the Field of the Self are awareness, choice, and accountability. Together, they form a cycle of learning. It is a communication loop, rich with the possibility of ever-increasing effectiveness.

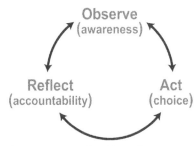

Figure 3.4. Cycle of Learning

- **Awareness**: the ability to awaken your consciousness to the physical sensations, emotions, and thoughts that determine the quality of your inner state, your "self." Awareness makes you conscious of your inner state and helps you accurately assess the state of others. It is the first step in establishing a leadership presence.
- **Choice**: the ability to accurately perceive the choices available to you and make the best choice possible. Choice is where awareness comes alive, where you take action and make a difference. Your leadership presence takes form in the choices you make.
- **Accountability**: the ability to fully acknowledge that the results of your choices are the results of your choices, to make corrections when necessary, and to learn from your experiences without pointing fingers or blaming others. Accountability is the ability to reflect on your actions, take ownership of the results, learn, and move on. Leaders who take accountability for their actions establish a compelling presence.

Chapter Four

The Discipline of Awareness

Purely emergent leadership works fine for organisms with little conscious-ness or sense of self, such as bacteria and insects. But with a sense of self, different individuals develop emotional investments in different outcomes. Conflict becomes inevitable. As life evolved, consciousness, conflict, and differences of opinion, desire, and need made leadership much more complex. Purely emergent leadership was no longer sufficient. Intentional leadership became necessary to maintain cooperation and collective action.

SPIRIT MEETS SCIENCE

Throughout the centuries in which scientists and mathematicians were study-ing the world in ever-greater detail, exploring how everything from the vanishingly small to the unimaginably immense works, another group of researchers and explorers turned their attention in the opposite direction—to the inner lives of human beings to study the spirit, or soul. These individuals had minds as deep and powerful as those of the scientists and mathematicians, and they applied themselves to their study with equal rigor. But their methods were radically different. While scientists and mathematicians sought to take the human observer out of the equation and understand how the world works independently of us, spiritual seekers sought to ignore the rest of the world and learn how human beings function by studying their inner states. To be clear, I am not talking about religion, though many spiritual masters come from reli-gious traditions. You can follow whatever religion is meaningful to you, or not follow one at all, and still draw on the lessons of diverse spiritual traditions.

Our hyperconnected world is bringing these two previously distinct avenues of study together. For scientists, the baffling discoveries of the nineteenth and twentieth centuries forced them to acknowledge the role consciousness plays in the acts of observation and analysis. They realized you cannot study the world outside of yourself without studying your inner world. How they observed the world and interpreted their observations was not just a function of the mechanics of the world, it was equally a function of the consciousness of the observer. As scientists' observations became ever more detailed and accurate, they realized their mental models played a role in everything they observed. You don't experience the world directly. Your experiences are the product of your mind interacting with the world. You can't separate your mind from the world; your mental models are profoundly influenced by your inner state.

Similarly, teachers in spiritual traditions are coming to understand that human beings only exist in context. If you want to live a full and meaningful life, understanding the way the world works is as essential as knowing your inner life. The hyperconnected world is bringing all of this together, and none too soon because you can't lead effectively in a hyperconnected world without being a whole human being, in touch with both your inner life and the outer world.

To some, this may sound like the pop psychology and pop spirituality that conflates misinterpretations of science with misinterpretations of spiritual traditions. Quackery is alive and well and thrives on the internet, where sham scientists and sham spiritual teachers make considerable money leading people down blind alleys. That's not what I'm talking about. The scientists and mathematicians I reference were and are rigorous thinkers and leaders in their fields. So were and are the spiritual teachers. Their teachings are based on careful study and analysis of the inner lives of people, no less rigorous than the analysis of the scientists and mathematicians studying the external world. Just as scientists and mathematicians devoted themselves fully to their practice and study, enlightening the intellect, spiritual teachers devoted themselves fully to the rigorous and difficult path of studying the human spirit. They were no slouches; these were not new age dabblers looking for platitudes to secure an easy path to emotional comfort any more than Einstein was a snake oil salesman. They are as committed to understanding the inner lives of people as scientists and mathematicians are to understanding the mechanical workings of the universe. Where scientists and mathematicians teach us how to master the external world, spiritual teachers teach us how to master the self.

Here's what a few of them have said:

- Rumi, Islamic poet and scholar: "Yesterday I was clever, so I wanted to change the world. Today I am wise, so I am changing myself."
- Abraham Maslow, American psychologist and author: "What is necessary to change a person is to change his awareness of himself."
- Thirteenth-century Zen master and philosopher Dogen Zenji: "To study the way is to study the self. To study the self is to forget the self."
- Psalm 46:10: "Be still and know that I am God."
- Marianne Williamson, American spiritual teacher, author, lecturer, and activist: "No one will listen to us until we listen to ourselves."
- Rabbi Rambam: "Kabbalah is known as the teaching of the hidden because it can only be grasped by a person to the degree that he is able to alter his inner qualities."

All of these point to the primacy of the Field of the Self as the origin of everything else in human life. My own self-awareness practice is rooted in Zen Buddhism. I was drawn to Zen in my adolescence because I wanted to see the world clearly and without distortion from my inner state. I have a strong analytical mind but realized early on that my intellect would not be sufficient for that journey. Zen meditation is a highly evolved and refined practice aimed at direct experience and ultimately transcendence of your inner state. I had no idea what I was getting into, but I have been blessed with some gifted teachers whose patience has guided me well.

Leading in a hyperconnected world demands as much spiritual discipline as it does intellectual rigor. Leaders must become masters of themselves in all three minds—the physical, emotional, and analytical—not just the intellect. When I said that leading in a hyperconnected world is not for the faint of heart, I meant it. It requires far more than intellectual rigor and a drive to succeed. It requires fully cultivating your finest qualities as a human being and overcoming your darkest tendencies. That is the path of a Field Leader.

This reflects an emerging challenge and opportunity for today's organizations: more and more employees are looking for more than a paycheck. This shows up in the millennial generation (Vesty, 2015). They are looking for meaning and a sense of purpose in their work. In a study commissioned by the Career Advisory Board and conducted by Harris Interactive, more than seven in ten millennials ranked meaning as one of their top three essential factors when looking for a job, and three in ten ranked it as the single most important measure of a successful career. But only 11 percent of their managers thought meaningful work was important to millennials. This is a huge gap in perception, and it's costing companies money. When millennials don't find work meaningful, they are apt to move on to a job where they do (Unruh, 2018).

SELF-AWARENESS

Self-awareness is the fundamental first step for cultivating the Field of the Self. The deepest and most powerful practices human beings can employ are self-awareness practices. They tap your greatest resources and release your greatest potential. They are also the most difficult and often take a while before you see the fruits they bear.

Self-awareness begins with a careful self-examination, observing your inner state without judgment to see how it influences your behavior. If you aren't aware of your inner state, you can't change it. If you are aware of it, you can change it—with practice. Self-awareness is, therefore, the fundamental first step for cultivating the Field of the Self. Spiritual traditions are a rich resource for learning to study and manage your inner state.

If you've encountered spiritual masters, you may have noticed they have a presence that reflects an inner state of calm imbued with great strength. In their actions, they have tremendous fluidity and adaptability while never compromising their core principles. They are like giant sequoias. Their inner state projects a presence that is at once massive and unassuming. They can bend with the wind because they have deep roots that hold them steady. That is the leadership presence called for in our hyperconnected world. Leading in this world does not require you to become a fully enlightened spiritual master or a saint any more than you must become an advanced scientist or mathematician. But you must be on the path to develop your whole self with humility, courage, and a commitment to self-transcendence and service to others. This is as essential as a well-developed intellect capable of drawing meaning from data. You must be a whole person.

To be aware of something means to have a conscious perception of it, to take note of it, and to have a mental model you can observe and test. Conscious perception is different from thinking. Thinking about joy is different from experiencing joy. The skills of self-awareness are, therefore, different from the skills of scientific analysis. Scientific analysis is primarily a discipline of *thinking* about things; awareness is primarily about *consciously noticing and experiencing* things. Thinking can be a distraction from awareness. To develop self-awareness, you must focus on consciously experiencing your inner state. Once you have developed the capacity to experience it, you can begin working on it. That may include thinking about it, but thinking is far from the only path to understanding and managing your inner state. In fact, it is often the least effective path.

Your awareness at any point in time is actually much less than you probably realize. Researchers have found the processing capability of the conscious mind appears to be between 50 ("Information Theory," 2018) and 120 (Levitin, 2015) bits per second. That's less than it takes to track what two people are saying at the same time. And it appears we can only hold somewhere between 4 (Cowan, 2001) and 7 (Saaty and Ozdemir, 2013) discrete "chunks" of information in our consciousness at one time. (A "chunk" might be a person, a color, an object—anything you might hold in your mind as a discrete "thing" in your world.) In other words, you are always much less conscious—less aware—than you think. The brain does a remarkable job of moving information in and out of consciousness and rapidly shifting what you are aware of in any given moment, thus giving the illusion that you are aware of much more than you actually are.

One hundred and twenty bits of information per second is pretty slow processing, considering your body is sending about eleven million bits of information to your brain every second. So your conscious mind processes at most about one one hundred thousandth of what's coming in. The rest gets handled beneath the surface.

The challenge, then, is to have more control over where your attention actually goes—what is loaded into your consciousness and what is left out—so you can accurately perceive what is happening at any point in time and make the best possible choices in any situation. If you approach this as an intellectual exercise, you will quickly become overwhelmed. Your intellect will never be able to parse all those incoming flows of information and decide where to focus. For that, you need spiritual discipline, and that is where wisdom traditions come in.

CULTIVATING SELF-AWARENESS: THE PRACTICE OF CENTERING

As you develop self-awareness, you will become more and more attuned to the dynamic quality of your inner state, and you will begin to discover where and how you can influence it. Current leadership literature is full of references to self-awareness and centering. To be centered means to be in balance. If you are off balance, you are easily knocked over; if you are balanced, you can respond to perturbations with equanimity, grace, and strength. To be centered means your body, emotions, and intellect are unstressed, clear, and aligned. There is no internal churn; you know where you stand and can respond quickly to whatever happens. You adapt readily to circumstances without giving ground on your purpose and principles. You maintain calm and equanimity in the midst of stressful challenges—a vital leadership capability.

When you are centered, your core communication loop is alert and alive with energy, taking in information from all three minds and sharing it among them, but with a kind of remove—you observe this happening, no mind dominates any other, and you don't engage in changing what is happening with any mind. In this state, there is no inner turmoil or struggle, there is just awareness. You may move off center to engage in intentional thought or analysis of sensations, emotions, and thoughts, but if you are skilled at centering, you will return to center quickly.

People who are not familiar with centering practices often think being "centered" is a state you get to and then stay in. Nothing could be further from the truth. I once watched a fifth-degree black belt martial artist demonstrate her skill by fending off several students attempting to attack her at the same time. She moved like the wind, and no one laid a hand on her. I later asked her how she managed to stay so centered in the midst of such intense, nonstop challenges. She smiled and said, "Oh, I don't. I'm constantly getting off center, but I get back really fast." An Olympic figure skater I spoke with put it a little differently. She said, "People watching us think we go from one move to the next, from a spin to skating backwards on an outside edge to a flip and so on. What they don't see is between every move, every time we shift from one position to another, we go to a point of balance. If you miss the point of balance, you fall down." Long-term meditators will tell you if you expect meditation to give you a fully centered life all the time, you will end up living in frustration and disappointment.

Centering is something you practice, and mostly you practice returning to center, not staying there, because staying there can be quite difficult. When your body moves, emotions stir, or thoughts arise, you may quickly move off center. When that happens, you want to get back as quickly as possible so you can accurately perceive what is happening around you and respond in the most effective way possible.

Bill Russell was a center for the Boston Celtics. A five-time winner of the NBA Most Valuable Player Award and a twelve-time All-Star, Russell led the team to eleven NBA Championships, the most of any player in NBA history (Rose, 2017). In his memoir *Second Wind*, he describes experiences when two opposing teams would spontaneously enter into a heightened state of awareness. He writes:

> At that special level, all sorts of odd things happened. The game would be in a white heat of competition, and yet somehow I wouldn't feel competitive— which is a miracle in itself. I'd be putting out the maximum effort, straining, and yet nothing could surprise me. It was almost as if we were playing in slow motion. During those spells, I could almost sense how the next play would

develop and where the next shot would be taken. Even before the other team brought the ball in bounds, I could feel it so keenly that I'd want to shout to my teammates, "It's coming there!"—except that I knew everything would change if I did. My premonitions would be consistently correct, and I always felt then that I not only knew all the Celtics by heart, but also all the opposing players, and that they all knew me. There have been many times in my career when I felt moved or joyful, but these were moments when I had the chills pulsing up and down my spine. (Russell, 1978)

How do you know when you are centered? It's not an easy state to describe because it is not an idea; it is something you experience. It's like trying to describe hearing a great piece of music. But when you talk to people who have practiced centering techniques, there are many commonalities. They report that when they are centered, they feel calm but energized, their mood is light and open, their thinking is clear, and they aren't pulled off balance by unexpected events or outbursts of emotions in others. Their breathing is slow, deep, and regular. Other people experience them as clear headed, focused, caring, and effective. Meditation is one of the most common practices people use to achieve this state.

When Mary Barra became CEO of GM in January 2014, she took the helm of a stodgy, bureaucratic company with a culture of denial and finger point-ing run by an old boys' network (Colvin, 2015). It had just come to light that, for over ten years, managers and employees had known some GM cars had faulty ignition switches. By the time the crisis was behind them, it would be revealed that over one hundred people had died in accidents caused by those switches (News, 2017). The cost to GM would exceed four billion dollars (Isidore, 2015). The challenges Barra faced were daunting.

Self-awareness, connection to purpose and principles, and a calm center were essential for Barra to salvage GM. In videos of her testimony to the US Congress, where she was grilled relentlessly on the ignition switch problem, she never gets rattled. When you listen to her in speeches and interviews, she never goes off center and she never compromises her purpose and prin-ciples. She is straightforward, holds her ground, and is clearly committed to taking accountability for the problem and making sure nothing like it ever happens again.

By all accounts, Barra thoroughly remade GM's culture and turned the company around. By 2016, GM was reporting record profits and had em-barked on bold plans that reimagined the company, shedding unprofitable businesses and focusing on ride-sharing markets, electric cars, and autono-mous vehicles. She has accomplished this in part by fostering open, honest dialogue throughout the company. She encourages conversations in which people identify behaviors that need to change and commit to developing new behaviors (Reingold, 2016). In short, she exemplifies self-awareness, a centered presence, and all the qualities of the Field of the Self demanded of a leader in a hyperconnected world.

An internet search on how to develop self-awareness will provide you with more articles, blog posts, and websites than you could read in a lifetime. But most if not all of them boil down to a handful of simple methods:

- Centered breathing
- Meditating
- Journaling
- Listening openly to how others experience you

While these may seem distinct, in fact, they work in concert, each extending and deepening the others. The effective leaders that I know use most or all of them. The first three—breathing, meditating, and journaling—are practices in the Field of the Self. I provide guidance for starting these practices in chapter 5. The fourth, listening to others, lives in the Interpersonal Field. I explore the practice of listening to others in section 3.

The goal of self-awareness, then, is to manage your core communication loop and arrive at a centered inner state from which you can focus your attention where it is needed and respond efficiently and effectively to whatever situation you are in. That is an essential capability for establishing the presence of a Field Leader. Let's see how that's done in each of the three minds.

AWARENESS OF THE THREE MINDS

To manage the three "minds" from which whole thinking emerges, you must first be aware of them. You must learn to consciously note what is happening in all three minds.

- Physical Mind—The signals your body is sending—muscles that are tight or relaxed, the quality of your breathing, your posture and facial expression, your heart rate, the feeling of your feet on the ground
- Emotional Mind—Your emotional state—excited, frightened, joyful, calm
- Analytical Mind—Your thoughts—clear, focused and directed, scattered, churning, silent

Self-awareness also includes observing how these three minds constantly interact and influence one another—the core communication loop I described earlier.

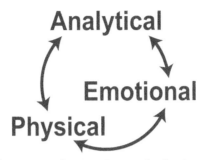

Figure 4.1. The Core Communication Loop

Because the three minds are so interconnected, you cannot develop deep awareness in any of them without developing awareness in all of them. Your inner state is highly dynamic. The more you study it, the more you will see it never stands still. This is one of the intersections of science and spirit: masters of both traditions understand that everything is dynamic, constantly changing. This is as true of your inner state as it is of the external world.

Self-awareness is the tool that enables you to go off autopilot and notice when the usual pattern of your core communication loop isn't serving you. As you observe your emotions, they calm down; as you observe your breathing, it becomes deeper and steadier; as you observe your churning intellect, it becomes quieter. The simple act of self-awareness alters your inner state because it regulates the inner communication loops.

As your self-awareness skills grow, you will be able to make these adjustments faster and with greater ease. The more you practice awareness, the more freedom you will acquire. You learn to notice in real time when your patterns of interactions with yourself and others start to break down and to address that immediately rather than letting unproductive behaviors propagate. The boss who habitually blows up and creates fear and chaos with their people can find ways to lead more effectively; the team member who is always late can notice their impulse to squeeze in that one last email, lower the impulse before it takes over, and get to the meeting on time. The salesperson can notice that they are not resonating with a particular customer and explore other ways of engaging them. I have often seen that organizations whose people develop heightened self-awareness have a rate of learning and sustainability that far outstrips organizations whose people don't have it.

Many people have described to me the experience of leaving a meeting with a vague sense that something was left unclear. On a subtle level, they knew the lack of clarity could lead to problems down the road. Nothing was said about it either in the meeting or afterward. Yet when asked, many people who were in the meeting will say yes, upon reflection, there was a sense something needed clarification. The awareness was sitting just below the threshold of consciousness. Typically, people report that once they become aware of these almost conscious sensations, they discover actions to take that they would otherwise have missed.

Chapter Five

Whole Thinking
and the Physical Mind

Being out of touch with our body limits our capacity to learn and evolve, and it dramatically reduces the possibility of meaningful relationships, as well as an authentic spiritual presence—surely all foundations for a fulfilled, satisfying life.

—Richard Strozzi-Heckler

Just as the four fields all start in the Field of the Self, everything that happens in the Field of the Self starts in the "mind" of the body—which I am calling the physical mind. The physical mind shines in its ability to sense the world and to interact with the world—to take action. All action happens through the physical mind. Thus, if you are not able to center the physical mind, your actions will be less than optimal.

When I first met Joseph, he was struggling with Margaret, whom he had inherited as an employee when a team from the marketing department had been absorbed into the IT group. With the move to IT, Margaret's job changed considerably, and she was struggling. In the marketing group, Margaret had been in a very tactical role. She could list out her tasks for the day, lay down a plan of attack, and check them off as she got them done. In Joseph's group, she was in a more strategic position. She was expected to set direction for complex projects and deal with constantly changing circumstances. There were no daily tasks she could check off. As I got to know Margaret, it became evident that she was very task oriented and took great satisfaction in checking off tangible accomplishments. She was neither comfortable with nor drawn to the more fluid and less tangible world of strategic thinking.

Joseph told me that he felt he had behaved poorly toward Margaret, and his behavior may have been part of the reason she was struggling. As we talked, it became clear that while Joseph's self-awareness was not high, he did realize that his behavior was, at times, hurtful to others.

Like many leaders with whom I have worked, the behaviors that had helped Joseph advance to his current position were now holding him back. Joseph had always demanded high performance from his teams and didn't hesitate to let people know when he was disappointed or unhappy. That had resulted in a string of successes that moved him up the organizational chart. But with a team of high performers whose jobs demanded creativity and collaboration, his aggressive style was not working. "And," he said, "it doesn't fit with my Christian values. The problem is I don't know any other way to get results, and I won't sacrifice performance for kindness. That would be a failure to serve the company, and I won't compromise that. But I just feel there has to be a better way. I don't want to go home anymore feeling bad about how I treated someone."

There were a few things I noticed about Joseph right away. He was tall, solidly built, and had a deep and commanding voice. He tended to lean forward, especially when he was getting frustrated. This gave him a little more height but also threw him off balance. I conducted part of our first session standing. With his permission, I would occasionally approach him, place my hand on his sternum, and push gently. He would immediately stumble backward. I suggested to him that though he was thinking he needed to learn to manage other people better, he actually had to start by learning to manage himself better. We had to begin our work in the Field of the Self.

The first thing I taught Joseph was how to breathe. You might be thinking, "We all know how to breathe; we'd be dead if we didn't." You're right that we all know a way of breathing. But we don't all know how to breathe well.

In the Field of the Self, centered breathing is the foundation of managing the physical mind. Many people find this practice has a surprising impact on virtually everything they do. In some situations, it can literally save your life. Soldiers being prepared for battle, SWAT teams, emergency responders, and others who routinely have to function at their peak ability in high-stress situations are taught combat breathing (Kennedy, 2011). It is similar to the centered breathing practice I taught to Joseph.

Your diaphragm is a muscle that lays horizontally beneath your lungs and above your belly. If you've ever watched babies breathe, you will have noticed their bellies gently rising and falling with each breath. Even when they are stressed and cry out, you can see their bellies move. Their bellies move because their diaphragm moves down when they breathe in, causing the belly to move out and creating more room for the lungs to fill with air. When they breathe out, you can see their bellies move in as the diaphragm moves up and pushes air out of the lungs. This is the most natural way to breathe—the way we are designed. But as adults, most of us have lost that natural way of breathing: our breathing has become shallower and faster. We have to retrain ourselves to breathe properly.

Modern science is providing new evidence for what spiritual teachers have been telling us for millennia: centered breathing is foundational to mastering the Field of the Self. Here's what I taught Joseph:

> Find a quiet place where you can be undisturbed for about ten minutes. Stand quietly and let your thoughts settle. Close your eyes and do a brief body scan: focus your attention on the top of your head and relax any tension there. Then slowly move your attention down through your body, relaxing any tension you discover. When you have reached your feet and relaxed your entire body, place one hand on your belly with your thumb over your navel. When you breathe in, the area under your hand should move out, all the way down to your little finger. When you breathe out, that area should move in. If this does not happen naturally, it means your body has forgotten to use your diaphragm when breathing. If that's the case, you have to retrain it. Intentionally expand your belly with each in-breath, and contract it with each out-breath. With practice, this will become natural once again. I directed Joseph to spend five minutes each day in this practice.

Breathing this way affects your entire being. It seems simple, and it's hard for some to believe it can make much difference, but it can significantly alter your inner state. With proper breathing, you can regulate your brain rhythm (Herrero et al., 2017), manage stress (Harvard Health Publishing, 2018), lower your blood pressure, relieve anxiety, heighten your awareness (DiSalvo, 2014), and realize a variety of other positive mental and physical health effects (Bhasin et al., 2013). Centered breathing has been shown to lower the levels of cortisol and adrenaline, the stress hormones (Kim et al., 2013). This is the breath of leadership.

When I first asked Joseph about the problems with Margaret, he immediately replied that he was terribly frustrated with her. "She just doesn't seem to try. The things I ask her to do aren't rocket science, but she futzes around and spins her wheels and never makes progress. I wonder if she's just lazy or maybe not very bright." There was disdain in his voice. I could see his frustration and anger rising up.

Joseph understood that Margaret's new role was quite different from her old role. But his habit of pushing people for high performance was so strong he couldn't see any way of responding to her other than demanding better performance. The idea that Margaret was, in fact, behaving in the only way she could, given who she was and how she operated, was not something he was ready to absorb.

I sensed Joseph needed to change his inner state before he could change how he saw Margaret. Logic would not suffice, so I chose not to challenge his view of her. I began by working with him in his physical mind. We returned to the standing practice I described earlier, in which I would check how grounded and centered he was. As he spoke about his frustration with Margaret, his breathing became faster and higher in his chest, and he leaned forward. I placed my hand on his sternum and pressed, and he would stumble backward. As he became aware of this tendency, he began to notice when his breathing and posture shifted, and when I approached, he would begin diaphragm breathing and correct his posture. He found that when he did this, he no longer lost his balance.

I asked him to start monitoring himself and to keep a journal in which he could jot down his self-observations. Specifically, I asked him to make notes of any physical sensations—changes in his breathing, posture, muscle tensions—that he experienced when he encountered Margaret or thought about her. And when he found his breathing shortened and his weight was forward, I asked him to shift back to a grounded stance and practice diaphragm breathing.

When I saw him a couple of weeks later, I asked him how it was going. He smiled ironically and said, "It's a lot easier to get centered when you're here to help." He paused, then said, "I'm noticing these habits of frustrated behavior with a lot more people than Margaret. And I'm seeing how they lead to the behaviors I want to change. But I don't see any way to do that. Am I supposed to just let people not perform? Most of the time, I still just launch into criticizing and demanding. When I catch myself and reestablish my breathing and my balance, I just draw a blank. I don't know where to go, and if there's one thing I hate, it's not knowing what to do. I got where I am by taking action and pushing others to do the same. I'm not going to give that up."

I asked him to be patient and told him we'd explore alternative choices a little later in our work together, but for now I wanted to know more about what else he was observing in himself. "Not much," he said. "I think even when I do the breathing you asked me to do, and get more balanced or grounded, I'm still tense and my mind is distracted. And I feel so strongly I have to *do* something that my usual behavior just pops out."

I told him he was making progress, that in our first sessions he hadn't had the ability to articulate his inner state so clearly. And the feeling of drawing a blank was actually a good thing because it showed he was creating a space for new choices to appear, choices he hadn't previously seen. Before he could discover new behaviors, he had to decouple from the inner state that drove the old behaviors.

I asked him to continue what he was doing—recentering when he caught himself off balance, adjusting his breathing, relaxing tense muscles, observing his inner state, and making notes about what he observed. And I asked him to add one more practice: when he found himself frustrated to the point of becoming angry or disrespectful, he should stop the conversation and tell whomever he was talking to that he needed some time to reflect. He could take a few minutes on the spot to settle himself, or he could schedule a follow-up meeting. Joseph acknowledged this would be pretty uncomfortable for him, especially the part about leaving things unresolved, but he was game to give it a try.

I saw him again a couple of weeks later and asked him how it was going. He replied, "It's been very hard to pull back and not be reactive. But I'm also noticing there's a part of me that's good with that because I'm choosing not to behave in ways I end up regretting."

In summary, centering in the physical mind can be achieved through diaphragm breathing in which you feel your lower belly move out when you breathe in and move in when you breathe out. Developing a physically centered inner state involves three steps:

1. Become still and notice your body, tuning in to where it holds tension, where it is relaxed, and whether you are balanced or off balance.
2. Use diaphragm breathing to become physically centered. Placing your hand on your belly may help you feel the movement of your diaphragm.
3. Relax any tension and keep returning to a point of balance and diaphragm breathing.

Chapter Six

Whole Thinking
and the Emotional Mind

The heart has its reasons, of which reason knows nothing.

—Blaise Pascal

Rene Descartes was a contemporary of Galileo. As one of the leading thinkers in the Age of Reason, he was committed to eliminating all aspects of thought other than pure logic. While brilliant, his rigid commitment to logic was what the neuroscientist Antonio Damasio referred to as *Descartes' Error* in his book of that title (Damasio, 1994). Descartes viewed emotion as a barrier to understanding and a source of complexity and chaos. Damasio's work suggests that rather than being sources of complexity and chaos, emotions are nature's mechanism for managing them. Rather than opposing rational thinking, they make it possible. In evolution, the emergence of rich social structures and complex organizations arrive with the appearance of organisms capable of experiencing emotions. It may well have been that the emergence of the emotional mind, and the uniquely human ability to marry emotions with physical sensing and intellectual reasoning, made human cultures and organizations possible. While Descartes's logical reasoning was brilliant, his error was turning his back on other ways of knowing.

While unmanaged emotions can create chaos, well-managed emotions can mitigate it. Field leadership involves establishing emotional relationships— relationships that are not motivated by logic, though logic can help to explain them. Descartes, Galileo, and their contemporaries did not understand this, but they were not all wrong. Emotions can only manage complexity and avoid chaos when you can center your emotional mind. Otherwise, they often will create chaos. The Age of Reason thinkers were trying to avoid the risks of engaging emotions, but they failed to see their potential.

Managing your emotions is essential to establishing an effective leadership presence. Just as the physical mind shines in its ability to sense the world, the emotional mind shines in its ability to take those sensations, create meaning from them, and direct your actions. Mastery of the emotional mind is called emotional intelligence. Emotional intelligence has been recognized as a vital leadership skill and a critical aspect of corporate culture for over three decades. A vast marketplace provides books, training, and coaching services to develop emotional intelligence in leaders, managers, and employees. Study after study has shown that when properly developed, emotional intelligence pays off (Goleman, 2005). In one study, incorporating emotional intelligence assessments into executive recruiting led to an 88 percent reduction in the number of executives who left for other jobs within two years of being hired. In mid-level jobs, those with the highest emotional intelligence are twelve times more productive than those with the lowest emotional intelligence and almost twice as productive as average employees (Cherniss, 1999). Salespeople with high emotional intelligence outperform those with average or low emotional intelligence (Rojell, Pettijohn, and Parker, 2006).

A 2015 study in the journal *Pediatrics* examined the performance of twenty-four teams of physicians and nurses. They found that when a team experienced even mild incivility prior to interacting with patients, it resulted in profound, even devastating, effects on patient outcome (Riskin et al., 2015). Research shows that interactions characterized by low emotional intelligence interfere with working memory capacity, which is where cognitive processing necessary for planning, analysis, and management of goals occurs (Engle and Kane, 2003). In a study published in *Harvard Business Review*, researchers collected experiences from thousands of employees across multiple companies at all levels of the organization chart. They found that 98 percent reported experiencing uncivil behavior, and significant percentages of those individuals reported costly side effects. These included deliberately diminishing their work effort, reducing the time they spent at work, intentionally decreasing the quality of their work, losing time worrying about the incident, avoiding the offender, and more (Porath and Pearson, 2013).

Of the three minds, the emotional mind is the most powerful driver of your behavior, the choices you make, and the actions you take (Martino et al., 2006). Leaders who fail to cultivate emotional intelligence pay a high price. If it were easy to develop, emotional intelligence would be prevalent throughout most organizations. But it is not easy.

UNDERSTANDING EMOTIONS

To investigate the emotional mind, consider what emotions are and how they affect your inner state and mental models. From a purely biological perspective, you could say emotions are defined by the levels of hormones in your bloodstream, the mix of neurotransmitters in your brain, your heart rate, respiration, and a slew of other biochemical and neurological factors. But emotions also interact deeply with your thought processes and physical sensations. They are, after all, one of the three minds through which the core communication loop runs. Your body, emotions, and intellect are always talking to each other, often unconsciously. Because emotions alter your inner state, they alter your presence with others and thereby alter your effectiveness as a leader.

Emotions are powerful architects of your softwired mental models, changing them rapidly and dynamically as you go about your day. Strong emotions narrow your field of view and focus your attention on whatever triggered them, amplifying that event and diminishing your awareness of other events. This can cause you to selectively ignore important information—especially information that might contradict the legitimacy of your emotion. This can distort the Field of the Self, impairing your decision making and putting relationships at risk. If someone says something that angers you, everything you observe about that person will be filtered through your anger, and your mental model of that person will be distorted. Joseph's frustration and anger distorted his perception of people who brought him disappointing news.

I asked Joseph if he could name the emotions he experienced when his disrespectful behavior was triggered. Specifically, I asked if he could name any emotions other than frustration or anger. He thought for a moment. "That's a really good question. Emotions aren't something I usually pay any attention to. I don't know . . . why is this important?" I explained to him that we often have emotions of which we are not aware. When that happens, the emotions influence us without our noticing. That's what caused him to behave in ways he would later regret. By becoming aware of his emotions, he could have more choice over how they influenced him. I asked him to begin jotting down whatever he noticed about his emotional mind as well as his physical mind.

If you want to change habits, beliefs, and impulses that diminish your leadership presence, centered breathing and awareness of your emotions are the places to start. The next step is centering your emotional mind.

ACCEPTANCE: THE PRACTICE OF
CENTERING THE EMOTIONAL MIND

When you experience strong emotions, your core communication loop will likely run at full speed. With uncomfortable emotions, your analytical mind may strive to dominate your physical and emotional minds. But as your analytical mind replays the events that led to the emotions, your emotional mind will be triggered again by the memories, which can then trigger the physical and analytical minds, and the cycle repeats.

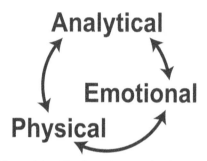

Figure 6.1. The Core Communication Loop

Eventually, this cycle will weaken and fade away, but it can leave a residue of stress, resentment, shame, or sadness that continues to diminish your energy, creativity, and capacity for joy.

Regulating the core communication loop when your emotions are heightened is not easy, but you can learn to do it. People often think they must control emotions, and they equate control with suppression. To maintain a healthy Field of the Self, emotions must be experienced and accepted. Suppressing them creates a toxic state of internal tension that negatively affects your physical and mental health. It also creates a numbness. Numbness inhibits your ability to notice *any* of your emotions and use them effectively, and it inhibits your ability to accurately notice and interpret what other people are saying and doing. When you do not honor your emotional life, you lose your emotional intelligence. Life becomes deadened, and you can begin to feel like a robot, going through the motions with no joy or engagement. Your Field of Self and the presence that emanates from it become stagnant. Leaders who exhibit no joy or engagement will inspire none in others.

I prefer the phrase "managing" to "controlling" emotions. Managing emotions respects the fact that they are real and require attention while also asserting your right to not be controlled by them. Managing them means entering into a partnership with your emotions, calming them when necessary but not ignoring or denying them. Just as centered breathing does not deny the reality of your physical response to circumstances, centering your emotions does not deny their reality or importance.

As you become aware of your emotions, you can begin the centering practice of the emotional mind, which is acceptance. Just as diaphragmatic breathing calms and centers your physical mind, acceptance can calm and center your emotional mind.

Acceptance is a tricky word. You might think it's the same as approval, but it's quite different. Approval is a judgment; acceptance is nonjudgmental. Approval is an inner state that says, "I like what happened. I will support the actions that led to it happening." Acceptance is an inner state that says, "I accept that I cannot change what happened and will not focus my time or energy on resisting that truth." When I speak of acceptance, I am simply saying it is fruitless to burn up time and energy complaining or in some way resisting the truth that someone said or did something you don't like.

Joseph struggled with the notion of acceptance. He told me, "When people don't perform, I just have a hard time accepting that. It's my job to keep them in line and let them know they need to step up." Joseph was interpreting acceptance as approval, or at least acquiescence. Refusing to accept something you cannot change leads to resentment, an inner state in which your core communication loop gets stuck repeating its thoughts and feelings in a vicious cycle, as though harboring those thoughts and feelings will somehow make things better. It's a waste of time and energy. This is a toxic state for anyone, and it is especially toxic for leaders because emotions are contagious. You will, intentionally or not, spread your resentment around, diminishing performance in your peers and those you lead. A distorted, uncentered Field of the Self creates a distorted, uncentered leadership presence.

As Joseph's self-awareness grew, he realized his core communication loop was reinforcing his anger, his belief he should not "suffer fools," and his unwillingness to accept that the things that happened had happened. With practice and coaching, he learned to manage his core communication loop and intentionally center his inner state. He did that with centered breathing, meditation, and developing the habit of asking himself, when he became upset and resentful, "What do I have to accept in this situation so I can move on and become productive?" With these practices, he began to see new possibilities. Acceptance shifts your focus from the past to the present and future. Joseph discovered new choices for how he could respond in emotionally challenging situations. He became curious rather than resentful. He became a coach instead of a boss. And he learned to cultivate emergent as well as intentional leadership.

This was not an overnight fix. Joseph worked for months to develop greater self-awareness. Changing his behavior took longer. It's easy to write about it as though he learned a few things, made a couple of adjustments, and everything was fine. But it didn't go that way. His path was full of bumps and potholes. He wrestled considerably with his emotional reactions to disappointment, and in those first months, he frequently got thrown far off center and resorted to his old behavior. In time and with practice, though, he learned to catch himself, to recenter, and to get back on track faster, eliminating chaos, establishing a powerful leadership presence, and reducing stress for himself and others.

Acceptance is not a concept or an idea. It is an internal shift, an emotional release, and a change of heart. It is a state of being, not a state of thinking. Acceptance centers you emotionally and enables you to experience your emotions and learn from them, rather than allowing your emotions to drive your behavior. With practice, you can use emotion to establish the leadership presence you want.

Clearing distortion out of your Field of the Self—your inner state—can be humbling. The biggest change for Joseph came when he saw that his most important struggles were with himself, not with others. Over time, the quality of his team meetings changed dramatically. Team members no longer avoided bringing problems to Joseph, and they were no longer concerned with having their direct reports in meetings with him. In fact, they began to look for opportunities to do so. And when it occasionally turned out that someone was truly underperforming, Joseph handled it with professionalism, respect, and compassion.

Trying to change your behavior without changing your inner state is difficult. We've all experienced this. When you're angry with someone, listening openly and responding to them with curiosity is difficult at best and often impossible. Listening openly and responding with curiosity doesn't fit with who you are in the moment. But changing your inner state leads naturally to new behaviors. When you are calm and centered, listening openly with curiosity is easy.

Like many leaders with whom I have worked, Joseph initially thought that eliminating emotion and focusing on facts was the way to lead. Focusing on facts and clear thinking are critically important to field leadership. But it is equally important that you manage your emotions effectively, allowing them to reveal what is important without allowing them to drive your core communication loop. The steps to doing that are:

1. Use diaphragm breathing to become physically centered.

2. Reflect on what emotions you are experiencing. As they trigger physical reactions, recenter physically.
3. Ask yourself: What memories, thoughts, or physical sensations keep triggering this emotion?
4. Ask yourself: What do I need to accept to become centered emotionally?

The steps are simple but not easy.

Chapter Seven

Whole Thinking and the Analytical Mind

We should take care not to make the intellect our god: it has, of course, powerful muscles, but no personality. It cannot lead, it can only serve.

—Albert Einstein

I suspect that the great thinkers of the Age of Reason were so drawn to the analytical mind because as Einstein said, it has powerful muscles. Those powerful muscles could restrain the unruly chaos of the body and emotions, enabling mathematicians, scientists, and philosophers to make sense of an otherwise incomprehensible world. As they mastered the intellect, its muscles grew, unleashing the Age of Reason and then the Industrial Revolution, the Information Revolution, and now the Age of Connection. But for leaders, and especially Field Leaders, the analytical mind needs the personality of the physical and emotional minds to know how to wield that power effectively.

The power of the analytical mind comes from several capabilities that dramatically extend those of the physical and emotional minds. I think of them as the power tools of the analytical mind. They are:

- Curiosity—the drive to discover, learn about the world, and understand how it works. Curiosity engages all three minds. We all know the intense physical and emotional engagement that comes with studying and learning something that fascinates us. But the capability to satisfy curiosity lives largely in the analytical mind.
- Doubt—the ability to reflect on and question the validity of your mental models. The analytical mind can do this because, unlike the physical and emotional minds, it can hold conflicting views at the same time. It can consider the view it doubts and compare it to alternatives. This is where

you can override the softwired mental models created by your physical and emotional minds and your past experiences and even question the hardwired mental models programmed into your genes.

- Reason—the powerful capability that Galileo, Descartes, and their successors developed into a fine art: the ability to study mental models, formulate questions, design and conduct experiments, and develop new, intentional mental models, and the ability to imagine a desirable future and develop plans to get there.

These capabilities work closely together, each depending on the other. Curiosity feeds doubt, doubt feeds reason, reason feeds curiosity. And reason enables you to reflect on what you know, examine mental models, consider new ones, and test alternatives. These power tools become even more powerful with the capability to record what we have learned and share our insights and beliefs with others through the communication loops of a hyperconnected world. We can be curious about, doubt, and reason about what other people tell us.

But as neuroscientists have revealed, the analytical mind also has some drawbacks. For one, it is quite slow compared to the physical and emotional minds (Kahneman, 2011). Because the analytical mind is slow, it is useless in crisis situations in which split-second decisions are required. That is the tradeoff it makes for having the time to reflect, study a situation, take in more data, and explore different paths of logic and their potential outcomes.

Contrary to popular belief, the analytical mind does not make decisions on its own. It analyzes, but it does not decide. The actual process of deciding involves complex networks of communication loops that connect many parts of the brain (Bechara, Damasio, and Damasio, 2000). The analytical mind certainly plays a role, but it is far less than is commonly believed. This is hard for some leaders to accept because they like the feeling of control that comes from believing decisions are made with their intellect alone. But the emotional mind plays a significant role. It has to because decisions are made based on what you care about, and caring is fundamentally emotional. The physical mind influences both the analytical and emotional minds through the core communication loop. I explore the decision-making process in greater depth in chapter 9. Without the physical and emotional minds communicating effectively with the analytical mind, the analytical mind is adrift, making poor decisions with little awareness of the outcomes of those decisions (Damasio, 1994). Curiosity, doubt, and reason can only be exercised effectively in the context of the physical and emotional minds. We need all three working in concert.

SELF-REFLECTION

A fourth power tool of the analytical mind is self-reflection. The physical and emotional minds together construct mental models based on their direct experience of the world. They do this quickly and with little or no reflection, accepting their mental models without question. By default, the analytical mind endorses the mental models formed by the physical and emotional minds. But with well-developed self-awareness, the analytical mind can examine these models, doubt their validity, exercise curiosity about them, and form questions and experiments to test their usefulness. This is extraordinarily powerful; it is what led to the enormous explosion in human knowledge and capabilities beginning with the Age of Reason.

In addition to reflecting on mental models, the analytical mind can consciously, intentionally examine the activity of all three minds—including itself—and of the core communication loop that connects them. It can notice when your breathing is shallow or rapid, and it can notice when you are churning emotionally. It can even notice when the mind is filled with spinning, distracting thoughts. By focusing attention on your inner state, your analytical mind can engage your whole self in centering practices. This gives you the power to shift the state of all three minds and manage your core communication loop. This ability for self-reflection integrates all three minds and gives rise to whole thinking. Self-reflection is perhaps the most remarkable feat of which our brains are capable. It breathes life into Field Leadership and the Spectrum of Leadership and gives you the ability to choose where you want to be on the spectrum at any point in time—assuming, of course, you have developed the appropriate centering skills.

Chapter Eight

The Practice of Meditation

While the analytical mind has the capabilities to guide you to whole thinking, it does not do so naturally. Just as it is necessary to center the physical and emotional minds to tap their potential, it is necessary to center the analytical mind to tap its potential. Where diaphragm breathing centers the physical mind and acceptance centers the emotional mind, silence centers the analytical mind. Silencing your analytical mind is difficult—perhaps impossible—to do unless you can also arrive at center in the physical and emotional minds. Silence stops the incessant chatter of thought, enabling you to accurately assess your situation without bias or emotional sway.

Silencing the analytical mind does not mean you give up thinking. It means that when your thinking is ineffective, returning to silence can help you get back on track, back to focusing on what's important and not being distracted by what isn't. One of the most effective practices for doing this is meditation.

Meditation is an ancient practice. Archaeologists believe that people were likely meditating at least seven thousand years ago (Puff, 2013); some believe it goes back much further (Jaffe, 2007). It emerged in all major religions and in cultures around the world (Simonnes, 2014). In modern times, it has developed as a powerful tool for increasing the quality of life and human effectiveness in the secular world. It is in widespread use in businesses of all sizes and types, where it consistently enhances leadership as well as the bottom line. Goldman Sachs, Google, General Mills, Apple, and Medtronic are examples (George, 2014).

Meditation programs are also showing great value in the military. As described in the *New York Times* article "The Latest in Military Strategy: Mindfulness," Major General Walter Piatt was commander of the coalition forces in Iraq in the fight against ISIS. He is a battle-hardened soldier whose job often involved fighting intense battles. But his job also often involved establishing working relationships with tribal leaders who were wary and mistrustful. He began many of his days meditating silently in front of a palm tree. That's how he prepared himself immediately before entering a delicate diplomatic meeting with a local tribal leader in Iraq. Before the session, he said, he meditated in front of a palm tree and found himself extremely focused when the conversation began. In the *New York Times* article, he described the meeting this way.

> "I was not taking notes. I remembered every word she was saying. I wasn't forming a response, just listening," he said. When the tribal leader finished, he said, "I talked back to her about every single point, had to concede on some. I remember the expression on her face: This is someone we can work with."
>
> In the end, he said, mindfulness allowed him to "reduce conflict by better understanding."
>
> "I'm not saying, be soft," he added. "I'm saying, understand how compassion and empathy can be used for real advantages. Peace takes a lot of hard work." (Richtel, 2019)

Major General Piatt didn't use intentional leadership with the tribal leader. Rather, he created the context for emergent leadership. He prepared himself using the disciplines of the Field of the Self to engage in emergent leadership in the Interpersonal Field. What emerged was a conversational dance between them, one that could not have been planned or predicted but brought them to the best result possible.

An article in *Harvard Business Review* (Seppälä, 2015) reported numerous benefits of meditation for leaders, including:

- Greater resilience
- Improved ability to reduce anxiety and manage stress
- Increased emotional intelligence
- Enhanced creativity
- Stronger relationship skills

Neuroscience tells us why. Researchers around the world have been using advanced brain imaging technology to observe what happens in your brain when you meditate. Meditation enables neural capabilities that are essential for Field Leadership. In "The Mind of the Leader" (Ricard, Lutz, and Davidson, 2014), these include:

- Increased activity in areas of the brain associated with the ability to remain mentally present and clearheaded in the midst of uncomfortable, even painful, situations.

- Increased activity in regions of the brain associated with the ability to maintain focus in the presence of distractions and to return to focus quickly when you become distracted.
- Diminished responsiveness to stimuli in regions of the brain that give rise to anxiety and depression.

Advanced meditators are able to engage all of these effects at will. This is where the masters of spirit and of science are finding common ground, exploring together the power of the human mind and showing us how to tap its potential. As the body of research grows, the power of meditation becomes increasingly grounded in scientific data. There are good reasons it's showing positive results on the bottom line.

Many practices fall under the umbrella of meditation. Every religion has its own version, others have emerged in psychology, and the proliferation of teachers and practitioners continues, giving rise to new variations. The longest running and most evolved practices are those found in Buddhism, in which meditation has been practiced and studied intensely for 2,500 years. Because Buddhist practices have spread around the world, constantly adapting to new cultures, the practices have been distilled to the point that they can be applied in any context. They are the basis for most of the meditation practices in vogue today. Because Buddhism is a nontheistic religion (that is, it does not claim a relationship to a god; the Buddha explicitly stated he was no more than a human being), anyone can study its teachings and learn its practices without changing their religious beliefs.

The most common meditation practices fall into three categories: focused attention, compassion, and mindfulness (Ricard, Lutz, and Davidson, 2014). While with practice each of these will center all three minds, they also correspond to the centering practices I describe for the three minds. Focused attention typically focuses your attention on your breath, and as you have seen, regulating your breath is the way you center in the physical mind. Compassion meditation is aimed at cultivating a sense of compassion for those with whom you interact. Compassion is closely related to acceptance—the center of the emotional mind. And mindfulness meditation, which is also referred to as open-monitoring meditation, correlates to silence in the analytical mind.

HOW TO MEDITATE

The most common practice introduced in leadership and corporate settings is often referred to as mindfulness meditation, but it is really a combination of focused attention and mindfulness. It is a simple practice. As with any new practice, you have to stay with it for a while before it becomes a habit and before you see its benefits. Here's an approach to getting started:

- Find a quiet place to sit where you won't be disturbed. It can be anywhere that is convenient. One leader I coached chose to do it every morning in the office parking garage. She was away from the hustle and bustle of home and hadn't yet entered the hustle and bustle of the office. Others find a quiet place at home or reserve a conference room at work.
- Use a timer. A couple of problems arise without a timer. You may be distracted checking the clock to see how long you have been meditating, and you may be more likely to give up when it gets difficult even if the time is not up. A timer helps you give yourself fully to the practice.
- Set the timer for however long you intend to meditate. Ten minutes is a good starting point. If ten minutes is too long for you, try five. As your practice deepens, you can choose to extend this. Some people also decide to meditate twice during the day, often once in the morning and once later in the day.
- You can sit in a chair or on a cushion on the floor. If you are on a chair, adjust the height so your thighs are parallel with the floor; this alleviates stress that could otherwise develop in your legs. Your back should be straight and your body relaxed. If you are in a chair and need back support, you can place a cushion between your back and the back of the chair.
- Rest your hands on your thighs or on your lap.
- Start your timer. Many people prefer to close their eyes; you can choose to keep them open if you like. Now bring your attention to your breath and practice diaphragm breathing. Your attention should not be intense and laser focused. Rather, just let it rest lightly on your breath. Some people find it useful to count their breaths, starting over when they get to ten.
- Your mind will inevitably wander. When it does, just accept that it wandered and bring your awareness back to your breath. Some people find it useful to label that experience by saying "thinking" to themselves as they come back to their breath. If emotions come up, don't resist them and don't engage them. Just accept them. If it's helpful, you can label that "feeling." If your breathing changes by getting shallow or rapid, accept that and return to diaphragm breathing.
- When your timer goes off, take another moment to settle. Reflect on how each of your minds reacted to the timer going off. Then get up, take a stretch, and get back to your day.

Real mastery comes when you can be fully present and centered in all three minds at the same time. Just as the physical and emotional minds can be quite unruly if left to their own devices, the analytical mind can fill with chatter, race from one thought to the next, and spin unproductively. It becomes centered when it becomes silent. This can be achieved through meditation.

As you monitor the state of the three minds, you will become aware that a thought triggers physical and emotional responses, an emotion triggers thoughts and physical responses, and a physical sensation triggers thoughts and emotions. As you develop greater self-awareness, you will be able to observe these interactions in real time and use centering practices to manage them. Regulating your breathing and becoming attuned to your physical presence will enable you to emotionally accept the current situation and quiet your mind. Acceptance will help settle your body and your thoughts. And silence in your thoughts will make acceptance and physical centering easier. Meditation trains you to regulate the core communication loop and bring all three minds into harmony.

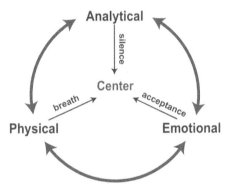

Figure 8.1. Centering in the Three Minds

As your meditation practice develops, situations that would normally throw you off center will be less likely to do so, and when they do, you will come back faster. You will maintain greater clarity of thought in the midst of turmoil, you will sense and focus on what's important in any given situation, you will sense what is happening to others in the moment, and you will see the most effective ways to respond to them. You will make the best choices available to you. This is what mastery of Field Leadership looks like.

Joseph experienced this with Margaret. When I began working with him, he found himself perpetually frustrated with her. His frustration would cause him to tense up and lash out. In response, she would resort to silence and resentment. As I coached Joseph, I encouraged him to practice a meditation in which he revisited one of these situations in his thoughts. As he experienced the frustration and anger, he learned to stay present with his feelings. He found this quite difficult and resisted the practice when I first suggested it, insisting the result would be that he would get angrier and angrier. He was sure it would be worse than a waste of time: it would drive him to more of the behaviors he was trying to avoid. But he agreed to give it a go.

It took time and hard work, but one day, he came in to our session in a state of calm I hadn't observed in him before. He said he'd been doing the meditation practice the previous morning, visualizing a conversation with Margaret that had been particularly frustrating for him, and in his visualization, he'd become quite agitated. But for the first time, he was able to observe the frustration rather than just engage in it. He described it as almost an out-of-body experience in which he felt both very frustrated and very calm at the same time, as though he'd split into two people: one his old self, the other a new observer of himself. And then, suddenly, he fully accepted Margaret for who she was. The frustration dissolved, and he had a sense of deep compassion for Margaret. He realized that an alternative to resisting her behavior was to truly accept it, trust that she was doing the best she could, and join her in trying to find a way for her to work more productively. He'd met with her shortly before our session, and for the first time, he felt he was able to genuinely understand her predicament. And, he believed, she sensed that for the first time he was on her side. His mental model of her and of their relationship had changed, and they both knew it.

Joseph and Margaret continued that conversation over the next few weeks. They decided the best solution was for Margaret to find a position elsewhere in the company that could leverage her strengths and provide work she found exciting. Joseph was a strong advocate for her, using his connections with HR and other leaders to find the best place for her.

The practice of meditation is simple, though some find it challenging to quiet their minds, center their breathing, and accept their situation. It takes time and practice. As much as you may want to center, what you get at first is more likely to be distraction. Letting go of the distraction can seem like an insurmountable task. One impulse is to think your way through it, but that is fruitless—it keeps you stuck in the analytical mind. Intellectual thought takes you off center, collapsing your awareness and keeping you in the communication loop of rumination. You may find yourself struggling strenuously, and seemingly fruitlessly, to stop. But the struggle is not fruitless, only long. Eventually, perhaps from exhaustion, perhaps from discovery, insight comes. Abruptly, the distance between intellectual thought and whole thinking collapses. Gradually you learn to move between the two with less effort. The struggle diminishes as intellectual thought releases its intense grasp and you no longer cling to "knowing" in the analytical sense. In its place you have a kind of pure seeing and being. This is the essential source of a leadership presence.

This is an emotional shift, an acceptance, a letting go. You no longer seek to be "right," you simply seek to see what is. This reveals a new kind of knowing that comes from whole thinking, one that sees and embraces the vital dynamic nature of life and works effortlessly with its energy. From this place, you accurately perceive the state of other people; you regulate your own responses to effectively influence (not control) them, and you accept them for who they are. You allow yourself to be influenced by others, but wisely—influenced toward greater insight and synergy. And in this dance of mutual influence, you grow in wisdom and become something greater, richer, and more effective than you were when you began. This is Field Leadership in its truest form.

ENCOUNTERING YOURSELF

The greatest challenge any of us faces is encountering ourselves. For many people, sitting still is one of the most difficult things they ever try to do. Just sitting still, breathing gently, and being present to their own selves can be challenging, even painful. I see leaders particularly struggle with this because their world is so focused on action and outward results. They've lost the connection between inner awareness and outward results.

Developing the Field of the Self requires clarity and centering in all three minds. You must throw out any ideas of mind over matter, of making decisions based only on data, of ignoring your emotional and physical minds—you must engage in whole thinking. The following questions are typical of what you might ask when engaging in whole thinking:

- What am I feeling physically and emotionally? What is it in me that gives rise to those feelings?
- What am I thinking? What is it in me that gives rise to those thoughts?
- How do my feelings and thoughts interact?
- How much of my inner experience accurately reflects the world, and how much of it is distortion from my personal biases, concerns, and emotions?
- Am I centered in all three minds? If not, what do I need to do to get centered?

As you develop your ability to center in the Field of the Self and engage in whole thinking, you will establish a presence of integrity, authenticity, and honesty. For an organization to thrive in a hyperconnected world, these must be the ground of its leadership and its culture.

Chapter Nine

The Discipline of Choice

Making effective decisions in an uncertain, complex, hyperconnected world is one of the most challenging responsibilities of leadership. It is the second discipline in the Field of the Self. We have long lived with a belief that decision making is primarily a logical process, but leadership and organizational science, psychology, and neuroscience are proving that to be false. Choice requires whole thinking—all three minds centered and working in concert.

How do human beings make decisions? Everything we have explored in awareness up to now lays the foundation for the answer. Awareness enables you to become intentional about your inner state and your mental models. It prepares you to act. Choice is the discipline of taking action; it is where all the elements of awareness come alive as you make decisions. Your physical, emotional, and analytical minds are all deeply involved in choice, even if you are not aware of their activity (Lacasse, 2017). But you can only make intentional choices about things of which you are aware. If you are not aware of your own moods and beliefs—for example, you are angry or believe someone has a hidden agenda—then you will have no choice about how your anger or mistrust affects your behavior. Likewise, if you are not aware of another person's moods and beliefs, you cannot interpret their behavior accurately and make wise choices about how to interact with them.

As you have seen, the physical and emotional minds make many decisions on their own, and they make them fast. They rapidly generate interpretations like "safe" or "dangerous," "like" or "dislike," and those feelings generate high-speed decisions. Recall the near car accident I discussed in chapter 3. This is great in life-or-death situations in which fractions of a second can make the difference. But it's not so great in a world that doesn't conform well to our ancient, hardwired mental models. In certain kinds of problems, the physical and emotional minds notoriously fall down—in spite of their power to convince you of their rectitude.

The Monty Hall problem is a famous example. And it's one at which you will fail miserably without serious engagement of your analytical mind to come up with the right answer.

Monty Hall was the coproducer and original host of the TV game show *Let's Make A Deal*. Hall would select someone from the audience to play the game. As the player, you would be shown three doors and told that behind one door was a high-value prize—say a new car—and behind each of the other two doors was a dud—say a goat. You would be asked to choose a door. Let's say you chose door number one. Instead of revealing to you what was behind door one, Hall would open one of the other doors, say door number two, revealing a goat. So now you knew one of the doors you didn't pick—door two—had a goat behind it. Next, Hall would give you the opportunity to switch doors: you could either keep whatever was behind door one, which you had already chosen, or you could switch to door three, which was still closed.

How will you make this decision? Members of the audience may be screaming which door to pick, perhaps you believe three is your lucky number, or your intuition tells you that it makes no difference which door you choose. All of that is driven by your physical and emotional minds, and it's all useless. It turns out your analytical mind can answer this question. But it must apply real rigor to its thinking. On first blush, it would be easy to reason that there are two doors, so it makes no difference—each has a 50/50 chance of being the right door. In fact, two times out of three, you will win if you switch doors. There is a rigorous mathematical explanation for why this is true, and it is born out in experiments and computer simulations, though the analysis is difficult. The contestant who can do the analysis will always make the best choice.

In the Age of Reason, thinkers like Descartes believed you could make decisions with just the analytical mind. I sometimes hear the echo of Descartes when leaders say, "Just give me the facts, then I'll decide." Facts are important. They enable you to establish the material state of your world; they provide you with data for analysis and reasoning, and they provide a common foundation with others on which to explore perspectives. But facts alone are never enough to arrive at a decision because the meaning and value of data are heavily influenced by your emotions. Without meaning and value, there is no basis for decisions. Even after fully understanding the Monty Hall problem, your choice is based on what you desire. If you desire the car, you should switch. If you desire the goat, you should not switch. It takes whole thinking to make the best choice.

Neuroscientist Antonio Damasio is one of the world's leading researchers in the area of emotions, reasoning, and decision making. He studied individuals whose emotional centers had been severed from the analytical centers of their brains due to illness or injury. He found that they became unable to make effective decisions. They were able to reason perfectly well; they could analyze complex situations and come up with appropriate predictions of the outcomes of different choices. But when they had to actually choose, they were at a loss. Though they appeared as thoughtful and intelligent as before their brain injury, after their injury their lives fell apart. They could not stay focused on tasks, made bad investments and lost all their money, and were susceptible to failed relationships. They could not engage in whole thinking.

Whole thinking leverages all three minds to come to intentional, conscious decisions, using each mind to balance the others. That doesn't mean that with whole thinking you'll always be right, but it does mean you have given it your best shot, and you'll be well positioned to learn from the outcome. Without accessing all three minds, your ability to choose effectively is severely limited (Kahneman, 2011) because you will be missing valuable information. Your mental model is deficient.

As Damasio's work shows us, the physical and emotional minds are essential for effective decision making because they imbue data with meaning and value. But they are unable to analyze data, consider different perspectives, or question their own mental models (Slovic et al. 2004)—all essential capabilities of the analytical mind for complex decision making. As the Monty Hall problem shows us, in a complex world, the analytical mind is equally important. Complex decision making requires heightened awareness of your inner state so you can manage the interplay of the three minds. With sufficient awareness, you can tap the meaning and value that your physical and emotional minds ascribe to events while avoiding the distortions they can create through their rapid primitive interpretations. And you can allow sufficient time for the ponderous analytical mind to do its work and converse with the physical and emotional minds.

Let's take a look at how the three minds work together. An event occurs—say the near car accident I described in section 1 in which another driver ran a stop sign and shot across your path. Your physical mind responds far faster than you can possibly be aware, as shown in figure 9.1.

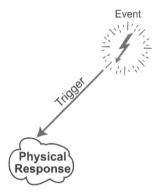

Figure 9.1. The Physical Mind Responds First and Fast

Almost instantaneously, your core communication loop kicks in and starts a conversation between your physical and emotional minds, as shown in figure 9.2.

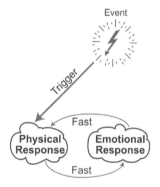

Figure 9.2. The Physical-Emotional Communication Loop Is Fast

Your emotions heighten your physical response, which in turn drives your emotions into higher gear, which further heightens your physical response. By now you've already begun to move—muscles throughout your body have tightened, your breath is shallow and rapid, your foot is moving toward the brake, you are turning the steering wheel. The car passes in front of you, the accident is averted, and finally your analytical mind joins the conversation, providing logical analysis to determine what to do next, as shown in figure 9.3.

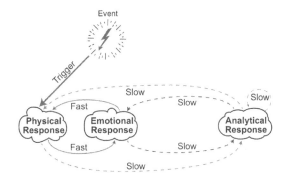

Figure 9.3. Communication Loops with the Analytical Mind Are Slow

In dangerous situations in which extremely fast responses are necessary, this works well. But the vast majority of decisions you make don't require that speed. When talking with another person your physical and emotional responses may trigger you to say something you'll later regret. A more thoughtful response, mediated by your analytical mind, may be far more effective. But that requires overcoming the fast, emotionally compelling loops and making room for the slow, analytical loops. That cannot be done with willpower alone. The physical and emotional minds are stubborn and will not yield to the lumbering logic of your analytical mind. They will, however, yield to centering practices, which open them up to a more effective dialogue with the analytical mind. And with sufficient practice at centering, the physical and emotional minds will stay centered and respond more effectively, even in the midst of life-or-death events. That is why so many martial arts include meditation as a fundamental practice. This is hard, soul-searching work. As I have said, leadership in a hyperconnected world is not for the faint of heart.

A METHOD FOR DECISION MAKING

David, the CEO of a global professional services firm, was on a video conference with Alice, the head of his European operations. David had invested considerable time and energy over the previous year developing his ability to engage in whole thinking and instilling in his leadership team an appreciation of its importance. David was considering acquiring a firm in Germany that offered services complementary to his firm. He'd asked me to sit in on the video conference.

His question to Alice was, "How do you feel about that?" After a brief pause, she went into a monologue that lasted about ten minutes, in which she shared her thoughts on aspects of the new approach and its strategic implications. She shared data related to the German firm, its services, and its customer base. And she shared her analysis of how they might intersect with their own services and customers. It was articulate but dry, and in the end, it wasn't clear where she stood. David restated his question: "That was helpful. And what I'd like to know now is how you feel about it, not what you think about it."

This elicited a much longer pause on Alice's part. After reflecting, she said, "You know, it makes me anxious. While we have some data, there's considerable uncertainty in it. I worry it will disrupt some exciting projects we have going, and it could have a negative impact on our European employees who are engaged in those projects. And because it represents a shift in how we are seen in the marketplace, I have some fear that our customers and investors may become confused about where we're going. I guess I'm really not excited about it."

David replied, "Alice, thank you, I appreciate your honesty. And I learned more in the last few minutes than I did in the previous ten. We'll keep talking; we may not move this forward."

It's not that there were no analytical thoughts in Alice's second response, but they were framed in an honest expression of her emotional state, and that framing brought out significant aspects of her response that were not accessible when she responded primarily with her analytical mind.

Before reaching a decision, David had further conversations with Alice and other members of his team. Alice became clearer about her thinking. As she centered emotionally, she realized her reservations were real and supported by the data she had analyzed as well as her sense of how her team and the firm's customers and investors would experience the acquisition. As David listened to Alice and others and reflected on his attraction to the acquisition, he realized he had an emotional desire to do something big and exciting. But the timing wasn't right, and the pleasure of excitement is not a sufficient foundation for making substantial business decisions. As he accepted this, he felt an emotional release, felt very centered, and was able to get back to the business of running the company.

FIELD JOURNAL: A STEP-BY-STEP APPROACH

Decision making isn't a process; it's a conversation among your three minds that takes place through your core communication loop. It also often involves communication loops that arise in the Interpersonal Field as you explore possibilities with others, as it did for David in his conversations with Alice and other members of his leadership team.

What follows is one approach that can guide you in making decisions. It is not a rigid process but rather a series of reflections for engaging in your inner conversation, engaging others in conversations, and thinking about what you learn. Which reflections you choose to engage in and the sequence in which you do so are up to you. You may loop back and forth between two or three of them or you may find just one of them is useful in your particular circumstance. Use them creatively as a set of discovery tools.

Your response to each reflection will influence your responses to the other reflections. You don't complete one step fully and move on to the next. Rather, you start reflecting on one activity, take notes, then reflect on another, then loop back or move on in whatever order makes sense to you.

Engaging in this internal conversation starts with centering. So as you go through the following reflections, stay tuned to your inner state, and when you go off center, use the three practices of breath, acceptance, and silence.

Preparation: To begin, identify the decision you are facing. Articulate the question. For David, the question was whether to acquire the German firm.

Organize your data. Consider what additional data you need to make an effective decision. David needed to know what his leadership team members thought and how they felt about the idea. And he needed more data about the German firm, the market implications, and the potential impact on his firm's culture.

Center yourself. Notice what is happening in your inner state. Use diaphragm breathing; accept whatever you must to calm any emotional turmoil; and meditate. The value of centering is that it gives you access to curiosity, doubt, and clear-headed reasoning, the power tools of the analytical mind. The opposite of being centered—physical tension, emotional turmoil, and spinning thoughts—all suppress those capabilities.

Reflections: When you are centered, pick up your Field Journal and engage in the following reflections. Depending on your circumstances, some of these may be more or less relevant to the decision you are contemplating. Use your Field Journal to record your thoughts and feelings as you engage in these reflections.

Reflection 1: What is the decision? Briefly describe relevant elements of the current situation and the decision you must make. Notice what happens to your inner state as you engage in this exercise. If you find yourself getting pulled off center—breathing gets short or rapid, emotions come up that distract you, thoughts start to spin—bring yourself back to center. As David did this practice, he became increasingly aware of his attraction to the excitement of the acquisition and saw how that was distorting his ability to question its wisdom.

Reflection 2: Ask yourself what you deeply care about and define the broader purpose within which this decision fits. If you cannot connect a major decision with deeply held values, then you will find yourself adrift with no way of navigating all the possibilities. David deeply cared about the long-term health of the firm and the well-being of its employees and customers. He saw the market was shifting, and it was not clear that the German firm's services would fit with where the market was going. He also saw the importance of maintaining the firm's culture and not overwhelming the staff who were already engaged in intense projects. Again, notice what happens in each of your three minds as you explore the larger purpose. If you are pulled off center, use your centering practices to return.

Reflection 3: Define the outcomes you want to create with this specific decision. A way of asking this question is the phrase "for the sake of what" would I do this? For David, this included the possibility of strengthening the company's foothold in Europe, having an expanded customer base, and expanding the firm's service offerings. As in reflection 2, he realized his desire for something big and exciting was distorting his ability to assess the importance of those outcomes and the likelihood this acquisition would actually produce them.

Reflection 4: Look at the data and use your analytical skills to draw conclusions. If the data is complex, run spreadsheets and statistical analyses. Jot down your thoughts and check them out with others.

Reflection 5: Engage others who might provide useful insights, reflections, and data.

Reflection 6: Consider how this decision will enhance the lives of those you serve. This includes customers, employees, communities in which you do business, partners, and others.

At some point, having gathered all of this information and done all of this reflection, you must decide. This involves all three minds of your inner state, and it is sometimes quite challenging. In the end, you have to *feel* right about whatever decision you make. Emotional centering is essential here. Once you have decided, you must make peace with that decision and move forward. Second guessing and regrets will not serve you.

FIELD JOURNAL: YOU ALWAYS HAVE CHOICES

When I conduct workshops on mastering the Field of the Self, I often hear people say something like, "I have to take my daughter to soccer tonight" in a tone of voice that reveals resentment and a sense of lost opportunity for the other things they could be doing. As they develop greater awareness, they recognize they do, in fact, have choices. This leads to two important realizations. First, believing you don't have a choice puts you at risk of resentment or hopelessness, which leads to internal stress, loss of joy, and underperformance. Second, this mood strains your relationship with those around you. If the best choice you can make is to do something other than take your daughter to soccer, then you can handle it in a way that mitigates damaging your relationship. On the other hand, if you fully choose to take your daughter to her soccer game, you can enjoy your time with your daughter and be fully present.

In every circumstance of life, you have choices. They may not be the choices you want, but they are choices nonetheless. Even people living under the most oppressive circumstances in prisons and concentration camps have choices. People lying on their deathbeds have choices. You can choose the attitude you have toward your death, and you can choose how you behave as your death approaches. This realization is both empowering and humbling if you have the courage to embrace it. It is humbling because you must accept that you don't have full control over your life. It is empowering because it awakens your sense of agency. No matter your circumstances, you have the power to choose and to influence how your life unfolds.

Try this simple exercise in your Field Journal:

1. Think of a circumstance in your life when you often say, "I have to . . ." (Fill in the blank with whatever it is you believe you have to do.)
2. Repeat to yourself a few times, "I have to __."
3. Make a note about how that statement affects your inner state; note the reaction you have in each of your three minds.
4. Ask yourself, "What choices do I have?" List them in your journal. Don't edit as you go—put down every choice you can think of, even if it is impractical or something you know you wouldn't do. The parent whose daughter needs a ride to a soccer game might include the following:
   • Take her to the soccer game and stay for the game
   • Drop her off and get on with other things, then pick her up at the end
   • Ask someone else to drive her
   • Arrange for a cab or ride-sharing service to take her to the game
   • Ask her to find a friend she can ride with
   • Tell her she will have to miss the game
   • Get her to the game late

When you have your list, go through the choices one by one and reflect on how each would feel. You might eliminate some quickly, but give yourself the freedom to acknowledge that each of them is a choice. When you eliminate one, say to yourself, "I will not do this." This is a way of exercising your power to direct your life. Make a note of how this affects your inner state—your physical mind, emotional mind, and analytical mind.

Consider the consequences for you and anyone else involved in each choice that you can't easily eliminate. Pay attention to all three minds as you think about each choice. Note what you observe in yourself.

When you have settled on what you will do, say to yourself, "I choose to . . ." Notice how different it feels to say "I choose to __" rather than "I have to __." It can be an interesting experiment to try a few times both ways—"I have to" versus "I choose to." Make a note in your field journal of what you observe in yourself in each of the three minds.

There are, of course, circumstances over which you have no control. You have no choice about whether or not it is raining outside or the choices others might make. But even in those circumstances, you do have choices about how you will feel and behave given those circumstances. Awareness of your emotional reaction to events, and the ability to center emotionally by accepting what you cannot change, enables you to see clearly the choices you do have. It is freeing to move from "I have to" to "I choose to," but only if you truly accept that you are choosing freely.

Aisha, a manager I coached, frequently found herself disagreeing with Paul, another manager. These disagreements invariably ended in conflict. Aisha and Paul were stuck in a habituated communication loop that always produced the same result. Aisha saw only two possibilities for these conversations: remain mostly silent and resentful and don't tell Paul what she thinks, or tell Paul what she thinks, which always leads to conflict. Aisha sincerely wanted this dynamic to change, but she could not see that there were other options. When I pointed out to her that her range of options was pretty narrow, she asked me what other options there were. Rather than answer her question, I taught her the meditation practice described in chapter 8. She began meditating for ten minutes a day, seven days a week. Another centering practice I taught her was to pause briefly before she spoke, giving her time to center and become aware of her inner state before speaking. The pauses were usually brief enough that they did not create a gap in the flow of her conversations but made her aware of what she was about to say and enabled her to make a choice before speaking. The meditation practice enhanced Aisha's awareness of her inner state; the pause practice enabled her to make use of this awareness when she was in conversations.

These practices paid off quickly in Aisha's relationship with Paul. Her first step was accepting that Paul would be pushy and would insist that his view was the only right view. Accepting this, she was able to center herself emotionally. When she was stuck in silence and resentment, her emotional state shut down her analytical mind. But as she centered emotionally, a new choice appeared: to engage her analytical mind in curiosity. She began asking Paul questions to better understand his perspective and concerns. She left these conversations with insight. With that shift, their relationship changed from mistrust and adversity to gradually growing trust and respect.

The most powerful choice Aisha discovered was to talk to Paul about the tension in their relationship. By the time she discovered this choice, the tension had already begun to dissipate, but this conversation catapulted their relationship to another level. Because they were able to talk honestly about how they had both contributed to the breakdowns in their conversations, the trust between them grew exponentially. They continued to find themselves periodically in conflict about something on which they needed to work together, but they recognized the brewing conflict early and could acknowledge it, nipping it in the bud rather than allowing it to grow.

As you have seen, logic and data are insufficient for navigating complexity, and a hyperconnected world makes everything more complex and less predictable than it was in the past. So the question looms: how is a leader in a hyperconnected world to make decisions?

The answer is to think like a scientist *and* a mystic. As a scientist, develop your analytical skill and challenge yourself with questions that require rigorous analytical thinking. Walter Frick, a senior editor at Harvard Business Review, advises leaders to learn basic probability to sharpen their decision-making skills (Frick, 2018). As a mystic, develop your intuitive skill through centering practices like meditation.

The first step is developing emotional fortitude through acceptance, the centering practice of the emotional mind. Accepting that you cannot ever have complete information, and logic alone is insufficient for overcoming complexity, opens your mind to new possibilities. It frees you from the anxiety and paralysis that can come when you feel you have to "get it right." In anything but the simplest cases, you will never have that certainty, so stop worrying about it. If you are anxious and fearful that you might make the wrong decision, you will have a far more difficult time accurately perceiving your choices and making a good one. Daniel Kahneman, Nobel prize–winning psychologist and author of *Thinking, Fast and Slow*, says that if he had a magic wand, the first thing he would eliminate is overconfidence. In other words, instead of striving for certainty, accept uncertainty and go forward with humility and courage.

Seeing, acknowledging, and making the best choices is not always easy— in fact, at times it can be gut wrenching. You may have deep-seated beliefs and emotional reactions that reject some choices before you even consider them. Your friends, family, and community may exert pressure on you to conform to their beliefs and emotions. And in organizations, the cultural norms and power structure may work against you. Accurately seeing the available choices and making the right choices often require courage, wisdom, and fortitude. These emerge from the centering practices introduced in the discipline of awareness. The discipline of choice relies as much on your spiritual self as on your intellect.

Chapter Ten

The Discipline of Accountability

The problem with juggling is that the balls go exactly where you throw them.

—Ron Graham, professor of mathematics at UC San Diego, former
president of the International Jugglers Association, and sometime
performer with Cirque du Soleil (Cole, 1999)

For the past two decades, the Gallup organization has followed employee engagement in the United States and around the world. They have consistently found that only 32 percent of employees in the United States describe themselves as "engaged" in their work lives. Worldwide, only 13 percent do (Mann and Harter, 2016). Organizations everywhere are finding their employees do not find meaning in their work and do not have a high level of concern about the quality of their work. Lack of engagement translates into high employee turnover, suboptimal productivity, missed opportunities for innovation, and more (Bersin, 2014). Employee engagement, on the other hand, creates positive business results (Sorenson, 2013).

In a world with such low employee engagement, it is no surprise that in my work with leaders and organizational culture, the word "accountability" comes up all the time. I am told that people are not accountable and people must be "held accountable." Organizations say they want "cultures of accountability." But few define accountability or say how they will know when they achieve it.

Accountability and engagement are close cousins; accountability is the manifestation of engagement. If an employee is engaged, they find meaning and purpose in their work, care about the quality of their work, and will be accountable for the results they produce.

While it is common today to use the terms *responsibility* and *accountability* interchangeably, I draw an important distinction between them. Responsibility is easy to define. Being responsible means carrying out the tasks explicitly defined in your job description, because of promises you made, or because of social expectations. In a sense, it means being true to your word and conducting yourself with integrity. But responsibility goes no further than that. You can be responsible in your job while not caring about anything beyond meeting the requirements for a paycheck.

Accountability is harder to define because it is not so much a concept as an inner state, one that involves caring about something and being committed to having a positive impact regardless of whether you are responsible for an outcome. Accountability is an orientation to your life, your choices, and the results of those choices. Being accountable means being consciously connected to what you care about and choosing to look honestly at the effects of your words and actions on furthering those things. When understood this way, accountability is a choice you make.

What you care about may go far beyond what is expected of you in your job description or the roles you play in various aspects of your life. For example, with the exception of the CEO, no one in an organization is responsible for the overall health and well-being of the organization. But anyone in the organization can take accountability for contributing to its overall health. When they do, the choices they make every day will be made in the context of their effect on the whole organization.

As a simple example, I often go for walks in a park near my house. Because it is against the law to litter, it is my responsibility to throw any trash I might have into trash bins. But it is not my responsibility to pick up other people's trash. However, as someone who cares about the quality of life in my community and about the well-being of our parks and green spaces, when I see trash on the walking path, I pick it up and put it in a trash bin. It would be easy to walk on by, perhaps thinking to myself, "They need to get someone to clean this area up more often," or, "What a jerk someone was for trashing the park." But as a person who chooses to take some accountability for the well-being of the park, I stop and take care of the problem. If it becomes a recurring problem, I may go a step further and contact the park board to discuss how they might address the problem. Thus, it is possible to be accountable for things for which you are not responsible, and you can be responsible without being accountable.

Accountable employees are always looking out for the greater good and are emotionally connected to the mission of their organization. They are willing to sacrifice personally if it serves that mission. They don't engage in blame or finger pointing. Finger pointing is an avoidance tactic; it moves the focus from you to someone or something else. That's the opposite of accountability. Accountability brings the focus to you and to the issue at hand. Choosing accountability means taking a stand for something.

The disciplines of awareness and choice are the necessary prerequisites, the foundation, for accountability. Without awareness and a broad view of possible choices, accountability cannot emerge. For Aisha, awareness broadened her perspective from defending her turf to the larger issue of how she could have a productive relationship with Paul. As she turned her focus inward, she saw how her emotional state affected her interpretation of Paul's behavior. That helped her to see how she contributed to the pattern of fruitless arguments and revealed choices other than silence and defensiveness. With these new insights, she chose to take a stand for forming a productive relationship with Paul and to become curious instead of defensive when he said something that troubled her. This was a highly accountable choice because it focused on changing herself rather than blaming Paul for the problem.

Whenever you change one element of a communication loop, the entire loop changes. The communication loop that kept recurring between Aisha and Paul was one of a power struggle and defensiveness. When Aisha responded to Paul with genuine curiosity instead of defensiveness, she changed the loop. In that new loop, his historical pattern of aggression and loudly repeating what he had already said no longer made sense. He became more thoughtful and respectful. Aisha's accountability led to a new and more productive communication loop.

This may sound easy. It often isn't. Systems driven by communication loops tend to maintain stability, so inertia always resists change in established systems. No matter how committed you are to changing a pattern, habituated communication loops may kick in to maintain the status quo. That is why accountability is so often raised as a desirable state in organizations and yet is so rarely achieved. It requires persistence to stay the new course long enough for new results to manifest and for new communication loops to become the norm. Aisha had to first overcome her internal communication loops that raised her emotional resistance to Paul's behavior. Then she had to overcome her behavioral patterns of responding to Paul with defensiveness. For Aisha and Paul, there were plenty of speed bumps along the way, but with persistence and coaching, they were able to shift to a new and more productive pattern.

This notion of accountability is powerful because it connects you to what you care about and gives you the sense of power that comes with knowing you are making choices freely. People who are connected to what they care about and choose their actions freely are wholeheartedly engaged and therefore far more effective than people who are just punching a time clock for a paycheck.

I have worked with many organizations in which blame and finger pointing were the norm and accountability was absent from the culture. This sometimes shows up as an attitude of "everyone for themselves." These toxic behaviors are common in underperforming organizations. In fact, one of the reasons I am asked to work with organizations is because they have struggled and failed to make the transition from blame to engagement and accountability.

Consider the communication loops that occur in organizations in which people avoid accountability. You see something outside your area of responsibility that is not going well. That stimulates your core communication loop to cause you to look away and pretend you didn't see it or, worse yet, to gossip with others about someone who's not doing their job. Pretending you didn't see something may influence others to also pretend not to see. Engaging in gossip can reinforce communication loops that spread the gossip further. In such an environment, people will feel unsafe, trust will be low, and accountability is nearly impossible.

Compare this to the communication loops in organizations in which people consistently choose to be accountable. You see something outside your area of responsibility that is not going well. You practice awareness, noticing your response to the situation and the interpretations you form about it. You may be angry, defensive, or worried. You notice how your emotions and your beliefs affect the choices you perceive, and you practice centering, letting your emotions settle down so you can see a broader set of choices. Then you act: you make a choice, either addressing the issue yourself or bringing it to someone else's attention. In organizations with a culture of accountability, others respond to your action, considering ways they can help. Perhaps you need support in raising awareness of the issue. If others don't understand your concern, they ask questions to clarify; perhaps they step in to take care of the issue themselves. In all of these cases, the scope of everyone's concern is bigger than their own area of responsibility and their own identity. The scope of their concern is the overall mission around which everyone is aligned. These are the behaviors of Field Leaders and of those who follow them.

Accountability, when seen as an inner state, challenges you to take risks. It is easy to just think, "That's not my problem." It is much harder to risk taking an action. "That's a problem, and because I care about the success of the enterprise, I am willing to speak up." All kinds of uncomfortable experiences could spring from that simple act. You could be told you are out of line or you don't know what you're talking about. People could label you as nosy or intrusive. Or you could discover that your perception was off, what you saw as a problem wasn't a problem, or that it was already being handled. Remaining silent and saying nothing risks none of that; it feels safe.

Except it isn't. Remaining silent is actually riskier, just not in such a socially visible way. It's risky because by remaining silent, you collude with everyone else who fails to speak up in a conspiracy of silence that perpetuates blame, finger pointing, and avoidance, the opposites of accountability. And you sacrifice your integrity, perhaps the greatest risk of all. In choosing silence, you choose to live with the knowledge that, day after day, you fail to do what you know is right, you fail to live up to your potential to be the most valuable contributor you can be. You live with a lifelong accumulation of small disappointments in yourself. It's certainly easier in each moment to choose silence, but the price for you is a life lived half-heartedly. The price for your organization is that it fails to thrive.

Anyone who sits through a meeting with some awareness that important concerns are being left unspoken or unaddressed plays a part in the aftermath of the meeting: the wasted time, increased costs, emotional disappointments, and injured relationships that result from the collective silence.

People who choose to cultivate an inner state of accountability make two distinct choices. The first choice is to speak up and take a stand when they sense the need, even if they know they may stumble and be less than perfect in their speaking. The second is to acknowledge the ways in which they have contributed to a problem. Accountability is soul-searching work. As a Field Leader, your responsibility is to cultivate accountability in yourself, role model it for others, and develop a culture in which those you lead also choose to be accountable.

If you accept my definition of accountability as a choice to cultivate a particular inner state, an attitude that shapes your behavior, then the notion of holding someone other than yourself accountable is meaningless. As a leader, you can only hold people responsible. I realize this flies in the face of how the word is used dozens of times every day. But when you speak of holding someone accountable, you lose the distinction of accountability as an inner state, and it becomes synonymous with responsibility. I prefer to speak of holding people responsible, meaning there are consequences for their failure to fulfill the tasks they have promised to fulfill. That leaves alive the vitality of accountability as an inner state that you actively cultivate in yourself and, as a leader, in others.

ADOPTING THE DISCIPLINE OF ACCOUNTABILITY

I worked closely with a logistics company, coaching several of their executives and senior managers. One of them, we'll call him Carl, managed a team that served as a hub for coordinating the activities of several other teams.

Carl's job was complex, interacting with numerous other leaders, and his team interacted with several other teams. Carl was an effective manager, and as the company adopted a field approach to leadership, he reached out to strengthen his relationships with other leaders. Together they were working to develop Field Leadership skills in themselves and in the teams they led.

I asked Carl what he saw as his larger purpose in the organization, what difference he would like to make in his tenure at the company. He reflected for a while, then said, "I just don't see myself that way. I don't see myself as someone making a big difference in the company. That seems really ego-centric. I don't have that kind of vision." But Carl also expressed frustration at the slowness with which some other leaders were adopting the methods of Field Leadership. He wanted them to show up wholeheartedly embracing the stronger relationships and greater transparency that Field Leadership requires, and when they didn't, he saw the impact it had on his team.

As he got clearer about those concerns, I suggested he did have a vision for the company, and it was an important one. It didn't involve his ego, but it did involve things he cared deeply about: the well-being of his employees, his relationships with other leaders, and the long-term health of the company. As Carl absorbed this, he began to see that if he didn't take a stand for the changes he knew would benefit the company, he would be letting himself, his team, and the company down. That required Carl to engage people throughout the company, including senior executives, about Field Leadership and understanding accountability as a personal choice. These conversations have not always gone easily, but he embraces the notion that difficult conversations are far better than silence.

An accountable person always asks:

- What did I do that contributed to the outcome?
- What should I keep doing because it led to a desirable outcome?
- What could I have done differently to make the outcome better?

They focus on their own agency, their own power, and their own commitment to address challenges and opportunities. An accountable leader also looks at how to cultivate accountability in others.

To practice the discipline of accountability, you must be aware of what you most care about and what your most deeply held values are. You must be aware of the impact you want to have on the things you care about—in other words, the difference you want to make—and you must commit to working toward making that difference.

FIELD JOURNAL

In your Field Journal, list all the things you can think of for which you are responsible at your job. These are the things that are explicitly defined in your job description, things on which your performance will be directly measured.

Now reflect on and jot down qualities or goals you care about achieving in the organization for which you work. What you come up with may or may not be in your job description. That doesn't matter; what matters is becoming aware of what you care about. Think of these qualities or goals as "differences you want to make." I'm not talking about wanting to move up the organization chart or get a pay raise. Those may be important to you personally but have no impact on the success or failure of the organization. Think of the difference you want to make in terms of the organization's success. Consider a point in the future when you are no longer with the organization and reflect on what others could acknowledge as your contribution, how the organization became better because of the work you did.

Reflect on how it feels to consider being accountable on this scale. In your journal, write down your thoughts, emotions, and physical sensations as you think about taking on this level of accountability. Consider why it matters to you and how it would feel to achieve this level of impact. Write down what resources you would need and what practices you would have to adopt.

Recall that your Field of the Self is the expression of your inner state; it establishes the presence you have with others. Leaders who cultivate an inner state of accountability establish a presence of accountability. That is the first step in cultivating a culture of accountability in which those you lead also develop that inner state. As that happens, emergent leadership becomes possible. Leaders and followers alike can adapt quickly to any point on the Spectrum of Leadership, giving rise to emergent leadership where appropriate and intentional leadership when called for.

Interlude Two

Taming Complexity with Rules

Because nature had to deal with complexity long before humans arrived, we should take a look at how nature manages it and how those lessons apply to leadership today. Nature had billions of years to experiment and the entire planet for a laboratory. With those resources, she was able to birth a remarkable solution to meeting the challenges and opportunities of complexity: what scientists call "simple rules." Simple rules are guidelines for behavior that enable organisms to make the right choice at the right time and to establish cooperation and collective action without complex analysis or micromanaging.

An elegant example is a flock of starlings. Though they consist of thousands of birds, these flocks navigate across the sky as one organism. All the birds move in concert, the flock as a whole rising and dropping, turning and swooping in one continuously unfolding, highly coordinated movement. They do this under constantly changing conditions—shifts in the wind, the arrival and disappearance of predators, changes in the weather—adapting perfectly to each new situation. At every point in time, each bird is managing its relationships with its neighbors, adjusting its behavior in ways that optimize the performance of the flock as a whole.

We know a great deal about the biology and structure of birds, and we understand the mechanics of flight. But mechanical thinking sheds no light whatsoever on how the birds in a flock of starlings manage to cooperate so effortlessly. The flock is a complex system. Its behavior is unpredictable because it is constantly monitoring its dynamic environment and adapting, second by second, to changing conditions. Mechanical thinking doesn't address that kind of challenge. Flocks of starlings need a different kind of solution, just as do organizations that need their leaders, employees, and other stakeholders to collaborate effectively in a hyperconnected world.

We don't know for sure what the actual rules are for starlings, but computer simulations successfully mimic their flocks with just these three:

- Collision Avoidance: avoid collisions with nearby flockmates
- Velocity Matching: attempt to match velocity with nearby flockmates
- Flock Centering: attempt to stay close to nearby flockmates (Reynolds, 1987)

Remarkably, these simulations show that not only are these three simple rules sufficient, but each bird only needs to pay attention to its seven nearest neighbors for the entire flock to function (Young et al., 2013).

The first rules that appeared in living systems were encoded directly in DNA and made it possible for the orderly complexity of life to appear on Earth. These rules live in biochemical communication loops. They are hardwired, never changing throughout an organism's lifetime, evolving only through genetic changes from one generation to the next. In organisms with more advanced central nervous systems, like humans, softwired rules also exist. As with softwired mental models, softwired rules can be changed and can be overridden. We can exercise the discipline of choice (Johnson and Lam, 2010).

The appearance of rules made cooperation and collective action possible, giving rise to emergent leadership. As organisms became more complex and consciousness developed, intentional rules and thus intentional leadership appeared. The nature of rules, how they are established, and how precisely they are defined varies dramatically at different points on the Spectrum of Leadership. At the intentional end, they are many, detailed, and specific. We are quite good at developing such rules, as evidenced by the reams of policies and procedures in organizations everywhere. But we are only beginning to understand how to apply broad simple rules at the emergent end of the spectrum in our organizations.

RULES IN THE FOUR FIELDS

The simplest example of a rule is one that tells bacteria, when their energy is depleted, to move toward an environment that will reenergize them (Taylor, Zhulin, and Johnson, 1999). These types of rules preserve the cell and enable it to propagate. They are the most primitive kinds of rules in living systems. As I conceptualize the four fields, this is where the Field of the Self was first established.

At some point, bacteria became "aware" of other bacteria, and a new level of complexity appeared: the complexity of two organisms interacting and cooperating to improve their chances of survival. The Interpersonal Field was born (Braga et al., 2016). Over time, these rules evolved further to enable co-operation and collective action among groups of cells (Reid and Latty, 2016). This was another leap in complexity, giving rise to the Field of Teams. As these larger groups of bacteria began to interact, the Enterprise Field emerged (Choi, 2015).

Simple rules allow rapid decisions in complex environments in which detailed policies and procedures can be paralyzing. Simple rules also enable rapid course corrections.

With human beings, rules function best when they are internalized. When people accept a rule as their own, they don't have emotional resistance or resentment toward it, and they don't waste mental resources thinking about it. Like a softwired mental model, they simply follow it. Rules imposed from outside and never internalized lead to rigidity, apathy, and bureaucracy; rules that are embraced and internalized lead to adaptability, engagement, and creativity. The challenge for leaders is to develop rules that people internalize. In fact, that is what leaders are striving for when they encourage people to be accountable and for everyone to exhibit leadership. Leaders want individuals to take personal ownership of the outcomes of their actions and the well-being of the organization.

Before stoplights were invented, traffic police stood in the middle of intersections and directed traffic, telling people when to go, when to stop, and when to turn. People internalized and accepted the authority of the traffic police, and traffic flowed without incident. The rule people internalized was, "Do what the police officer tells me to do." That system operated at the intentional end of the Spectrum of Leadership, with an authority figure making decisions for the community of drivers.

Once stoplights were invented, we learned another simple rule: stop on red, go on green. This rule requires no leader or director; it operates toward the emergent end of the spectrum. The orderly flow of traffic emerges naturally from it.

This rule is also internalized. And like all effective simple rules, it serves as a guardrail on behavior. It doesn't give a lot of specifics—how far in advance to start slowing down if the light is red, how to judge the likelihood of a green light turning red—it just tells me not to run a red light. Within that limit, I'm free to handle how I drive.

The stoplight rule is an example of an intentionally designed rule imposed by an outside force but internalized to the degree that it becomes automatic. While there are social consequences for disobeying it, it is effective not because of the authority of the law but because it is internalized. I have on occasion found myself sitting at a red light late at night, with no other cars in sight in any direction.

Although I believe there will be no consequences for running the light, deciding to do so is difficult. I viscerally resist because the rule is deeply internalized.

A business example comes from Mary Barra, the CEO of GM. A couple of simple rules are evident in how she leads: keep it simple, and empower people.

Before becoming CEO, Barra had headed up human resources at GM. When she took that post, GM's dress code was written in painful detail, attempting to cover every possible circumstance in which there could be a question about how one was to dress at work. It was ten pages long. This was at the extreme intentional end of the Spectrum of Leadership. Barra replaced the ten pages with two words: "Dress appropriately." In one action, she shifted the dress code from the extreme intentional end of the spectrum to the emergent end where rules are few, simple, and broad.

When Barra implemented her two-word dress code, she received an angry email from a senior director complaining that "dress appropriately" was insufficient. He wanted intentional leadership—rigid, detailed, command-and-control instructions. She called him and asked him to explain his concerns. He ran a large area of the company in which government officials sometimes showed up on short notice. He was concerned that having people in jeans would not make a good impression. Barra listened to his concerns, then asked him to talk to his team and work it out. This sent a signal that he was not being given an order but rather was invited to participate in determining how the rule would be defined in his area. Not long after, he reported that his team had met, shared ideas, and decided that the few individuals who meet with government officials would keep dress pants in their lockers (Grant, 2018). He and his team had internalized the spirit of the rule and found a solution that gave people freedom and autonomy to dress comfortably while also being prepared for surprise visits from government officials. He had asked for intentional leadership, but what was most effective was emergent leadership.

Barra used intentional leadership in establishing the simple rule of "dress appropriately." What "appropriate" meant in different contexts was then handled at the local level, without the need for higher levels of the company to intervene or control with complex policies and procedures. As people internalized the rule, orderly patterns of people dressing appropriately emerged throughout the company. That is how emergent leadership works. There is no leader; leadership emerges from the collective behavior of the community. In a 2018 interview, she commented, "To me, the big 'a-ha' was that you need to make sure your managers are empowered because if they can't handle 'Dress appropriately,' what other judgment decisions are they not making?" (Grant, 2018).

If you accept that leadership is the means by which people develop the ability to cooperate and take collective action, then the job of the leader is to create an environment in which people do. Simple rules operate at the emergent end of the Spectrum of Leadership and provide broad behavioral guidelines that apply in many circumstances. They loosely constrain choices. People then have a sense of autonomy and the freedom to be creative in how they address challenges and opportunities while not going so far as to violate the broad goals of the organization. The detailed policies and procedures that characterize the intentional end of the spectrum apply to specific, repeatable processes. When carrying out repetitive tasks in a stable and predictable environment, policies and procedures can ensure efficiency. But in complex, dynamic environments, overly specific policies and procedures create rigidity—the opposite of the adaptability required in such environments. Organizations today need leaders who create environments in which leadership operates along the entire spectrum.

THE POWER OF SIMPLICITY

How much can we learn from nature's simple rules? How powerful are they? We are just beginning to learn what they are capable of, but already mathematicians, scientists, and engineers are finding they can solve vexing problems. Physarum polycephalum is a large single-celled bacterium that can spread itself out over a large area in its search for food. But as it explores, it withdraws from areas with no food, leaves behind thin tentacles in areas of moderate food, and large tentacles in areas where food is dense. The result is a network of tentacles that provides the most efficient possible transport route between areas where food is found. It creates large tentacles to transport large food sources and smaller tentacles for smaller food sources. And it is fault tolerant, meaning if one route is disrupted or damaged, it can quickly adapt to use another route for the same food source.

A cross-functional group of researchers from fields including engineering, electronics, biology, and mathematics joined forces to see how they might apply Physarum's skill to human problems. They recognized that the problem Physarum solves with its food-hunting strategy is the same problem cities face when they want to design a transportation network. Around large metropolitan centers, people want to travel between areas with high, moderate, and low density. And there are physical barriers that make it difficult or impossible to build a railroad track or a road.

On a large, flat surface, the researchers replicated the conditions around Tokyo, placing more Physarum food in areas where the population was dense and smaller quantities of food in areas with a small population. They created conditions Physarum would avoid—where there were physical barriers that would make it difficult or impossible to build railroad tracks or roads. Then they put a Physarum cell down on the board and watched what happened.

In a short period of time, Physarum had spread itself out to cover all the areas it could reach. It then retracted itself from areas where there was no food and thinned out the tentacles to areas of low food density. It left larger tentacles with greater transport facility leading to areas of high food density. In short, it had mapped out the optimal design of a transport network in and around Tokyo (Tero et al., 2010).

The experiment has been replicated with transportation networks in cities, states, and countries around the world. The resulting networks that Physarum create often replicate what is already in place. When they don't, Physarum's solution is often better than what humans created (Adamatzky, 2016b).

Two immediate benefits can be seen in these experiments: Physarum could provide a very cost-efficient mechanism for designing transport networks, and it could be used to determine whether existing transport networks are as efficient as possible. The researchers who conducted the initial experiment are now working on understanding the rules Physarum follows and replicating those in software.

We have only begun to scratch the surface. Nature has solved many problems that are fundamentally similar to problems we are facing today. Simple rules gleaned from nature's examples are being applied in the design of telecommunications networks, robotics, warehouse automation, medicine, business strategy, leadership, culture, and much more.

RULES LIVE IN COMMUNICATION LOOPS

Rules live in communication loops. When I see a traffic light go from green to red, it triggers a muscular impulse. If I ignore that impulse, it sends a signal to my emotional center that I'm getting into a dangerous situation. The emotional response of fear will amplify the impulse to move my foot. The longer I wait to put my foot on the brake, the stronger my fear grows, and the stronger my fear grows, the stronger becomes the urge to brake.

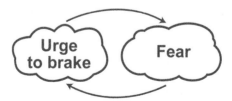

Figure Interlude 2.1.   Physical-Emotional Response to Stop Light

In the same way, walking into work at GM wearing worn-out jeans would likely trigger an emotional response that you were not dressing appropriately, triggering an urge to dress differently. The more inappropriate your clothing, the stronger your discomfort. In a culture of accountability, people follow rules because they have internalized them and have a visceral need to follow them. They also know that within the boundaries of the rules, they are free to behave in whatever ways they believe will best serve the enterprise. In a culture of command and control, the elegant system of emergent leadership that nature created is short circuited. Command-and-control rigidity blocks the internalization of rules, crushes creativity, and renders accountability all but impossible. Accountability requires choice, and rigidity takes choice away.

Donald Sull and Kathleen Eisenhardt described the use of simple rules to solve complex business problems in their 2012 *Harvard Business Review* article "Simple Rules for a Complex World." They describe ALL, a railway company in Brazil that took over a nationwide network of freight lines that were in terrible disrepair. A fifth of the bridges were near collapse, ancient locomotives were still in use, and the organization was in serious financial straits. The railroad was in such poor shape that it was used for only about a quarter of the shipments for which it should have been used. The problems were complex, but the company's leaders decided to implement simple rules rather than bureaucratic policies and regulations. Sull and Eisenhardt wrote: "ALL's CEO assembled a cross-functional team to develop simple rules for prioritizing capital spending. Any proposal, the rules said, should:

- Remove obstacles to growing revenues
- Minimize up-front expenditure
- Provide benefits immediately (rather than paying off in the long term)
- Reuse existing resources."

These simple rules enabled people throughout the company to exercise creativity and take accountability for their actions while staying within the broad guidelines defined by the executive team. Within three years, revenues had increased by 50 percent. When the company went public several years later, it was Latin America's largest independent logistics company. It was renowned for its culture and was considered one of the best employers in Brazil (Sull and Eisenhardt, 2012).

The internet is perhaps the most striking example of simple rules and how complexity's wild side can unleash limitless possibilities. When the internet was being established, four simple rules were laid down to guide its development:

- If you divide the network into subnetworks, each subnetwork must be able to function on its own. And if you build a network outside the internet, it should be possible to connect it to the internet without making any changes to it.
- If a message fails to get to its destination, the sender will wait for a brief period of time, then resend it.
- The devices that connect different parts of the network together will do nothing but pass data along. No information will be stored at the connection points.
- There will be no global control. In other words, the internet can grow and adapt freely in response to human needs and desires without constraint. (Leiner et al., 1997)

Adhering to those rules gave rise to all the wild possibilities of the internet. Simple rules can create effective emergent leadership, even in organizations that epitomize intentional leadership, like the US military. In a *Harvard Business Review* article, Daisy Wademan (2017) describes how the military improved the performance of soldiers by addressing the challenges families faced when soldiers are deployed away from home. A senior leader in the government's office of Military Community and Family Policy told her, "The number one reason for military professionals not being battle ready is worry about the people at home." So they developed a set of simple rules to enhance the ability for soldiers to maintain connections to their families. The rules are:

- Prioritize predictability. Ensure that when soldiers are not deployed away from home, their work schedules are consistent and reliable, so they do not miss planned family events.
- Keep work routines consistent. Maintain a moderate level of work or structured activity after a soldier returns from a long deployment. This was found to create a better balance in family connection than lots of unstructured time.
- Advertise and destigmatize the family resources the military offers. Soldiers sometimes felt that using family support and mental health resources was a sign of weakness. To counter this belief, the military developed advertisements and visual reminders of the resources and encouraged leaders to discuss them openly with their staff.
- Connect working parents to each other: families with similar challenges and stresses are often the best support resources.
- Be present while away. Military families were taught how to create a sense of a soldier's presence even when the soldier was away on a long deployment. For example, placing photos of the entire family in conspicuous

areas, keeping around toys that children enjoyed playing with the absent parent, and playing music the family enjoyed together all served to create a sense of the absent soldier's presence in the home.

- Don't talk. Do. Children often connect with parents best through activity rather than by talking.

These rules, while simple and broad, have served effectively to increase the sense of connection that soldiers have with their families and thus allow them to focus more on their work, especially when they are deployed for long periods of time. Wademan points out these same rules could be effective for businesses to support working parents.

RULES IN A COMPLEX HYPERCONNECTED WORLD

Emergent leadership depends on people taking accountability for the results of their actions. If they do not—if the culture is one of keeping your head down, just doing your job, and blaming others when things go wrong—then emergent leadership will fail. Emergent leadership can only be cultivated in an organization in which trust is high and individuals feel safe making decisions and taking risks. Mary Barra cultivated that sense in the manager who felt threatened by her broad dress code rule. The employees at the Brazilian railroad had to know it was safe to try different approaches and do things differently than in the past.

There are three critical insights leaders must grasp in order to establish effective rules:

- Rules must be internalized so that people have a visceral feel for when they are breaking a rule.
- As you move toward the emergent end of the spectrum, rules must become broader and less specific. They should serve as guardrails that leave room for creative problem solving within the boundaries of the rules. They do not attempt to provide specific actions for every possible scenario.
- For emergent leadership, rules do not always follow logic; they are intuitive guidelines for behavior. You can't figure out how they will work in advance. You have to use your best guess—your intuition—then try them out. If they don't work, see what's not working and modify them. That's how nature does it.

The mechanical thinking of the Age of Reason and the process thinking of command-and-control leadership provide rigid rules for specific actions with no room to adapt to circumstances and no individual empowerment. The process version of a rule for starlings might be "Always stay twelve inches away from your neighbors." If starlings rigidly followed such a rule, their flocks would collapse in chaos.

The management and organizational development literature of the past decade is filled with references to the need for employees to be empowered, find work meaningful, and be accountable for business results. None of that can happen in a rigidly intentional leadership environment because empowerment, meaning, and accountability require freedom of choice and the opportunity to be creative. In its desire to eliminate the potential for chaos, extreme intentional leadership often goes too far in diminishing the potential for creativity and adaptability.

Simple rules don't give you the confidence about certain outcomes you can get from detailed, rigid policies and micromanaging. But they do free up creativity and cultivate attitudes of accountability, which are far more valuable in a dynamic world than rigid rules and policies that may be outdated before they are even printed. In any case, the confidence of certainty is a myth. Science, spirituality, and business have all demonstrated that life is and always will be uncertain. The nearer we get to nature's wild side, where possibility and chaos are close neighbors, the less certain the future seems and the richer the possibilities become.

While many simple rules address specific challenges, like designing a railroad network or establishing a dress code, there are even more fundamental rules that nature established over the eons of evolution that led to modern humans. Those rules are reflected in the disciplines of the four fields. They emerged from nature's endless experiments; they are the rules the mystics discovered in their exploration of the human spirit. They appear in myriad cultures, modern leadership literature, and studies of other conscious animals that exhibit intentional leadership (Conradt and Roper, 2003). They are the ancient rules of cooperating with others and contributing to collective action in ways that further the well-being of the community, rules that tell us to be trustworthy and accountable. These ancient rules are universal and are the foundation of all the other rules we create.

Section III

THE INTERPERSONAL FIELD

Chapter Eleven

From the Field of the Self to the Interpersonal Field

Once individual organisms existed, simple rules made cooperation and collective action between them possible, thus creating the interpersonal and team fields. The Interpersonal Field is the product of two individuals interacting with each other. When two organisms enter into an interpersonal relationship, the relationship is greater than the sum of the parts. The Interpersonal Field is richer and more complex than the sum of the two Fields of the Self from which it emerges. It is a new kind of entity.

From an evolutionary perspective, this was an extraordinary transformation that created vast new possibilities for complex living systems. In the Interpersonal Field, two organisms can communicate, cooperate, and take collective action without being in physical contact with one another. For humans, the hyperconnectivity of the internet makes it possible for interpersonal relationships to exist among all individuals on the planet.

In section 2, you saw that perceiving and managing your inner state and cultivating those abilities in those you lead are critical competencies for effective Field Leadership. In the Interpersonal Field, you must add to these capabilities, learning to sense the inner state of others and empathizing with them. Empathy is the ability to understand what another person feels and thinks from their perspective. It does not mean agreeing with them, and it is not feeling sorry for them. Rather, it is understanding their inner state—what they experience in their physical, emotional, and analytical minds—and how that leads to their beliefs and behaviors.

Just as your Field of the Self emerges from your core communication loop, the Interpersonal Field you establish with another person emerges from the communication loops between the two of you. The Interpersonal Field is as rich and varied as all the relationships you have with other people. The quality of the Interpersonal Field is dependent on the quality of the Fields of the Self from which it emerges. If the Fields of the Self are off center and distorted, so will be the Interpersonal Field that emerges from them.

In section 2, I explored the internal communication loops that arise among your three minds and define your inner state. Those are powerful communication loops; they make possible your consciousness and personality. In the Interpersonal Field, communication loops grow more numerous and more complex because they now arise between individuals. The complexity of the Interpersonal Field includes the complexity of the individual Fields of the Self plus the complexity of the interactions between two individuals.

Just as there are three disciplines in the Field of the Self, there are also three disciplines in the Interpersonal Field: honesty, integrity, and trust. The three disciplines of the self enable you to manage your inner state; the three interpersonal disciplines enable two people to manage the state of their relationship.

Business leaders are increasingly realizing that we have shifted from an economy driven by processes and operational efficiency to a relationship economy. Recall from chapter 2 the difference between complicated and complex phenomena. Complicated phenomena can be understood and managed with pure logic—the purview of the analytical mind. Complex phenomena are the product of communication loops; logic fails to explain them or predict their behavior. The analytical mind is thus insufficient to understand and manage them.

Business processes are complicated. Human relationships are complex and have replaced business processes and operational efficiency as the drivers for competitive advantage. This is not to say that business processes and operational efficiency are no longer important—they are absolutely essential. It's just that they are no longer sufficient to compete successfully. Without excellent business processes and operational efficiency, you don't have a chance: they're the price to get in the game, but they won't win the game. Winning will come to organizations that excel in relationships. And because today work itself is complex, requiring cross-functional teams and extensive collaboration, even operational efficiency depends on effective interpersonal relationships. In this economy, relationships drive everything. And the disciplines of the Interpersonal Field—honesty, integrity, and trust—determine the quality of relationships.

The Interpersonal Field is, for many, the most challenging of the four fields. It is so challenging because, to our neurobiology, it feels the riskiest. Establishing interpersonal relationships often requires significant vulnerability. You reveal yourself to others, letting them see how you feel and what you think. Especially as a leader, you must take accountability for how your behavior affects others. That doesn't mean you are responsible for how they respond to your words and actions. But it does mean you must strive to behave in ways that maximize the likelihood that others will respond well.

The Interpersonal Field is also challenging because managing the dynamics of the Interpersonal Field is more subtle and complex than managing the Field of the Self. In the Interpersonal Field, you have to deal with words and actions generated by others, and you must navigate not only the inner state of your thoughts and emotions but also the external state of your relationships with others. Their behavior is beyond your control and can trigger your three minds in many ways, upsetting your inner state. Communication loops in the Interpersonal Field can be harder to discern and manage consciously. For all these reasons, managing your inner state is essential if you are to establish effective interpersonal relationships. You don't want inaccurate mental models or emotional hijacking to impair your ability to communicate effectively and build strong relationships.

WE ARE NOT AS SEPARATE AS YOU MIGHT THINK

People usually think of themselves as distinct, separate individuals. They operate in the world autonomously from others, make their own decisions, and direct the course of their lives.

Many biologists today believe a beehive is best thought of as a single living superorganism composed of thousands of individual organisms (Tautz and Heilmann, 2009). The superorganism is greater than the sum of its parts, capable of complex behaviors that individuals within the superorganism could not conceive, much less perform. In a similar way, two people interacting create a relationship that is more complex and richer than the two individuals separately. They become one system defined by the communication loops of their relationship. You can think of an interpersonal relationship as a superorganism.

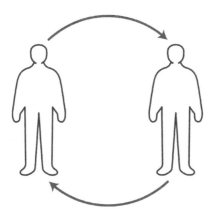

Figure 11.1. A Superorganism: Two People Form One Relationship

This might seem far fetched, but consider that you—your body, your physical self—is a collection, or community, of many billions of individual cells, many of them radically different in form, function, and behavior from the rest. Furthermore, your body also consists of your microbiome—billions of bacteria that live in symbiotic relationships with the parts that are genetically "you." And in addition to all these cells and bacteria, the living "stuff" that makes up you, there are billions of chemical molecules—water, proteins, hormones, and many more—that are essential to who and what you are. And we call all of this "you" and think of "you," this vast collection of cells and bacteria and molecules, as an individual organism, an individual being. And consider how we refer to two people in a romantic relationship: they are a couple. A group of people who are aligned on a task and work together to achieve that task are a team. People who live near each other are a neighborhood. Collections of neighborhoods are towns or cities. Whenever people interact with each other, they form relationships that create a new "superorganism" that transcends the individual selves, similar to the superorganism of a beehive. In this sense, organisms are not defined by physical boundaries but rather by relationships through which individuals cooperate and take collective action.

Where you draw the boundary around an organism and whether you consider it a superorganism is a matter of how you look at it. There is no one "right" way. Individual people, interpersonal relationships, teams, and entire organizations can be understood as organisms or as superorganisms. If you look at an entity—say, a person—as an individual, then to you, that person is an organism. They are also superorganisms made up of the cells, bacteria, and molecules of which they are composed. And when they interact with others to form relationships, teams, and so on, they are members of superorganisms that are greater than themselves. What distinguishes one from the other is that superorganisms are more complex and have an intelligence that transcends that of the individuals by themselves. With awareness, you can experience that in the Interpersonal Field and in the Field of Teams. Interpersonal relationships and teams bring you into something that transcends you as an individual.

So when you enter into a conversation with another person, it may be useful to think of the Interpersonal Field you have created as a living organism. If you treat an interpersonal relationship as a living organism, each party must honor the relationship and take accountability for its health and well-being, transcending their individual personal concerns for the sake of the whole. This is one reason that behaviors like finger pointing and blame are so toxic. They break the organism of the Interpersonal Field down into its parts, losing the intelligence of the whole.

It is one thing to talk about beehives as superorganisms, but that is a far stretch from the complexity and sophistication of the interpersonal relationships observed in higher organisms and, in particular, in human beings.

What made possible the rich variety and subtlety of human interpersonal relationships? At some point in evolutionary history, the limbic system of the brain began to develop. The limbic system is the source of emotions, and with emotions, interpersonal relationships took on a depth and breadth that would forever change life on the planet Earth. With emotions, organisms can change each other's inner states in complex ways (Lewis, Amini, and Lannon, 2001). When someone looks at you a certain way, you may feel love; if they look at you another way, you may feel fear. This ability of two individuals to alter each other's inner states deepened the connection between them, making the superorganism of the interpersonal relationship stronger and more powerful. As the limbic system evolved, the rich tapestry of human emotions became possible. Interpersonal relationships became vastly more complex, creating families, communities, businesses, and societies.

With these capabilities, the size and complexity of human systems has no limit. As long as you can sense and communicate with another person, you can change one another's inner states. Interpersonal relationships, teams, and enterprises can proliferate wildly.

All of this happened organically, with no one aware of what was emerging in human society. Today, scientists and spiritual masters together are giving us at least a basic understanding of these forces that shape everything we do. And we are learning just in time because in our ignorance of how nature works, we have created systems that do not work well at all and, in some cases, are doing grave harm. The vast inefficiencies so many organizations experience in their operations and the seemingly perennial and intractable problems of getting tens, hundreds, thousands, and tens of thousands of people to cooperate and take collective action all require that we use these insights, this new knowledge, to adjust our ways of thinking, deciding, and leading. And the Self and Interpersonal fields are at the root of it all.

In today's workforce, because of the deeply collaborative nature of work in a hyperconnected world, relationships are your number one concern. All work today involves relationships—one's relationship with one's manager, coworkers, direct reports, customers, vendors, and others. Relationships have become the lifeblood of work. If relationships are not strong, everything done through them—cooperation, communication, teamwork, cross-functional efforts—is compromised. Relationships are also paramount in the marketplace. Customers today have the freedom to obtain products and services from any provider anywhere on the planet. If they aren't happy with their relationship with you, they can quickly go online, read reviews of other providers, and switch. In a hyperconnected world, customer relationships are the lifeblood of business.

Chapter Twelve

The Discipline of Honesty

Leaders frequently tell me that they want to promote honesty in the workplace and want a culture of honesty. But rarely do they take the time to reflect on what the word actually means. Often they assume it means "saying what you think," "speaking your mind," or "not lying." There's some truth in all of these, but from a Field Leadership perspective, there's a lot more to honesty.

The disciplines of the Field of the Self—awareness, choice, and accountability—are focused on managing your inner state. They involve introspective practices to enhance your effectiveness both personally and professionally. Developing those disciplines is largely done in the space of your inner life. But they prepare you for the disciplines of the Interpersonal Field.

Awareness of yourself is, in a sense, a practice of becoming honest with yourself. In awareness practices, you peel back the layers of physical sensations, emotions, and beliefs that prevent you from fully and accurately observing your inner state and becoming centered. Self-awareness reveals to you who you are at your core and what you care about. The more you practice self-awareness, the more honest you become with yourself. That is how honesty works in the Field of the Self.

In the Interpersonal Field, honesty reveals your inner state to others and lets them see who you are at your core. From this perspective, interpersonal honesty is more than saying what you think because your inner state is composed of more than thoughts. As you saw in section 2, your physical and emotional minds play major roles in your inner state. Interpersonal honesty is the revealing of yourself, your inner state, to another person. This immediately opens up a much larger conversation than simply saying what you think. Telling someone your surface opinion but not revealing your deeper beliefs or emotions is a shallow level of honesty. Real honesty requires courage, commitment, and a willingness to be vulnerable and to trust others to respect what is true for you. And of course, if you want others to respect your truth, you must begin by respecting theirs.

This understanding of honesty clearly links it to awareness; you can only reveal to others those things of which you are aware. The more honest you become with yourself, that is, the more you allow yourself to see yourself fully, the more honest you can be with others. So honesty is a journey in awareness and vulnerability; it brings with it a good dose of humility as well because it requires that you let others see your flaws as well as your brilliance.

While it is easy for leaders to say, "We'll build a culture of honesty," it's not so easy to do. In a culture of honesty, you can't cover up blemishes or pretend to believe something you don't and still call yourself honest. And you must accept honesty from others. You must want those you lead to tell you what they think and how they feel about you as a leader. You want their honest revelations about how their work is going, how effective their relationships with others are, and what they need to succeed. You must hear all of that with respect and openness. That level of honesty is at the heart of Field Leadership.

PERSONAL VERSUS PRIVATE

I sometimes hear people resist talking about emotions in a business environment. They object that emotions are personal and therefore shouldn't be brought into the workplace. It's important to distinguish between "personal" and "private." Emotions are often both personal and relevant at work. Your inner state—how you feel and what you think—affects your relationships at work and your ability to perform your job.

On the other hand, *private* matters relate to parts of your life that are outside of work. You only share those matters with another if you have a relationship with them that extends into the private sphere of your life. If you have formed a friendship with someone at work, you may choose to talk about private matters, but that is in the context of friendship, not work. It is important to make sure the person you are talking with is comfortable with the conversation and will honor your privacy when talking to others.

So it is absolutely appropriate to protect privacy in the workplace. Privacy is where you set up boundaries that say, "This part of my life is not relevant to the conversation we're in and is not to be shared with you." The nature and quality of your relationships with family members, how you manage your finances, and what you do with your free time are all examples of private matters you may not choose to reveal to others. On the other hand, your emotional state and your thoughts in a business meeting are personal but very appropriate to share. In fact, it is appropriate for others to expect you to share those, not because they are nosy or prying but because your emotional state and thoughts directly affect how you interact with them and can reveal valuable insights. If you are not willing to share with others how you feel, you hinder their ability to understand and interact with you.

Daniel Goleman, the author of the books *Emotional Intelligence* and *Primal Leadership*, says:

> leaders cannot effectively manage emotions in anyone else without first handling their own. How a leader feels thus becomes more than just a private matter; given the reality of emotional leakage, a leader's emotions have public consequences. (Goleman, Boyatzis, and McKee, 2002)

That was written in 2002. Since then, organizations have become vastly more connected, with everyone influencing everyone to a degree not imagined before. What Goleman said then about leaders applies today not only to leaders. Emotional leakage happens with all of us in every relationship we have, so your emotional state, while personal, is not always private. Your emotions need to be acknowledged and sometimes discussed, not as a matter of criticism but in the spirit of managing them when they put performance at risk and leveraging them when they can improve performance. Field Leaders must establish environments in which this is routine.

CONVERSATION IS THE LIFEBLOOD
OF THE INTERPERSONAL FIELD

Interpersonal relationships are mostly developed and maintained through conversations. (I include email and voicemail exchanges, written communications, and other exchanges between individuals under the umbrella of conversations.) Conversations are interpersonal communication loops. They are how nearly all of our interpersonal exchanges happen. The quality of conversations determines the quality of leadership, team performance, individual contributor performance, and relationships with customers, vendors, and the rest of the world.

A critical capability for conducting effective conversations is the ability to distinguish opinions—your own as well as those of others—from facts. It is a vital distinction. In speech act theory, the word *assessments* is often used for opinions and the word *assertions* for facts (these definitions are derived from Speech Act Theory, which is an important body of work related to organizational performance). I have found this language useful and use it in this book.

Assessments express how you see something—your opinion or interpretation of a situation. They are neither true nor false in an objective way. As a simple example, I have at times found myself arguing with my wife about whether it's cold or hot in our living room. To me, it's cold. That's my assessment of the room's temperature. To her, it's hot. We're both right—for ourselves. There is no provable truth about whether the room is cold or hot.

Assertions, on the other hand, are statements of fact. They are definitively provable to be true or false. If my wife and I look at the thermostat and it says 70 degrees, we will both agree with the assertion that it is 70 degrees; we accept it as true. If I were to say it's 68 degrees, that would still be an assertion, but it would be false. This distinction is important because an assertion will always be either true or false, but an assessment can be changed. To continue my example, if I walk into the house in the middle of winter and it's 70 degrees, I may comment that it's warm in the house, whereas in the summer, I might describe the same temperature as cool. The distinction between assessments and assertions is a simple one, yet failing to distinguish one from the other leads to many of the communication and interpersonal breakdowns that plague organizations and derail performance. Developing the abilities to recognize the difference between them, to use them appropriately, and to help others do so as well are critical to Field Leadership.

Assessments are closely tied to your emotional mind, assertions to your analytical mind. That is why people get into passionate arguments about things like politics and religion. Two people may easily agree on what a politician said on a Sunday morning talk show. You can prove that—just look at the video. But they may have profoundly different assessments about what the politician meant or what motivated the politician to say what they did. Assessments simply reveal how you see a situation; they don't reveal an objective truth about the situation. Assertions, on the other hand, reveal an objective truth.

I see this play out in organizations every day. One person will say a project is going well, another that it is going poorly. They will argue endlessly, each trying to prove the other wrong, sometimes leaving the conversation unresolved and damaging their relationship. The powerful, albeit more difficult, choice would be for each person to be curious about why the other person sees the project the way they do. Curiosity engages others by defusing their need for defensiveness. They go from defending to engaging and explaining.

Knowing how to distinguish assessments from assertions and using them skillfully is vital for Field Leadership. In my work as an executive coach, I have often heard from leaders that this distinction is one of the most valuable skills they have learned.

Honest conversations are characterized by the ability to know what is true for you, to hear what is true for others, to respect both, and to commit to learning rather than to making your point or winning an argument. In an honest conversation, you take accountability for your own assessments without imposing them on anyone else, and you respect the assessments of others without feeling compelled to adopt them for yourself. This enables you to engage in conversations of discovery and arrive at a shared understanding rather than arguments that end in "agreeing to disagree."

Conversations about assertions are usually easy because they are about data. They operate mostly in the realm of the dispassionate analytical mind. Conversations about assessments are not always so easy because they are the complex product of all aspects of one's inner state—the confluence of all three minds. Emotions play a big part in assessments.

The following questions are simple but powerful ways to keep yourself centered and curious in a conversation that is rich with assessments:

- What's happening in my physical mind? Is my body relaxed or tense? Am I centered? Where is my breathing?
- What's happening in my emotional mind? Am I centered? What do I need to accept?
- What is the essential question, problem, or opportunity at the heart of this conversation?
- What assessments do I hold about this?
- What assertions can be made about this?
- What assessments are others holding?
- Why do I care about the assessments I hold?
- What leads me to hold these assessments?
- Why do others care about the assessments they hold?

These questions can help you get to a deeper level of honesty. They can cut through barriers that commonly derail performance and create mistrust and resentment. Just consider the impact of hearing someone say to you in a respectful tone, "Help me understand what leads you to that assessment," versus saying in an angry tone, "That's the stupidest thing I've ever heard." Clearly, the communication loops that each of these statements creates are worlds apart, and the behaviors that emerge from them are in stark contrast to one another. The former statement reveals your sincere desire to understand another's perspective. It has a good chance of leading to a productive outcome. The latter reveals your immediate frustration and anger, and it could well result in blame and avoidance of one another. And because what is said in conversations is often repeated, the effects might be amplified by all the interacting individuals in a workplace. The impact of a conversation can be dramatic, spreading through the rumor mill in a flash. It's the butterfly effect.

THE PERSONAL COST OF DISHONESTY

Organizations pay a high price for dishonest behavior. Internally, dishonesty erodes trust and engagement, resulting in a dispirited workforce. Externally, in the marketplace, dishonesty results in lost customers, lawsuits, and regulatory fines.

But individuals also pay a high price for dishonesty. Joshua Greene is a psychologist at Harvard University who is interested in moral judgment and decision making. In 2009, he and Joseph Paxton, at that time a psychology graduate student, published a paper on the differences in brain activity in people who lie versus people who tell the truth (Greene and Paxton, 2009). The paper is fascinating to read both because of the elegance of their experimental design and because of the results.

They found that when faced with an opportunity to lie, dishonest people consume more energy, engage in greater brain activity, and make slower decisions—whether they are lying or not. And that's just the tip of the iceberg. When someone tells a lie, the electrical conductance of their skin increases, their heart rate and blood pressure increase, their breathing accelerates, and other physiological changes occur (Bechara et al., 2005).

Biochemically, when people are dishonest, their cortisol level rises. Cortisol increases your blood sugar level to provide your body with more energy for a fight-or-flight response. But high blood sugar also leads to numerous chronic health maladies, including diabetes, stroke, heart disease, and more. Cortisol also suppresses your immune system and your appetite and sends signals to emotional centers in your brain that can trigger fear. Beyond the physical damage done by heightened levels of cortisol, your overall biochemical response to elevated cortisol puts you in a state of mind in which you are more likely to behave in ways that are retaliatory and unethical. In other words, when you are dishonest, your brain and body become tuned to take increased risks and engage in unethical behavior (Brink, Lee, and Carney, 2015).

The reverse has also been found to be true: when people engage in acts of even small honesty or virtue, positive emotions are elevated, anxiety is reduced, blood pressure diminishes, cellular aging decreases, and psychological well-being is enhanced (Brink, Lee, and Carney, 2015).

Dishonesty is costly, yet there are times when we all find ourselves being less than honest: it's part of the human condition. But with practice, you can train yourself to be more honest more often (DiSalvo, 2014). The disciplines of the Self and Interpersonal fields will help—if you are willing to do the work to master them.

LEVELS OF HONESTY

The process of becoming more honest involves shifting your attention from the person with whom you are interacting to yourself. As your self-awareness grows, you become capable of greater honesty. The Levels of Awareness and Honesty chart in figure 12.1 shows some of the major transitions on that journey.

	Awareness	Energetic Focus	Behavior	Example	Accountability
Honesty ↑	Aware of what you care about	Greater purpose/ the larger system within which you work	Engage, Connect, Understand	"I care about the difference this project will make in the lives of our customers."	Very High
	Aware of your part in the problem	Mostly on self	Own	"I acknowledge my behaviors that contributed to the problem."	High
	Aware of the need underlying your emotion	Equally on self and other	Reveal	"I want to feel valued on this team."	Moderate
	Aware of immediate emotion	Mostly on the other person	Blame	"I'm angry because of what you said."	Low
	Unaware – Blind, Automatic Reaction	Entirely on the other person	Attack/Defend	"I think you're a jerk."/ "It's not my fault."	None

Figure 12.1.   Levels of Awareness and Honesty

When you have very low self-awareness, you are limited to reactions that are driven straight from your emotions. If someone says something you find upsetting, you may respond by saying something like "I think you're a jerk." That may be all the honesty you are capable of. With limited self-awareness, your focus will be on the other person and what they said or did, and you will not choose to take any accountability for how the conversation evolves.

Depending on the level of awareness and honesty of the person with whom you are talking, they may respond in kind, giving rise to a communication loop of escalating anger and resentment. Such communication loops can go on for extended periods of time and often infect others, leading to diminished performance throughout the organization. At the very least, such conversations generally lead to people avoiding one another, which in itself is a kind of communication loop that prevents cooperation and collective action.

With a little more self-awareness, you have more choices. Your focus shifts to include at least some part of yourself, with a beginning recognition of your role in the conversation. Rather than responding with "I think you're a jerk," you might say something like "I'm angry because of what you said." Your behavior still has elements of avoidance and blame, but at least there is an acknowledgment of your inner state and a hint of accountability. This begins to open up the possibility of a real conversation that can resolve the disagreement and lead to understanding.

As you continue to shift your focus off the other person and onto yourself, you will find you are increasingly practicing acceptance—the centering practice of your emotional mind. With acceptance of the other person, you see more clearly how you can influence the conversation, and it becomes easier to take accountability for how the conversation goes. Your focus now is more balanced on both you and the other person. You become aware that beneath your initial defensive response was a need that felt ignored or threatened, and you are able and willing to reveal more of yourself. You might be inclined to say something like "I want to feel valued on this team. When you spoke, I felt that I was not seen as a valuable member of the team."

Heightening your self-awareness still further shifts your focus to be primarily on yourself, and you take a high degree of accountability for how the conversation unfolds. Eventually, you will get to something that is fundamentally true for you. And when you find that truth, you will be able to speak it in a way that is both fully honest and fully respectful of the person with whom you are talking. You will have left distracting sensations, emotions, and thoughts behind. You will be deeply connected to the greater purpose that motivates you in your life. You will strive to engage with and understand the other person's point of view, and you will seek common ground from which you can both strive to fulfill that purpose. At this level, you unleash truly creative collaboration, you build trust, and you establish a powerful leadership presence that will attract others.

Developing real honesty is a process of peeling back layers of emotions and beliefs that hide your true self and discovering what is at your core. When you peel back those layers and reveal your truth, you become authentic. This is the spiritual journey we explored in the Field of the Self. In the Interpersonal Field, that journey extends into your relationships, where you reveal yourself to others. This was the journey Joseph took in his relationship with Margaret.

In a way, this is the journey of a lifetime. No one ever achieves full and lasting self-awareness. No one fully transcends themselves and leaves all distracting sensations, emotions, and thoughts behind and stays fully connected to their purest sense of purpose. No one forms and manages relationships perfectly. But to become an effective Field Leader, you must strive to achieve the highest levels of self-awareness and interpersonal honesty of which you are capable, and you must learn to cultivate them in those you lead.

One of the biggest challenges with striving for honesty is that you will, at times, screw it up. You might have the perfect script planned out for what you will say to someone, and then it will come out all wrong. Or you will say it as you planned, but their response is completely unexpected and takes you so far off center that you fall into old patterns of being unaware and less than honest. Your emotions can hijack you, leading you into words and actions that you later regret. This kind of experience is inevitable for anyone committed to becoming more honest.

A good tip-off that you are settling for a shallow level of honesty is when you sense an element of disrespect, defensiveness, or hostility in your words or actions. In the short run, you may be able to achieve an immediate objective by being less than fully honest, but in the long run, it will catch up to you.

The good news is that the discipline of honesty also provides you with the tools to handle situations where you do screw up. The solution is straightforward. When you find yourself having slipped up on your level of honesty, you become honest about that. If you say things that, on reflection, you realize were not fully revealing of yourself, you go back to the person you were talking with, acknowledge that, and pick up the conversation again. *Any* level of dishonesty diminishes the quality of a relationship and prevents people from achieving their maximum potential for collaboration.

Another aspect of honesty, for leaders, is accurately and respectfully naming how you see your team performing. When there are thoughts and emotions that prevent people from engaging wholeheartedly, those thoughts and feelings will dominate the conversation until they are named and addressed. Learning to speak the truth and naming things that are often left unsaid, in ways that others will hear and address them, is essential for Field Leadership.

In a one-day workshop with the leadership team of a financial services company, we started the session with some simple games of coordination. The team was not very engaged and their performance reflected that—they were doing a pretty poor job of playing the games. At one point, I stopped them and asked how they thought they were doing. Elizabeth commented, "Not very well, but you know, I really don't care."

There was some laughter and friendly banter in response to this comment, and when that settled down, I said to her, "You know, I can see you don't care. And it's reflected in how you guys are doing in this game. And you know, that's really a good metaphor for the day. If you don't care, the day will go the way this game is going, with similar results. But if you do care, then really good things can come from it. I've played these games with thousands of people over the years, and I've seen people get real value from them because they committed to doing them well. They learned things about themselves in the process, things they carried back to work. I can't make today worthwhile for you. I can create a context where you can get a lot of value if you choose to care, but you have to make that choice."

I had reflected—albeit quickly—before making my comment, knowing it could create tension and conflict, and I spoke it carefully, in a light tone rather than a heavy-handed or confrontational manner. But I knew I had to name what was happening because if I didn't, it would create a background tone that would dominate the day. The mood shifted, and the day went well.

As high levels of honesty become the norm in organizations, the ability to have the straightforward conversations necessary to fulfill the mission of the organization increases. Collaboration happens more and more easily. When there are disagreements, they are surfaced quickly, handled respectfully, and are often the source of new ideas.

Honesty inspires honesty. It's harder to be dishonest with someone you know is being honest with you. When people are honest with one another, there is a high degree of trust. As long as the honesty is sustained, trust grows and the relationship can weather difficult conversations and challenging circumstances. Honesty spawns communication loops through which trust and performance grow.

HONESTY AND AUTHENTICITY

Honesty is not only closely related to awareness, it is also the foundation of authenticity. When you reveal yourself to others, they experience you as authentic. They know there is nothing fake about you; when you say something, you mean it, and you let them know where you stand. You do not manipulate others, and you have no hidden agendas; you are willing to be fully transparent and wholeheartedly respectful of others. You will establish a strong, attractive leadership presence, with loyal followers.

When you are less than honest, there is an incongruence between your inner state and your behavior. Dishonesty damages your leadership presence because people will sense that incongruence. They know when you are less than transparent. People gravitate toward leaders who are authentic; they avoid leaders who keep secrets and share less than they can.

Developing honesty with another person does not happen overnight. It typically grows gradually: as one person reveals more, it becomes safer for the other person to do so as well. In this way, over time, honesty grows. Trust and the capacity for cooperation and collective action follows.

The hard work of developing honesty requires soul searching, self-examination, and seeing—perhaps discovering—parts of yourself that may not fit with your self-image. And it requires risk taking, revealing more of yourself without certainty that it will be reciprocated. When you do this hard work, you create deep and lasting change; you establish powerful behavior patterns that are at once highly efficient and deeply human. That is how you transform yourself, your relationships, and the groups within which you live and work. That is how you establish the presence required for Field Leadership.

Chapter Thirteen

The Discipline of Integrity

The discipline of honesty is about awareness and transparency. Honesty is proportional to how much of yourself you reveal. The discipline of integrity is about alignment between your inner state and your words and actions. You cannot have honesty without integrity, and vice versa. When you say you will do something without fully intending to follow through, you are being dishonest. Holding a value but doing things that violate that value is a violation of integrity. When you lead people to believe you are trustworthy and working in their best interest and then you are manipulative and undermining their interests in your actions, you are lacking integrity.

The word *integrity* comes from the Latin *integritas*; it means wholeness, completeness, and purity. When you exhibit integrity, your words and actions align with your beliefs and feelings. Your outer behavior is in accord with your inner truth. Dishonesty—whether outright deceit, making misleading statements, or withholding information—is a violation of integrity. If you are lacking integrity, your essential wholeness and coherence have been disrupted. Your Field of the Self is distorted, and the choices you make are not coherent with your values.

Living a life of integrity is not easy. We all compromise our values at times. I am deeply concerned about the damage the human race is doing to the planet, yet some of my choices result in my consuming more resources than necessary. And there are times when I realize I have behaved toward others in ways that do not accord with the values I hold about human relationships. Growing your integrity is a lifelong practice, and perfection is never achieved.

The discipline of integrity involves aligning your actions with your core values. To have integrity, what you say and do must line up with what you know to be true, with how you feel, what you believe, and what you care about.

Most people want to live lives of integrity. Yet for all of us, it is easy to violate integrity in ways that seem small and insignificant in the moment. If you become careless and slip into routinely compromising your integrity, over time, the fabric of integrity in your life and in the organization where you work deteriorates. Those compromises add up, and you find yourself in a life and in an organization in which the accepted behaviors consistently skirt around real honesty and create a culture in which every individual sacrifices their integrity in order not to rock the boat.

I have repeatedly seen organizations in which the norm is for people to not speak what they believe, not acknowledge their emotional states with one another, and behave in ways that don't align with their core values. They have all kinds of reasons for these choices: "it wouldn't be tolerated," "people don't want to know," "we're not a touchy-feely kind of place." The end result is a culture in which integrity is not valued, dishonesty is the norm, engagement is nonexistent, and performance is consistently subpar.

The biggest barriers to integrity are often fear and lack of self-awareness. People are afraid their truth will not be tolerated, they will be mocked, or they will find themselves in conversations that are messy and difficult and that lead to strife rather than trust. Sometimes they are even afraid of their own self-judgments. All of these are very real possibilities. I have witnessed each of these conditions in various organizations with which I have worked.

I have also seen the price organizations pay for cultures in which integrity is not valued and honest conversations are not welcome. The quality of work in these environments is lackluster, people point fingers rather than take accountability for problems, and employee turnover is high. There is a strong correlation between employee engagement and an environment in which integrity is valued (Engelbrecht, Heine, and Mahembe, 2017). But perhaps the greatest price is paid by the individuals who succumb to such a culture and sacrifice their own integrity in order to conform. The introspection required for self-awareness is far more difficult in an environment in which you must keep your true self hidden. In an atmosphere in which dishonesty is tolerated and integrity is not valued, self-awareness may be too uncomfortable. A high level of self-awareness makes it more painful to ignore such behaviors. This creates a steady stress and diminishing of one's self esteem; the emotional toll can be significant. Cultures in which integrity is sacrificed may have functioned in the past, but it is the death knell for organizations in which interpersonal relationships drive performance.

A commitment to integrity means that when the going gets rough, you still operate according to your principles. You don't bail on the disciplines of the four fields in order to avoid difficult situations. Integrity is what ensures your actions are always coherent with your values.

Maintaining integrity requires effort. There are thousands of opportunities every day, usually small and in themselves insignificant, to compromise your integrity. You say you are committed to honesty, but are you willing to acknowledge your defensiveness when someone challenges you in a meeting? And are you willing to take accountability for the impact your defensiveness has on others? Each time you compromise your integrity, you erode it a little bit, and it becomes easier to compromise a bit more the next time you are in an uncomfortable situation. When you as a leader behave this way, you create a toxic environment for everyone you lead, and you teach them to behave this way as well.

Field Leadership requires that leaders establish integrity as a cultural norm. When everyone works to foster and maintain integrity and acknowledges when they slip up, the four fields stay healthy and vibrant. Distortion that appears in any field is addressed quickly before it becomes acceptable.

The lack of integrity manifests as a distortion in an Interpersonal Field. As a participant in that field, you can often sense when either you or the other person is lacking integrity. It is felt more than thought, but once felt, it can be studied with your analytical mind. You can check your own level of integrity with a simple question: *Is there something I care about, need, or desire influencing my behavior that I am not sharing with others who are affected by my behavior?*

If the answer is yes, you must examine carefully how that concern is influencing you, what is holding you back from sharing it, and how best to address the concern with integrity. Doing so often requires a challenging level of honesty in which you acknowledge the concern to the other person and, if necessary, acknowledge that you have allowed it to influence your actions.

You can use a similar question if you sense the other person is lacking integrity. You tell them what you sense, and you ask for an honest conversation to explain what you are sensing.

Such conversations are often difficult, but they are essential to maintaining healthy Interpersonal Fields. Without them, the ability to cooperate and take collective action is compromised, and trust is diminished. Which brings us to trust, the third discipline in the Interpersonal Field.

Chapter Fourteen

The Discipline of Trust

Trust is like the air we breathe. When it's present, nobody really notices.
But when it's absent, everybody notices.

—Warren Buffett

Of all the disciplines in the Self and Interpersonal fields, trust is the most external. Awareness, choice, and accountability live primarily in your Field of the Self. Honesty and integrity occur in the Interpersonal Field and are still significantly focused on what is happening inside of you. Honesty is about revealing yourself to others; integrity is about your actions being truly in sync with what you value and hold to be true. But trust is something that only arises in the space between people. Therefore, trust can only exist in the context of another person.

Honesty and integrity are the cornerstones of trust. Without them, trust is not possible. And without trust, cooperation and collective action are severely impaired. People must trust their leaders; leaders must trust those they lead; team members must trust one another, and customers and vendors must trust the organizations with which they do business. Field Leaders must ensure that trust is alive and healthy throughout the four fields.

It's sometimes difficult for leaders to know if they have the trust of those they lead. Compliance does not mean trust, nor does it mean respect. In fact, conflict and challenge are sometimes the earmarks of trust and respect. When there is sufficient trust and respect, people will risk conflict and challenge one another in the spirit of helping everyone to be their best. In the absence of trust and respect, people will avoid conflict altogether or engage in conflict in order to "win," that is, to have their point of view prevail without attention to the greater good for which everyone should be striving.

145

Most leaders assume they have the trust of the people they lead. This assumption is not always grounded and is fraught with risk. If asked, they may point to the lack of apparent mistrust as evidence that they are trusted.

In an article in *Forbes* magazine, David Horsager, author of *The Trust Edge: How Top Leaders Gain Faster Results, Deeper Relationships, and a Stronger Bottom Line*, said, "One of the biggest mistakes a leader can make is to assume that others trust him simply by virtue of his title. Trust is not a benefit that comes packaged with the nameplate on your door. It must be earned, and it takes time. As a leader, you are trusted only to the degree that people believe in your ability, consistency, integrity, and commitment to deliver" (Horsager, 2012).

One of the ways in which leaders build trust is by acknowledging their mistakes and apologizing when appropriate. But in a survey of over one thousand business leaders and employees conducted by the Forum Corporation, of the 250 employees that responded to the survey, only 23 percent said they trust their leaders now more than in the past, while fully 70 percent of employees and 74 percent of leaders said trust is more important now than in the past. Furthermore, when asked if their leader apologizes when appropriate, only 5 percent of employees said they always do, while 49 percent of the leaders said they do. Fifty percent of employees said their leaders rarely or never apologize, while only 2 percent of the leaders said this was the case. Clearly there is a serious disconnect between employees' and leaders' perceptions of their relationships (Smith, 2013).

When trust is lacking between any two people in an organization, the organization's performance as a whole is diminished. Trust will never be perfect between any two people, much less among the many diverse members of an organization. But striving to maintain trust as a cultural norm and keeping practices alive that build trust and repair it quickly when damaged are essential for organizations to thrive, especially in a relationship economy.

TRUST IS ALWAYS PERSONAL

Establishing trust, maintaining it, and restoring it when broken are among the most important responsibilities and sometimes the greatest challenges of Field Leadership. Without trust, relationships cannot thrive. But talking about trust can be challenging. I sometimes hear leaders say, in exasperation, they know trust is vital, but they don't know how to develop it in their people.

Trust is challenging because it is a deeply emotional topic and it always has a personal quality to it. Often it raises feelings of hostility, resentment, and defensiveness. It does not yield to the logic of the analytical mind. This makes it difficult to talk about, especially in organizations in which the disciplines of self-awareness and honesty are not deeply embedded in the culture. In such organizations, people often choose to avoid one another rather than address issues of trust.

One of the challenges of talking about trust is that there is no common language for it, and the minute it is raised, there is discomfort. This limits a leader's ability to establish trust and makes it particularly difficult to restore it once it's broken. Building, maintaining, and restoring trust all require conversation, yet it is often a topic that no one wants to talk about except in the abstract.

Because conversations about trust can feel intensely personal, they can exert a powerful influence on your physical, emotional, and analytical minds, distorting your Field of the Self. If you feel someone does not trust you, it can wear away at your self-esteem and make it difficult to be in a relationship with them. Likewise, if you do not trust someone, you may feel a persistent sense of anger and resentment toward them. Such emotions make it difficult or impossible to have an effective conversation about what is happening between the two of you. And when you don't have clear distinctions about what trust is, even if there is a will to have the necessary conversation, there may not be a way. For many people, trust and mistrust are vague emotional states they find difficult to express in words, and so they avoid conversations about them.

For all of these reasons, it is essential to create clear distinctions about what trust is and clear language about how to talk about it. These distinctions can significantly diminish the emotional charge of conversations about trust and can provide the means for navigating those conversations effectively.

TRUST IS A PRODUCT OF ASSESSMENTS

Recall the distinction between an assessment and an assertion. An assessment is an opinion or interpretation of something; an assertion is a statement of fact that can be proven true or false. Assessments spring more from your physical and emotional minds than your analytical mind, and they shape your soft-wired mental models and rules. They are thus powerful determinants of your behavior; it takes considerable self-awareness to manage them. We have all had the experience of fiercely defending our opinion no matter how compelling the evidence that it does not accurately reflect reality.

An assessment reveals much about the person who is speaking, often more than it tells you about the subject of which they are speaking. When I say that a room is cold, I am not really telling you about the temperature of the room, I am telling you how I experience the temperature of the room.

In working with clients to build a culture of trust, I introduce the notion that trust arises at the intersection of three assessments. If all three assessments are present, trust exists; if any of them are missing, trust does not exist. The three assessments are *sincerity*, *capability*, and *reliability*.

Sincerity is an assessment that others are being honest with you, that what they say is a true reflection of what they feel and believe. When you believe others are insincere, collaboration becomes difficult and sometimes impossible. Anything someone says is questioned, so lengthy explanations and rationales become necessary. And even with the explanations and rationalizations, the underlying motives and consequently the integrity of the speaker are questioned. This makes it impossible to establish alignment. On the other hand, when you believe that others *are* sincere in their words and actions, collaboration becomes easy and efficient. Lengthy explanations and rationales are not necessary. Conversations are focused on results rather than outing someone for having a hidden agenda or trying to prove them wrong in their point of view.

Capability is an assessment that a person has all the necessary resources to do what they say. They are sufficiently skilled and have the time, the tools, and everything else needed to fulfill their promises. It is quite possible for someone to be entirely sincere in their promise to do something yet, in reality, not have the necessary capability. A young project manager with only one year of experience in the business world may be entirely sincere in her offer to lead a large, complex project; her belief in her competence may reside in her lack of appreciation of what it will take to lead the project. The person setting up the project team may assess that the young project manager, while sincere, is not yet competent to lead such a project. Consequently, they would not trust the young project manager to lead the project.

Reliability is an assessment that, historically, a person has consistently done what they have promised. This assessment can only be made if you have some experience with the person or if you trust the assessment of someone else who has experience with the person.

TALKING ABOUT TRUST

Because trust is an assessment, and assessments are deeply rooted in your emotional mind, building trust, and especially rebuilding it once it is broken, is an emotional journey. The distinctions of sincerity, capability, and reliability are useful because without them, people tend to collapse all forms of mistrust into the assessment of insincerity. If you assess someone has been dishonest and intentionally misled you, it strikes a deep wound. Assessments of insincerity tend to be quite persistent because they suggest a fundamental dishonesty—a willful intention to mislead. Conversations about sincerity are often the most difficult trust conversations to have. If you can identify the source of mistrust as capability or reliability, it is easier to have respectful and rational conversations about those assessments and how to change them.

These three distinctions provide effective language for talking about trust and effective tools for identifying the cause of mistrust. The distinction of trust as assessment rather than assertion is particularly important because it defuses the personal aspect of mistrust: it is possible for me to tell someone I have developed mistrust in them and acknowledge my mistrust is a view I hold rather than a truth about them. Likewise, it is possible for me to hear someone tell me they mistrust me without my hearing their assessment as the truth about me. I can become curious about what they see in my behavior that gives rise to the mistrust, and together we can discover how to restore trust. Sometimes, it is simply a matter of better explaining your behavior; other times, it requires changing your behavior.

Having conversations about trust requires the ability to continually return to center and engage in deep honesty. Even when grounded in the distinctions of sincerity, capability, and reliability, trust conversations can be emotionally difficult. They don't always go smoothly, and sometimes they require revisiting the issue more than once. But they are far superior to the usual behaviors of avoidance and denial or heated conversations of blame and finger pointing.

Because trust arises at the intersection of two people, integrity is necessary in both parties to establish trust. If you believe someone is lacking integrity, trust is impossible because you assess that they are insincere. It takes integrity to inspire others to trust you; it also takes integrity to accurately assess that others are trustworthy. If you are lacking integrity, you are likely to assign malicious intent in others when it is not present, and you are likely to under- or overassess their sincerity, capability, and reliability if it serves you to do so.

When people trust one another, their conversations are efficient and their interpersonal relationships are strong. They feel safe asking each for other for clarification; they believe what is said to them is sincere and the person who is saying it is competent and reliable. Cooperation and collective action become seamless, and there is little wasted time or energy, driving organizational performance higher and higher. Furthermore, when there is a high level of trust, difficult circumstances become vastly easier to navigate because people have the necessary relationships to act quickly and efficiently.

In organizations in which trust is low, backbiting and power struggles are common. Everyone strives to get ahead on their own at the expense of others. Watercooler gossip prevails and drives the emotional states and beliefs of individuals, leading to wasted time and energy and a mood of resignation.

Issues of trust will inevitably arise in most, if not all, relationships. There are people who are fundamentally untrustworthy—they lie, they cheat, they manipulate, and they never acknowledge that they do so or take accountability for their behavior. Those people are few and far between. When you find yourself in a relationship with one of them, you must make the sometimes difficult decision of whether you will tolerate their behavior or end the relationship. In all other cases, with the right approach, issues of trust can be resolved and trust restored. But it takes skill, patience, and courage to do so.

Trust is a product of the disciplines of the Self and Interpersonal fields. It is fundamental to leadership; it is particularly fundamental to Field Leadership, in which the strength of interpersonal relationships is essential for organizations to thrive. Without trust, Field Leadership is impossible.

Chapter Fifteen

Conflict and Collaboration in the Interpersonal Field

Conflict arises in all Four Fields of Leadership, and it may be productive or toxic. You can feel conflicted in your Field of the Self, unable to decide among several possible choices, and teams and organizations conflict with one another all the time. But the place where conflict is most evident and most toxic is in the Interpersonal Field. If conflict in the Interpersonal Field cannot be resolved, resolving it in the Field of Teams or the Enterprise Field will be difficult or impossible. The disciplines of the Field of the Self and the Interpersonal Field provide a path to managing conflict and to turning it into a productive, rather than destructive, phenomenon.

RELATIONSHIPS COME FIRST, CONFLICT SECOND

If you experience challenging emotions when you think about having a conversation or when you are in one, your inner state is informing you that something must be addressed. The emotional challenge will take you off center, distorting your Field of the Self. And when there is distortion in the Field of the Self, there will be distortion in the Interpersonal Field. The mistake people often make is moving directly to discussing the topic or content of the conflict without first addressing the context of the conversation, which is the relationship itself.

The most fundamental rule for managing interpersonal conflict is to tend first to the relationship and then, only when the Interpersonal Field is healthy, turn to the content of the conversation. If you neglect the health of the Interpersonal Field, what is being left unsaid—how each of you is feeling, the assessments each of you is forming of the other, a lack of trust—will dominate the conversation. It will be difficult or impossible to make the conversation productive.

The first step in tending to the relationship is to tend to your inner state. Center yourself so that your Field of the Self is prepared to enter effectively into the Interpersonal Field. From a place of center, engage the person with whom you are talking using the disciplines of honesty and integrity. That is how you build the trust necessary for difficult conversations.

It may seem time consuming and inefficient to go to the relationship conversation first. After all, the point is to get work done, isn't it? But you can't work well with someone when the Interpersonal Field is distorted. The relationship creates the context for effective conversations. And your inner state determines the quality of the relationship. For effective collaboration, you must work the fields from the inside out. In doing that, you address distortion in the Field of the Self so it doesn't create distortion in the Interpersonal Field. And you address distortion in the Interpersonal Field so it doesn't inhibit your ability to have an effective conversation.

DON'T AGREE TO DISAGREE

When I coach people who are dealing with conflict, they invariably talk about it as something *outside* of themselves, as though it has a life of its own and is beyond their control. When they talk specifically about a conflict with another person, they talk about it as though the conflict either lives on its own in the space between them or in the other person. One CEO I coached, we'll call her Julia, insisted the ongoing conflict she had with Sarah, a member of her leadership team, existed entirely in Sarah. Julia knew their Interpersonal Field was not healthy, but she took no accountability for that. They often left their conversations "agreeing to disagree."

Agreeing to disagree is a common term. It's frequently accompanied by a tone of resignation or resentment. In fact, it sounds not so much like an agreement as a giving up, walking away in a state of hopelessness. This is a shame because it is often in disagreement that you have the greatest opportunity to learn from and about each other.

Disagreement is an opportunity to strengthen the Interpersonal Field. In disagreement, you can learn from one another through what each of you shares and the questions you ask. If you both ask skillful questions, and you are both open to hearing and reflecting on them and answering honestly, disagreement often dissolves as you discover common ground. Skillful questions cause you to examine your own point of view. Such self-examination can lead to new insights and a richer, deeper perspective than the one with which you started the conversation. Likewise, you can learn about the other person as they reflect on and answer your skillful questions.

In any work situation, there must be a fundamental shared concern in a conversation. At the very least, you are both committed to the success of the organization. Agreeing to disagree is most often a failure to stay connected to that fundamental concern throughout the conversation. You may end up holding different assessments about the best path to take, but if you are grounded in a shared fundamental concern, you will stay in the conversation long enough to fully understand how each of your points of view attempts to address that fundamental concern. From there, you can decide how best to proceed and agree on the path forward. The result of such conversations is learning, deeper understanding of the issue at hand, and stronger, more collaborative relationships. When you are skilled at having these conversations, you will more often seek out points of view that differ from yours rather than avoiding them. The challenge is to develop the interpersonal disciplines necessary for these conversations.

CONFLICT IS AN ASSESSMENT

While there are many ways of defining and thinking about conflict, I find it most useful to consider that ultimately it is how you define a situation—not just intellectually but emotionally, physically, and spiritually—that determines whether or not it is conflict. Someone else's conflict doesn't have to be yours, even if you're both in the same conversation. This reframing requires mastery in the Field of the Self.

When I asked Julia to describe her conflict with Sarah, she described Sarah's behavior, including her tone of voice. Julia held the assessment that Sarah was intentionally disrespectful and was certain that her assessment was right. Julia had struggled for several years with this relationship and felt quite stuck. Sarah was a valuable member of the team and brought considerable revenue to the company, and at the same time, Julia was close to saying she could no longer tolerate Sarah's disrespectful behavior and was thinking of letting her go.

What hadn't occurred to Julia was that she was as much a participant in the conflict as Sarah was—until I asked her whether the conflict would still exist if for some reason she left the company. She thought for a moment, then said "No. The relationship would no longer be there, so neither would the conflict." I then pointed out that she, therefore, must also be part of the problem. Every Interpersonal Field has two Fields of the Self, and both are responsible for the health of the Interpersonal Field. She paused and looked at me with a mixture of hostility and curiosity. Then she asked me to explain.

A relationship is in conflict *because you define it as such*. If another person is angry with you, you can react with anger as well, and you will be in conflict: each of you trying to prove yourself right, each of you trying to win at the expense of the other. But you don't have to respond with anger. If you have sufficient self-awareness and sufficient ability to manage your inner state, you can stay centered and curious. When you choose curiosity over defensiveness, conflict can become collaboration.

I asked Julia to reflect carefully on what she experienced when she met with Sarah. I had worked with Julia for over a year and had taught her the meditation technique I described in chapter 8. She meditated regularly, so she had some skill at self-awareness. After thinking for a minute, Julia said she became physically tense as soon as she knew Sarah was coming to talk with her, and when Sarah said things that Julia thought were disrespectful, Julia would get angry and argue the opposite point of view. I asked her how she thought Sarah felt in these conversations. Again she stopped and stared at me for a moment, then said she'd never thought about that.

One of the interesting things about self-awareness is if you are not self-aware, you can't be very aware of other people. Your own inner experience will continually generate distractions that prevent you from accurately seeing what's going on for others. Your interpretations of the event become distorted by all the inner noise. Self-awareness enables you to calm the inner noise so you can center and see what's actually happening more accurately.

Julia used her centering practices to reflect on what Sarah's experience might be. She realized it must also be stressful for Sarah to be in conversations with her, knowing she would be tense, defensive, and aggressive. With these insights, Julia decided to shift her behavior the next time she met with Sarah, to center and calm herself and to be curious about what was behind the things Sarah was saying. From that point forward their relationship improved.

CONFLICT AND THE BRAIN

The art of managing conflict is essential for Field Leadership. Some people think conflict management is about not reacting when someone says something you find disturbing. That's better than reacting poorly, but it's not sufficient. You must learn to react effectively. That means checking your fight-or-flight response, recognizing the inherent richness and opportunity in differing points of view, and moving to engage rather than defeat the person with whom you are talking.

Neuroscientists use brain scanning tools to observe activity in the brain. One of the changes scientists see in meditators' brains is a strengthening of the regulatory parts of the brain and a diminishing of the areas that trigger the fight-or-flight response (Zeidan et al., 2014). And as we saw in chapter 5, centering practices reduce adrenaline and cortisol, the stress hormones. Re-call Major General Walter Piatt, who used a meditation practice to prepare for his meeting with a tribal leader in Iraq, enabling him to stay centered and en-gaged throughout the meeting. In the same way, Julia's ability to change the nature of her conversations with Sarah came from her ability to center before meeting with Sarah and to stay centered during their meetings, preventing her physical and emotional minds from taking over her inner state. She used her meditation techniques to quiet the fight-or-flight part of her brain, inhibiting it from releasing adrenaline and cortisol into her bloodstream. With that taken care of, she could activate the parts of her brain that produce a sense of caring and curiosity toward others.

Julia did that by using the emotional centering practice of acceptance. Acceptance can be disarming, especially when the person with whom you are interacting is expecting resistance. Acceptance creates a space in which something richer and deeper than conflict can occur. Julia's curiosity and compassion were possible because she accepted Sarah for who she was in the moment of their meeting.

I have often observed that changing how one sees a relationship influences the other person to see it differently as well. Julia told me that as she stayed centered and expressed genuine curiosity with Sarah, she could see Sarah physically relax, her voice became less strident, and she became open to a genuine exchange of ideas. Julia's transformation of her Field of the Self led Sarah's to transform as well.

While brain scans tell us something about how this works in the meditator, an important question is why this had the effect it did on Sarah. After all, she was not a meditator and wasn't even aware that Julia was choosing to change the nature of their relationship. She certainly wasn't intentionally participat-ing in changing it.

Another area of brain research has shown us that something called *limbic resonance* occurs between two people who are interacting with one another (Lewis, Amini, and Lannon, 2001). The limbic system is composed of the areas of the brain that create and regulate emotions. Limbic resonance refers to the observation that when a person expresses an emotion—even subtly and unconsciously, through facial expressions or tone of voice—they will generate a similar emotional state in the person to whom they are talking. In other words, when someone is sending emotional signals to you, your brain is likely to resonate with theirs, reproducing in you an emotional state similar to the one they are experiencing. We've all experienced it, though you may not have known what it was. Think of a time you heard someone laughing loudly and found yourself smiling or even laughing. You also experience this when you are watching a movie. When you see someone in a film who is expressing sadness or joy, you are likely to experience the same emotion.

When Julia and Sarah both saw their relationship as a relationship in conflict, emotional resonance kept them in conflict. But when Julia changed her assessment and engaged Sarah from a state of respect and curiosity, emotional resonance led Sarah to change as well. This is how the Interpersonal Field emerges from Fields of the Self.

HONESTY, INTEGRITY, AND TRUST: CENTERING IN THE INTERPERSONAL FIELD

While Julia was able to center herself and develop more productive conversations with Sarah, she eventually realized that in their earlier conversations, she had been less than fully honest with Sarah. This meant that in those conversations, Julia had lacked integrity. She had not shared her own defensiveness and emotional reaction to what Sarah said. So eventually Julia came to talk directly with Sarah about their relationship.

This was a powerful step for Julia to take, requiring her to be vulnerable. But she was committed to cultivating Field Leadership throughout her organization, so she knew it was necessary. First, she told Sarah the relationship was important to her and she wanted it to be strong and collaborative. Then she acknowledged that her own past behavior had been less than exemplary, that she had allowed herself to become defensive and angry, and she apologized. She said she wanted to better understand what Sarah experienced in their conversations and asked her to reflect on that.

This became more than one conversation. Sarah needed to absorb what Julia had said and come to a decision about how far to trust her. She was cautious because in her prior experiences with Julia, Julia had sometimes been quite angry, bordering on what Sarah considered verbal abuse. But over time, Sarah came to trust Julia sufficiently to share her view of their relationship. They gradually built the trust they both wanted, and their conversations became far more productive.

As a Field Leader, it is your job to first develop your own mastery in the field disciplines, and then guide others to their mastery. You cannot intervene every time conflict erupts, but you can teach those you lead to manage it for themselves. This is not just a tips-and-techniques skill. It requires genuine care for those you lead and compassion in helping them deal with their inner state and their interpersonal relationships. You help them see their part in breakdowns and challenges because it's in their best interest to do so. If they can see themselves more fully, they will form better relationships, have greater confidence, and be more effective in their jobs.

Chapter Sixteen

Leadership in the Interpersonal Field

I have defined leadership as the means by which two or more individuals develop the ability to cooperate and take collective action. Any two individuals are likely to have differing desires and opinions about how their relationship should evolve, how they should cooperate with one another, and what collective actions they should take. In egalitarian relationships, such as those in a marriage, friendship, or peer relationship at work, decisions are often made with joint input and accommodation, and leadership is mostly emergent. On a moment-by-moment basis, intentional leadership may arise, but it will be dynamic, with influence shifting from one individual to the other. This often happens with no acknowledgment or even awareness.

In other cases, in which there is a clear power differential in the relationship, such as the relationship between employer and employee or manager and direct report, leadership may appear anywhere on the spectrum. Balancing emergent and intentional leadership is one of the challenges Field Leaders must constantly address. That requires the ability to sense and engage with the inner state of those you lead, which starts with awareness of others.

AWARENESS OF OTHERS

Field Leaders must have a high level of awareness of others—how they feel, what they believe, how they interpret their experiences—and the ability to use that awareness to cultivate effective, trusting relationships with them. This cannot be done with your analytical mind alone.

There are countless personality profiles and quantitative measures of individual differences that take an analytical approach to understanding human behavior in the workplace. These can be useful, but only in limited ways because all they provide is data about how an individual responded to an instrument's questions and an assessment of how to interpret the data. When you read someone's profile, the data mostly engages your analytical mind. Human beings are far more complex than such data can reveal, and managing interpersonal relationships is far more complex than the analytical mind alone can achieve. Human relationships are more art than science. Fortunately, there is another way.

As you have seen, your assessments and mental models of people shape your behavior toward them. Assessments and mental models arise mostly in your physical and emotional minds. If you are off center, your assessments and mental models will be distorted by your visceral reactions to what someone is saying, and your response to them will be less than optimal. But assessments and mental models are malleable; you can observe them and alter them through the disciplines of the Field of the Self and the Interpersonal Field. With centering practices, you can short circuit your primitive fight-or-flight response and use the interpersonal disciplines of honesty, integrity, and trust to establish open and respectful relationships, even with people you find difficult. By regulating your own inner state, you can influence theirs, helping them to come to a place of trust and shared purpose with you. This takes more effort and skill than reading a personality profile but is far more effective.

CULTIVATING PATTERNS IN THE SELF AND INTERPERSONAL FIELDS

Field Leadership involves a new way of thinking about and understanding leadership. It is holistic and systemic, and it requires leaders to develop deep personal and interpersonal capabilities. It often requires more soul searching than you may have done in the past.

A good way to begin is by changing some old habits and asking some new questions. One habit to change, in order to ask new questions, is the habit of asking conventional, analytical questions. Consider a team meeting in which you, as the leader, have been given bad news about a project. Conventional questions might be "Where in the process did we go wrong?" and "Who's responsible?" Those will pull you into an analytical mindset.

When you find yourself reacting quickly with analytical questions, center yourself and instead consider questions like the following:

• "What are the facts?" This is a data-gathering question, not an analytical question. Analytical questions attempt to analyze the data. The spirit of this question is to identify, without judgment, the actual events and choices that led to the present state. Starting with reality is always useful.

- "Why was that choice made?" This is not asked in the spirit of blame, but rather seeking to understand. If people feel they are being put on the spot, they will become defensive. If they feel you are seeking to understand them, they are more likely to open up.
- "How does each of us feel?" As you have seen, your inner state determines your behavior, and your emotional mind is a powerful determinant of your inner state. If people feel they must hide their emotions, they will be defensive. Recall that in the framework of the four fields, honesty is proportional to how much of yourself you reveal. If you want honesty, you must be prepared to ask and hear how people are feeling. Remember what I said earlier about conflict: if there is distortion in the Interpersonal Field, deal with that before dealing with the issue. You often have to start with how people feel and listen to them with compassion before they can open up.
- "What does each of us care about relative to this project?" This question can reconnect people to their emotional engagement with the project and their desire to see it succeed. As a Field Leader, it is your job to create an environment in which everyone feels they are all in it together and are all committed to the same outcome.
- "What are the vital relationships on this project, and how did those relationships influence the choices made?" This gets at the dynamics of the team and can reveal otherwise hidden influences that brought you to the current state.

The purpose of such questions is to reveal the context and the content of what led to the current state. The context—people's interpersonal relationships and the degree to which the disciplines of the four fields are practiced—often reveals patterns that result in recurring successes or failures. To solve recurring problems, you must find the recurring patterns—the behaviors and relationships—that give rise to them. These patterns exist in the Self and Interpersonal fields. If they remain hidden, they cannot be addressed. If an individual always points fingers, blames others, and fails to take accountability for the results of their actions, your job as a leader is to help them cultivate an inner state from which they make different choices. If two individuals do not trust one another, your job is to help them discover why and resolve the mistrust. When those problems are addressed, the recurring problems will come to an end.

LEADERSHIP DISCIPLINES IN THE INTERPERSONAL FIELD

- **Honesty**: Be transparent in all that you do and say. Honesty is proportional to how much of yourself you reveal. As a Field Leader, your job goes far beyond your technical expertise and decision making. Those are important, but at least as important is your ability to cultivate the disciplines of the four fields in those you lead. Begin by role modeling those disciplines with your own behavior.

- **Integrity**: If those you lead are confident that you are honest and your actions align with your principles, that you live the disciplines as well as preach them, they will see you as an authentic leader and will be drawn to you. Remember that cooperation and collective action are always choices people make. Your job as a leader is to inspire them to make those choices.
- **Trust**: Develop in yourself and in those you lead the ability to establish trust through honesty and integrity. And when trust is broken, the ability to accurately name the specific assessments that led to a lack of trust, to speak respectfully about those assessments, and to work to find ways to change them. Trust is built through honesty and integrity. It is also restored through honesty and integrity.
- **Speak up**: As soon as you know there's an issue or you sense a potential issue, name it. This sounds simple and obvious, but it can be surprisingly difficult. Naming issues invariably triggers emotions. There is risk of others becoming angry, of blame, of hurt feelings. But when issues are not named, they fester. Even worse, not naming issues can quickly become an acceptable behavior. Resistance to naming issues often stems from people not knowing how to do it well. The disciplines of the Self and Interpersonal fields can overcome that resistance.
- **Reflect on the other person's inner state**: When forming assessments of what someone else says or does or what their intention is, reflect carefully on what inner state they may be experiencing and engage them with empathy. This does not mean agreeing or approving; it means accepting that whatever their inner state is, it leads them to behave the way they do. For someone's behavior to change, their inner state must change. Helping those you lead gain mastery over their inner state is part of a Field Leader's job. Focus first on your concern for the relationship, then on your own behavior and how it contributes to the relationship, and only then on the other's behavior.

The Interpersonal Field persists over time and distance. This is so obvious that most of us take it for granted, knowing that our relationships with one another continue even when we are separated and not interacting. In some ways, Interpersonal Fields persist even after either or both individuals have passed away. My parents are both gone, yet my relationships with them continue to influence me in ways both mundane and profound, and the relationship they had with one another influences me as well.

In section 2, I described the spiritual aspect of the Field of the Self as a path of self-transcendence. This takes on richer meaning in the Interpersonal Field, where spirituality manifests as connection with others. In an Interpersonal Field, you have a heightened awareness of one another's concerns and inner states. Together, you discover insights and synergies that neither of you would have discovered on your own.

Interlude Three

Emergence

I introduced the word *emergence* in chapter 1 and have used it several times since. It's time to provide a deeper understanding of what emergence is and why it is so vital to leadership and the four fields. Emergence and leadership are deeply intertwined, and they become increasingly important as we move into the Field of Teams and the Enterprise Field. In this interlude, I explore that intersection and further explain the definition of leadership I offered in chapter 1.

HURRICANES AND WIKIS

When Hurricane Katrina struck New Orleans in 2005, the systems that were supposed to respond to disasters were overwhelmed. Much of the infrastructure that would be necessary for an orderly response was destroyed, and chaos ensued. But even as Katrina approached landfall, a small group of technology-savvy individuals were preparing to help.

Less than a year earlier, one of the largest tsunamis in history had killed over 225,000 people in Southeast Asia. As the disaster unfolded, a wiki named TsunamiHelp was created by a spontaneous group of volunteers. The purpose of the wiki was to provide a public clearinghouse for any information that might be useful. Within a week, it was the fourth most visited humanitarian website in the world (Wu, 2015).

One of the individuals who volunteered on TsunamiHelp was Rob Kline, a software programmer in Seattle, Washington. As Katrina grew in force ahead of landfall, Kline was following the news and growing increasingly concerned. It was clear that a disaster of unprecedented magnitude was about to occur. He reached out to others who had worked on TsunamiHelp. They quickly cloned its structure and named the new wiki KatrinaHelp. Rudi Cilibrasi, a student in Amsterdam, offered to host the wiki on a private server he operated, and KatrinaHelp was launched within hours of the hurricane striking New Orleans. Anyone in the world with internet access could contribute. On the main page, topic headings for Resources, Help, and News appeared, and beneath each, categories were created where people could add useful information. A sample of categories under Help on the home page includes ("Main Page," 2005):

- **Life and Death?** *Get Help Now!*
- **Missing & Found: Post** about missing & found persons; **find** more information
- **Help Offered**: **Hundreds of people** are offering to shelter refugees, make phone calls, and help in any way they can. **Please choose from one of the following seven areas you are interested in helping with:**
  1. Essential Goods & Services Offered
  2. Manpower & Volunteers Offered
  3. Housing Offered
  4. Counseling/Healing Services Offered
  5. Communications Offered
  6. Jobs Offered
  7. Transportation
  8. Other Help

The home page also had links to instructions for how to contribute to the wiki. People around the world began adding and updating information.

A wiki is a fundamentally egalitarian system for cataloging data. Anyone who has information they feel might be helpful can contribute. Anyone can edit it, and anyone can create categories of information. The wiki software creates an ongoing log of changes so that you can trace back to earlier versions if a mistake is made.

As New Orleans drowned, KatrinaHelp grew. People posted names of individuals who were missing and names of those who had been found. Software was added that could automatically match missing and found people. Addresses and directions to shelters, job opportunities, health and safety information, activities for children, and much more were added by individuals pitching in with whatever they had to offer. Four days after Katrina struck, KatrinaHelp was receiving a million hits a day, overloading Cilibrasi's server, at which point the Sitemeter hosting service took over and hosted it for free (Majchrzak, Jarvenpaa, and Hollingshead, 2007).

All this happened because vast numbers of individuals chose to follow an ancient rule hidden deep in our genes: when people are in need, reach out to help. It happened without anyone directing it, without a leader, and with a constantly changing cast of contributors. And it happened much faster and more effectively than the bureaucratic systems that were designed to respond to disasters. Rob Kline commented, "With the distributed nature of the Internet, you now have the ability for people with common interests to rapidly aggregate themselves and apply their nearly unbounded knowledge of different subjects into cohesive organization in a matter of hours. Because it's distributed, it's global, so when I have to go to sleep, someone else can pick it up and keep working on it" (Terdiman, 2005).

Groups that emerge spontaneously to address crises and disasters are being studied by scientists interested in human leadership, cooperation, and collective action. The term used to define them is *emergent response groups*. They are the spontaneous and temporary formation of superorganisms. Katrina-Help is a classic example of emergence.

THE NATURE OF EMERGENCE

As I stated at the beginning of this book, the term *emergent* is used to describe properties and behaviors of a system that occur at the level of the whole system and cannot be predicted or understood by understanding the parts alone. KatrinaHelp emerged with an elegant, well-ordered structure, offering up millions of pieces of information in an accessible interface with no planning or direction. While examples of emergent phenomena in human organizations abound, it is easier to study them in simpler contexts, so I will digress for a bit into natural systems that exhibit emergence before returning to leadership and human organizations.

I have written that flocks of starlings and insect nests are examples of emergence, but now I want to introduce a new creature: the lowly slime mold, a kind of primitive amoeba. Slime molds have been around for about one billion years (Tatischeff, 2019). There are many types. Meet Dictyostelium discoideum.

Dictyostelium is a single-celled organism that lives beneath decaying leaves and other plant matter on forest floors. Each cell normally lives as a single organism, independent and apparently unaware of any other Dictyostelium that might be in the neighborhood. They feed on bacteria and other organisms in the soil and reproduce through simple cell division. But when food runs short, a remarkable sequence of events unfolds. They give up their solitary lives, stop reproducing, and take on distinct roles. They become so-cial organisms that cooperate and take collective action.

This transformation begins with all of them coming together into a densely packed mound of cells that has a sort of tip at the very top. Surrounding cells continue to push into the center of the mound, forcing the tip to rise up, turn-ing the broad mound into a narrow column. Eventually, the column topples over. At this point, it resembles, superficially, a tiny garden slug. The "slug" then migrates to the surface of the leaves under which it has been living.

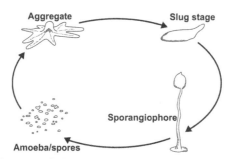

Figure Interlude 3.1.   Emergence in Dictyostelium

Once the slug gets to the surface, another transformation begins. Some of the cells begin to form a stalk that rises up from the middle of the slug. This is a complex process that ends with the cells on the outer surface of the stalk dying in order to provide a rigid structure for the stalk. Other cells form a disc that is firmly attached to the ground. This disc anchors the stalk so it doesn't fall over. Partway up the stalk, other cells form a kind of cup. As all of this is going on, still other cells take the first steps of turning themselves into spores. As they are turning into spores, they climb up the stalk and into the cup, where they complete their transformation into spores. Eventually, they form a bulbous mass of spores filling and rising above the cup. The cup prevents them from sliding back down the stalk and ending up on the ground. Above the bulbous mass of spores is another cup, upside down, that further anchors the mass of spores on the stalk. This whole structure is termed the *fruiting body* because it superficially resembles a tiny fruit-bearing plant, though biologically, it is vastly different from a plant.

When this process is complete, the undifferentiated Dictyostelium cells that were all identical and independent before food became scarce have transformed themselves into something resembling a small plant with a mass of seeds at the top. Those seeds—the cells that became spores—can then be carried by the wind or by passing animals to new, hopefully more fertile, territory. When the spores land, they return to their undifferentiated state as separate individuals and begin feasting on bacteria in the soil, unaware of one another until food once more runs scarce and the process begins again (Zimmer, 2011). These primitive simple bacteria transform into an emergent superorganism that exhibits all Four Fields of Leadership.

In emergent systems, the whole has capabilities greater than the capabilities of the parts, and not in a simple additive way. Five people together can lift a weight greater than any subset of them. But their strength is additive: what they can lift together is the sum of what they can each lift individually. There is nothing emergent about that. If you knew the strength of each individual, you could quickly calculate their collective strength. The behaviors and capabilities of Dictyostelium working together are much more than additive. They could never be predicted from studying individual Dictyostelium cells. In the same way, KatrinaHelp had capabilities far richer and more complex than could be predicted from knowing the individuals who contributed to it.

Emergent phenomena have been a source of mystery and fascination for eons. Thousands of years ago, the Greek philosopher and mathematician Aristotle puzzled over them, referring to their special properties in his writings on science and nature (Bogaard, 1979). Emergent phenomena give truth to the old saying that the whole is greater than the sum of the parts. We all know intuitively this is true, but many of us don't know *why* it is true. The mechanical thinking of the Age of Reason could not penetrate this question.

Only recently has the science of complexity freed us from the limitations of mechanical thinking and shed light on how emergence works. As you have seen, mechanical thinking is reductionist, which means it studies the parts of a system in the belief that understanding the parts will be sufficient for understanding the whole. But if the whole is greater than the sum of the parts, then mechanical thinking can never give insight into the whole. As scientists broke free of mechanical thinking and began studying complexity, they developed insights and methods to explore the whole and the parts together. From that work, they have begun to define common attributes that characterize emergent phenomena. It's a work in progress, but the following list provides some insight. In emergent phenomena (Addiscott, 2011):

- The whole is more than the sum of the parts—there are more capabilities and greater complexity in the whole than could be derived from all the parts separately.
- Neither the form nor the behavior of the whole can be predicted by studying the parts.
- The whole is coherent—it exhibits stability and order in the patterns of behavior of the whole and the interactions of the parts.

- The behavior of the whole emerges from the collective behavior of the parts. That is why it is said that, in emergent phenomena, the organization of the whole comes from the bottom up rather than the top down.
- The emergent behavior of the whole reinforces the behaviors of the parts that give rise to the whole. This is often referred to as downward pressure from the whole to the parts.
- The behavior of the parts is dictated by simple rules.
- The whole is leaderless, meaning no individual directs the behavior of the whole or the behavior of its parts.

Emergent phenomena evolved because they confer competitive advantage. A group of individuals can be a chaotic mob, but when they cooperate and take collective action, they become a powerful force, far more than the additive power of all the individuals in a mob. Emergence is how nature made it possible to transcend the limitations of individual organisms acting independently. To transcend those limitations, individuals had to develop the ability to cooperate with one another and take collective action. Cooperation means an individual agrees to behave in a way that helps out another individual; collective action means a group of individuals coordinate their behavior to achieve a common goal.

Consider Dictyostelium. Its transformation is a remarkable example of cooperation and collective action and explains why Dictyostelium are referred to as "social amoebas" (Eichinger et al., 2005). Before swarming into a mound, all the cells are identical. No particular cells are predetermined to become disc cells, stalk cells, or spores. It's just a matter of where they happen to be in the overall mass that determines their future. If a cell is near where the stalk needs to form, it becomes a stalk cell. Some cells die in the process, enabling others to go on to propagate the species. Without such cooperation and collective action, all the cells would starve and Dictyostelium as a species would likely cease to exist.

Cooperation and collective action are the prerequisites for orderly group behavior. Orderly group behavior gives rise to emergence and the competitive advantages emergence confers. Once cooperation and collective action were possible, emergence was inevitable. The question, then, is how did the abilities for cooperation and collective action arise? How did organisms make the leap from autonomous individuals to cooperating communities taking collective action?

For cooperation and collective action to happen, individuals must be able to exchange information and respond to information they receive—in other words, to establish interpersonal communication loops. Interpersonal communication loops are the means by which cooperation and collective action arise. The first such communication loops arose through the exchange of biochemical molecules in simple organisms like Dictyostelium. Later, more sophisticated means of exchanging information evolved.

Consider an ant hive. Most of the ants in a hive are foragers whose job is to find and harvest food. Initially, foragers wander randomly. When one of them finds food, it picks some up and heads back to the nest, switching from searching for food to harvesting it. As it makes its way back to the nest, it lays down a pheromone trail. Pheromones are powerful biochemicals that act as messengers between organisms; they are one of the most common forms of biochemical communication. When other ants pick up the scent of the pheromone, they move to it and follow it to the food source, where they also pick up some food and head back to the nest. As they travel down the trail, each ant adds more of the pheromone, amplifying the signal of the first ant. The initial signal is weak, attracting just a few additional ants, but as each ant adds pheromone it strengthens the signal, attracting more ants, who add yet more pheromone to strengthen it further.

Recall from interlude 1 that there are only five fundamental behavior patterns that can arise from communication loops. As ants add more pheromone to the trail, the communication loop follows the "growth" pattern, reinforcing the behavior that causes it to grow stronger. But pheromones evaporate quickly, and eventually the evaporation rate of the pheromone trail matches the rate at which new pheromone is being laid down. At that point the communication loop is in the "steady state" pattern, in which the strength of the pheromone trail neither increases nor decreases.

As food is taken back to the nest and the source diminishes, some ants switch back to foraging randomly for food. As fewer ants go down the trail, the pheromone evaporates more quickly than it gets deposited, and the signal gets weaker. The behavior of the communication loop has switched to one that is dying rather than growing. When the food source is gone, no more ants go down the trail, and the communication loop of the pheromone trail ceases to exist. When another food source is discovered, it all begins again.

The behavior of any particular forager ant also follows a communication loop, one it maintains with its environment. When the ant has not found food in its immediate environment, it forages. When the ant finds food, it harvests. This is an oscillating communication loop, moving between foraging and harvesting. On the environment's side of the communication loop, in an area where there are no ants, ant food can grow. When ants find food, they harvest it, leaving room for the environment to grow more food. The environment oscillates between having and not having ant food.

The behavior of an ant hive is highly complex and is regulated by communication loops on many levels. Ants don't follow logical processes; they follow simple rules that give rise to effective communication loops. From that emerges the hive, a superorganism that functions with remarkable efficiency, adaptability, and effectiveness. Communication loops make orderly complexity possible. This is why so much is written about the importance of communication in leadership and effectiveness in human organizations, in which communication loops determine the behavior, and thus the performance, of all four fields.

EMERGENCE AND RULES

Communication loops are necessary for emergence, but they are not sufficient. We have seen that left to their own devices, many communication loops will create chaos more often than order. So one more critical element must be added: the simple rules I described in interlude 2. The five possible behaviors for communication loops are growth, steady state, oscillation, chaos, and death. Left to themselves, many communication loops are more likely to lead to chaos and death than growth, steady state, or oscillation. But as we have seen, when individuals follow the right simple rules, communication loops can be held to patterns of growth, steady state, and oscillation. That is how the creative potential of complexity is realized. The whole can thrive while avoiding chaos and death.

So we must ask: how does nature arrive at the right rules?

For almost all of our planet's history, random genetic mutations have been nature's way of conducting experiments and coming up with new capabilities. Having billions of years and trillions of organisms with which to experiment, nature can afford lots of errors. Most of her genetic experiments are failures, but there are occasional successes resulting in organisms with new capabilities that confer competitive advantage. As these capabilities become established, they are refined and enhanced in subsequent generations.

For example, at some point, nature may have developed a rule for Dictyostelium that said, "When food runs short, move away from other Dictyostelium." This would also be mediated through a communication loop, but instead of bringing the cells together during a food shortage, it would have resulted in a scramble of cells moving away from one another. This rule would create chaos and ultimately death for all Dictyostelium that followed it, and the mutations that coded for the rule would have disappeared from Dictyostelium's genes. The rules I described earlier are the ones that survived. The communication loops of those rules have patterns of oscillation (the repeating pattern of feeding, swarming, and spreading spores), growth (when there is plenty of food and all the Dictyostelium cells feed and reproduce), and hold at a steady state (when spores form and wait until the right conditions arise before returning to a feeding stage).

Many of nature's successful experiments confer advantages that are purely physical, like more efficient biochemical processes, better vision, and stronger muscles. These confer mechanical advantages. But others are behavioral. For example, coral snakes prey on great kiskadees, a kind of bird common in Central America. Great kiskadees have evolved to instinctively avoid anything that has a color pattern similar to that of coral snakes. It's a simple rule that confers an advantage to every individual great kiskadee (Smith, 1977). Behavioral advantages are a big improvement over mechanical advantages because they enable rapid responses to changing conditions in the environment.

Another leap occurs when behaviors appear that confer advantages that are collective in nature. Army ants have developed the ability to build bridges across divides, enabling them to get to places that other ants can't reach (Hartnett, 2018). There are rules individual army ants follow that make this possible, but following those rules only provides survival advantages at the collective level. No individual ant can build a bridge, no matter how well it follows the rules. But when enough ants follow the rules, the bridge emerges. The benefit of these behaviors can thus only be observed in the emergent behavior of the whole. Emergence happens because it enables individuals to cooperate and take collective action in ways that benefit the whole, thereby giving the whole a competitive advantage (Choi, 2015).

When lots of individuals follow the right set of simple rules, they avoid chaos and death, collections of parts become wholes, and emergence arises. The cooperation and collective action of starlings is possible because of the simple rules they follow. Recall the Brazilian railroad company I described in interlude 2. Rather than spending lengthy hours laying out complex processes, procedures, and policies, they adopted simple rules from which emerged elegant solutions to their challenges. Contributors to KatrinaHelp followed the simple rule of helping people in need, and the simple rules universal to all wikis.

There are endless examples throughout living systems. Insect hives, human cities, the stock market, small entrepreneurial startups, cardiovascular systems, brains and central nervous systems, cells in your body self-organizing to heal a wound—the list is as varied as the forms that living systems take. In all these examples, extraordinarily complex behavior emerges when you look at the entire system. Yet you could never understand that behavior by looking at the parts alone. Communication loops and rules established over eons of evolution are followed again and again, evolving gradually, giving rise to steadily increasing complexity and endlessly evolving living systems.

Our hyperconnected world emerged from the vast complexity and capabilities of the internet. The internet arose from a small set of simple rules established by its founders, who then unleashed the technology on the world. Because people everywhere followed those rules as they added information and technology, the internet emerged. Within the universe of the internet is another small set of rules that guides the development of a wiki. Following those simple rules, millions of people around the world gave rise to Katrina-Help. None of them had any concept of what the overall structure and design would become, yet by following the rules, it emerged. This could not have happened with the extensively detailed, rigid, step-by-step instructions that spring from mechanical thinking and still characterize many modern-day business processes. Indeed, in the onslaught of Katrina, the engineered business processes that were meant to deal with disasters failed miserably. Emergent phenomena are the evidence all around us that the analytical thinking we have been addicted to for so long is severely limited in what it can accomplish and is insufficient for addressing the complex challenges and opportunities of a hyperconnected world.

EMERGENCE, LEADERSHIP, AND THE FOUR FIELDS

The phenomenon of emergence made possible the Spectrum of Leadership and the Four Fields. In the earliest stages of evolution, all that existed were simple single-celled organisms. They reproduced through cell division and lived their lives entirely independently of one another. The only field that existed was the Field of the Self. Evolution led to rules of behavior that enabled these simple organisms to cooperate and take collective action, making possible the Interpersonal Field. Complexity increased and capabilities expanded. Over millions of years of mutations, organisms became capable of cooperation and collective action on a larger scale, and the Field of Teams was born. Complexity and capabilities increased again, and in time, cooperation and collective action on a grander scale gave rise to the Enterprise Field. All of this was already present in primitive form in bacteria like Dictyostelium. They set the stage on which human life would eventually emerge in all its richness and complexity.

I believe that leadership began as emergent leadership through simple rules that enabled cooperation and collective action, thus affording some degree of competitive advantage in primitive organisms like Dictyostelium. Evolution built on those capabilities to give rise to more complex organisms in which a higher order of cooperation and collective action could emerge—still following simple rules, but now rules of behavior in complex multicellular organisms like insects, birds, and fish. That created the context within which yet another order of collaboration and collective action could emerge: the capabilities of consciousness, of foreseeing possible futures, resolving conflict, and making plans. With that, intentional leadership and all the complexity of human societies became possible.

The traditional view of leadership as entirely at the intentional end of the spectrum, constrained within one person and always taking the form of command and control, is too limited for a complex hyperconnected world. Intentional leadership is absolutely necessary at certain times and in certain places. But in other times and places, it is ineffective and counterproductive. The role of leaders must evolve to include the entire spectrum and to balance emergent and intentional leadership, using simple rules when emergence is called for and detailed policies, procedures, and directions when intentional leadership is needed.

Section IV

THE FIELD OF TEAMS

Chapter Seventeen

The Power of Many

Understanding Teams

Never doubt that a small group of committed people can change the world. Indeed, it is the only thing that ever has.

—Margaret Mead

DEFINING TEAMS

Nowhere can we better see the interplay of emergence and intention than in the Field of Teams. In the Interpersonal Field you can have a high degree of awareness of the entire relationship. When you join a team, the field is too large and too complex to have that kind of awareness. You can be intimately aware of your participation in the whole and quite intentional about how you contribute to it. You can see the results of team efforts, but no one can fully grasp how they were achieved.

Let's start by getting clear about what a team is. Recall that I have defined leadership as "the means by which two or more individuals develop the ability to cooperate and take collective action." Thus, leadership does not manifest in a group of individuals that do not cooperate and take collective action. And in my view, such a group is not a team.

I define a team as a group of individuals with a clearly defined shared purpose who cooperate and take collective action to fulfill that purpose. Thus leadership and teams are inextricably linked. And just as leadership exists on a spectrum from emergent to intentional, so do teams.

Emergent teams are looser than intentional teams. Their interpersonal relationships are generally weaker and more transient. Fully emergent teams, like the one that created the KatrinaHelp wiki, have no leader, and there may be no evident or stated shared purpose among the team members (Leuf and Cunningham, 2001). But leadership, nonetheless, is present because the team cooperates and takes collective action.

Intentional teams, on the other hand, are characterized by an explicit shared purpose—a goal to which everyone aspires and commits to fulfill. And they have a designated leader. My focus in this section is primarily on intentional teams.

Another way of defining a team is as a superorganism. I said in chapter 11 that an interpersonal relationship can be seen as a small superorganism. Teams are where human superorganisms really come into their own.

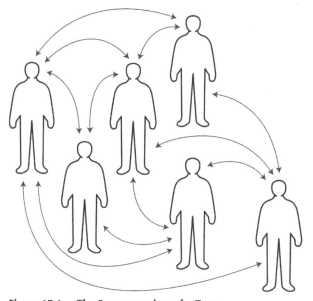

Figure 17.1.   The Superorganism of a Team

From section 2, you know that individuals can be aware of their inner state and therefore manage their Field of the Self. And from section 3, you know that both parties in an interpersonal relationship can be aware of the state of the relationship and can manage their Interpersonal Field. But this is not so simple in the Field of Teams. The superorganism of a team is shaped by forces that are greater than one individual can perceive. Your behavior can affect team members even if you do not directly interact with them. Your relationships with team members can affect other team members and the relationships they have with one another. There is a ripple effect from every action anyone takes that affects all others on the team, yet there is no one person aware of all of these interactions and their ripple effects. And whereas interpersonal relationships involve communication loops between just two people, in the Field of Teams, communication loops can involve more than two people. Team members must manage the Self and Interpersonal fields well because any distortion in those fields will be amplified in the Field of Teams. If team members do not have high levels of self-awareness, do not see and make effective choices, and do not take accountability for the results of their actions, they will not create an effective Field of Teams. Similarly, if team members' relationships with one another are not characterized by honesty, integrity, and trust, they will not create an effective Field of Teams. All of this leads to a level of complexity not present in, but dependent on, the Self and Interpersonal fields.

Both of these definitions of teams—as a group of individuals that cooperate and take collective action, and as a human superorganism—are useful. In fact, they are different facets of the same phenomenon: superorganisms are the product of individuals cooperating and taking collective action.

MEETINGS: WHERE TEAMS REVEAL THEMSELVES

I've observed team meetings with a lot of clients, and the quality and effectiveness of the meetings varies tremendously. In the worst case scenario, people fail to show up or they come in late, some leave early, there is no clear agenda, people distract themselves with text messages and emails, and everyone leaves feeling their time was wasted.

In the best cases, people leave energized and excited with a shared sense of purpose, a clear understanding of what each will be doing in the coming days, strong connections with one another, and the sense that they are all in it together. Each individual on the team is fully committed to the team's purpose; each knows what their contribution will be and what to expect of others. They have each other's backs: if they see a team member struggling or not performing as well as needed, they step in to see what they can do to get things back on track.

Most meetings fall somewhere in between. But many meetings that are considered well run and successful fall far short of the possible best-case outcome. These are meetings that have a tight agenda. However, they are not particularly energizing or inspiring, though people come prepared and they get through the agenda. In many organizations, that's the gold standard. Leaders in these companies are not tapping the potential of their teams to achieve the best-case scenario I described here. They may not even be aware of the possibilities.

The quality of team meetings reveals much about the quality of a team. Meetings are a great place to observe the field of a team and assess its health. In the worst-case scenario mentioned here, the team can hardly be called a team. There is no sense of cooperation, collective action isn't evident, and the relationships among team members are weak at best, dysfunctional at worst. The field of the team is weak and undeveloped.

In the more common middle ground meetings, there is dialog between team members and sometimes laughter. They are generally respectful, with the content of the meeting focused on individuals reporting the status of current milestones. There's usually an opportunity for people to ask questions and request help. The Field of Teams is not particularly strong—you don't have much sense of the team as a whole—but you can sense a functioning group.

In the best meetings, individuals have strong relationships with one another. They respect one another, and they know each other's strengths and blind spots. They provide feedback to one another and ask for and offer help. Everything they do is grounded in the shared purpose of the team. They see the forest as well as the trees. The Field of Teams is strong and obvious. Individuals sometimes finish one another's sentences; questions are inspired by genuine curiosity and are answered thoughtfully. Disagreements are handled respectfully and are seen as an opportunity to learn. Meetings are characterized by a mood of enthusiasm and engagement.

Another characteristic of great meetings is that they often blend intentional and emergent leadership. The meeting agenda may include highly intentional conversations that walk through elements of the project plan. Other parts of the meeting may be quite open ended and invite emergent conversations. In intentional conversations you can move through many agenda items quickly and efficiently; emergent conversations are where creativity and innovation show up. Field Leaders must be skilled at sensing when it is time to move up or down the spectrum, changing the balance of intentional and emergent conversation.

What makes the difference between great meetings and meetings that are merely average or mediocre? In my experience, the highest performing teams practice the disciplines of the four fields and manage their conversations using a model I will introduce shortly called the Cycle of Leadership. To the extent that a team does not follow these practices, performance is diminished. The difference is reflected in their meetings.

To be clear, not every high-performing team I have encountered understands the framework of the four fields or uses the language I offer in this book. But they live in the spirit of the framework and use language consistent with its principles and practices.

TEAMS ARE COMPLEX

The more communication loops there are in a system, the more complex it is. And as complexity grows, so does the potential for both chaos and creative new capabilities that can confer competitive advantage. Leadership makes the difference.

Relationships and communication loops proliferate on a team, and those relationships and communication loops interact with one another in complex ways. How those relationships and conversations are managed determines how the team will perform.

From a mathematical perspective, the relationships and communication loops on a team can be seen as a network. I'm going to provide a brief explanation of the science of networks, so we can better understand why the Field of Teams is so complex and what it takes for a leader to manage the complexity.

Consider that between two people, there is one relationship (see figure 17.2).

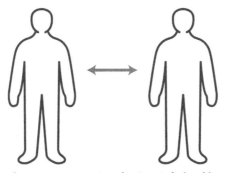

Figure 17.2.   Two People, One Relationship

With three people, there are three relationships (see figure 17.3).

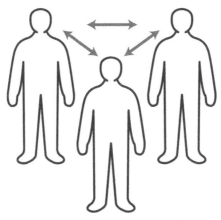

Figure 17.3.   Three People, Three Relationships

Adding one person to a group of two raised the number of relationships from one to three. What happens with four people? Now there are six relationships (see figure 17.4).

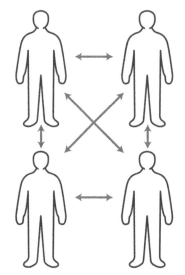

Figure 17.4.   Four People, Six Relationships

Adding one person to a group of three added three relationships for a total of six.

As the number of people on a team grows, the number of relationships grows faster, and it grows in a precise, mathematical way. Network science tells us that the number of relationships on a team with N people can be found with the formula shown in figure 17.5.

$$\frac{N \times (N-1)}{2}$$

Figure 17.5. Number of Relationships on a Team of N Members

Thus, for a team of eight people, there are twenty-eight relationships (8 times 7, divided by 2). For a team of ten, there are forty-five relationships. And there are more communication loops than there are relationships on a team because there can be multiple communication loops between two people, and one communication loop may involve multiple people. This is why leading teams is so complex. When you sit in a room with nine other people, what is most obvious is that there are ten people in the room. What you are not likely to notice is that there are ten people and forty-five relationships in the room, and all of those people and relationships interact through multiple communication loops. There's a lot going on under the hood of a team! The job of a Field Leader is to make sure all of this works for the individuals and the team. That can be a daunting task, especially if you approach it analytically. Fortunately, you don't have to.

Maria was the CIO of a manufacturing company. When she took over the role, her team of direct reports was demoralized and dysfunctional. The previous CIO had been an aggressive micromanager who operated at the far intentional end of the Spectrum of Leadership. People resented him and did not take accountability for problems. Projects were often late and over budget; the team was not trusted by other areas of the company, and they did not get along well with one another. Maria was hired to turn the team around. She had nine direct reports. That meant there were forty-five relationships that had to be managed, along with all the communication loops that those relationships generated.

Maria had worked with me in a previous company and asked for my help. In our previous work together, she had developed a strong leadership presence. In the first eight months in her CIO role, we introduced the four fields framework to her team and focused primarily on the Self and Interpersonal fields. Several members of her team resisted at first, but Maria persisted. She made it clear that she would support them in developing themselves and their relationships but would challenge any behavior that went counter to the disciplines of the four fields. In time, most of the team embraced the new methods; two people chose to leave and were replaced.

Maria had known for some time that the company would be implementing a new Enterprise Resource Planning (ERP) system. It would be the biggest project the IT group had taken on, and Maria knew they had to go beyond the Self and Interpersonal fields to become a strong team. It was time to introduce them to the disciplines of the Field of Teams and the Cycle of Leadership.

Chapter Eighteen

Team Disciplines and the Cycle of Leadership

Destri Lie has two conditions for her dancers: they must be good, respectful people, and their desire to dance must come above all else. For her, big egos have no place in the company, and a good personality is more important than flawless technique.

—Lydia Brosnahan, Walker Reader, Walker Art Center (2014)

The three disciplines in the Field of Teams are:

- Alignment: establishing a shared purpose that everyone on the team embraces.
- Engagement: establishing emotional commitment to the purpose and to relationships among team members and taking action to fulfill the purpose.
- Collective Learning: intentionally and routinely engaging in honest conversations to assess what has gone well, what could have gone better, and what is to be learned from both.

The disciplines in the Field of Teams create emotional bonds based on a shared purpose among team members, provide tools for executing effectively to fulfill that purpose, and provide practices for ongoing collective learning and continuous improvement. The disciplines dovetail tightly with the Cycle of Leadership. The Cycle of Leadership provides a means for bringing the disciplines to life and applying them to real-world problems; the disciplines provide vital practices for ensuring that the conversations in the Cycle of Leadership are honest, authentic, and effective.

THE CYCLE OF LEADERSHIP

The Cycle of Leadership reveals the life cycle of a project to be a network of conversations. It defines the important types of conversations in which leaders and teams must engage and provides a roadmap for using them to ensure successful projects.

Conversations are the lifeblood of teams. Everything happens through conversation, from the inception of a project through its completion. Yet often leaders fail to understand the distinctions among the relevant kinds of team conversations, each with a purpose and design. Without that distinction, all conversations blend into one type, resulting in confusion. A master chef would never think of equipping a kitchen with just one type of knife, yet this is what leaders do when they fail to recognize the role of each type of team conversation.

The Cycle of Leadership is also a diagnostic tool for understanding what happens when things go wrong, and for learning from experience. It provides a context within which the disciplines of the Field of Teams can be developed. In short, the Cycle of Leadership is a kind of Swiss Army knife for effective team conversations. And it works no matter the medium used for the conversation—live face-to-face meetings, emails, voicemails, and any other means of conversing. This was the tool Maria, in chapter 17, used to begin establishing the Field of Teams for her direct reports.

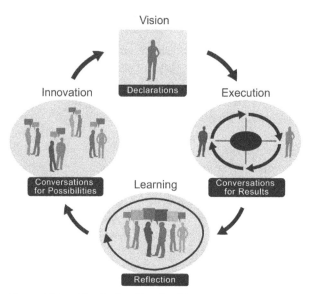

Figure 18.1.   The Cycle of Leadership

There are four kinds of conversations that occur in the Cycle of Leadership. When used skillfully, all of them strengthen the Field of Teams and lead to successful projects.

- **Conversations for Possibilities** engage team members and other stake-holders, tap collective wisdom, and begin defining purpose. They are the engine of innovation.
- **Declarations** define and publicly state purpose. Vision is established here.
- **Conversations for Results** get the work done: requests, offers, and prom-ises occur here. They are the engine of execution.
- **Reflection Conversations** review team performance and identify what the team did well and what they could do better with the intention of improv-ing future performance. They are the engine of learning.

Conversations for Possibilities

The Cycle of Leadership typically begins with Conversations for Possibili-ties. Conversations for Possibilities are the innovation engine of the Cycle of Leadership, where ideas are generated and purpose is explored. This is where Maria began her effort to bring her team together. Leaders often use Con-versations for Possibilities to open up dialogue about a direction or decision they are considering. Conversations for Possibilities are not about making decisions and moving to action; that comes later in the Cycle of Leadership. At this stage, the conversation is intended to accomplish three objectives:

- Tap the knowledge and wisdom of the team and other stakeholders and interested parties.
- Inform the team so team members can contribute and not feel blindsided when a decision is made.
- Begin establishing alignment and engagement.

Some people think of Conversations for Possibilities as traditional brain-storming sessions. Brainstorming as a means of tapping creativity and gener-ating ideas goes back to 1953 when Alex Osborn, an advertising executive, developed it (Osborn, 1953). He made great claims about its effectiveness, and it's been popular in business settings ever since. The problem is that it doesn't work. As commonly practiced, it actually inhibits creative thinking and produces subpar ideas. That's been known since at least 1958 (Taylor, Berry, and Block, 1958). While brainstorming sessions can generate vast numbers of ideas quickly, the quality of the ideas is generally poor. Adrian Furnham, an organizational psychologist who has studied idea-generating methods, wrote, "The evidence from science suggests that business people must be insane to use brainstorming groups" (Furnham, 2000).

Conversations for Possibilities are conducted quite differently, and the results they produce are richer, broader, and deeper. Research shows that having time to reflect on one's own, then gradually broadening the scope of individuals with whom you share your thoughts, leads to much higher-quality ideas than starting in a large group. Maria began having Conversations for Possibilities about the ERP project in one-on-one meetings with each team member. She started these conversations with the question "What contribution do we want to make to the company with this project?" rather than the more traditional question of "How will we accomplish this?" She asked them to think carefully about this question and to consider it with respect to the impact the project would have on the company, as well as the contribution they personally wanted to make to the project.

Starting with these questions had several effects on the development of the Field of Teams:

- Conversations focused on purpose rather than tasks. This caused greater introspection on the part of team members, and it laid the groundwork for aligning around a shared purpose.
- Contribution and service defined purpose rather than just the mechanics of implementing technology. This not only affected how the team thought about the project, it altered the Interpersonal Fields that team members had with their customers. Their customers——the other business units in the company—had historically viewed them as gatekeepers and road blockers, controlling what they could and couldn't do with technology. With this new approach, their customers viewed them as partners in solving business problems.
- Each team member articulated the contribution they wanted to make and shared it with the team. This strengthened and deepened the interpersonal relationships on the team.
- Each team member became aware of what the other team members were bringing to the project, what to expect from them, and how to help them. This enhanced their ability to cooperate and take collective action because they were more connected, trusting, and aware of one another.
- Each member's commitment and stature increased. Publicly declaring what each would deliver for the team gave team members a strong incentive to fulfill the commitment.

Maria's one-on-one conversations primed the team for coming together to share their thoughts in their first all-team project meeting. I facilitated that meeting and presented the Cycle of Leadership and the disciplines of the Field of Teams. Maria explained that these were the next developmental challenges in which she wanted the team to engage. I had them pair off and share their ideas one on one. Then I brought the pairs together and asked them to refine their ideas in groups of four. And finally, I brought everyone together into a team conversation. The whole meeting took about two hours.

These conversations progressed over several weeks, informally among individual team members and formally with the team as a whole. Ultimately, they crafted a powerful Declaration around which they were fully aligned, and they had a rich understanding of how each would contribute to the project and support one another.

Engaging the team in Conversations for Possibilities at the start of the project created dialogue far earlier in the process than was usual, yielding benefits throughout the project's life. For example, José oversaw all of the network operations for the company. He suggested that his network administrators sit in on meetings with customers to define their requirements. This was not the usual practice. Requirements were typically defined by a specialized group. Much later in the process, those requirements would be communicated to others, including José's team. Having the network administrators attend the early conversations with customers gave them a direct experience of their customers' real needs. They were able to start planning network requirements far earlier in the project, and in some instances they were able to influence business requirements in ways that reduced the load on the network.

Declarations

Declarations are at the heart of the Cycle of Leadership. A Declaration is a commitment to a future state; it describes where you are going and what you are going to achieve. Making effective Declarations that inspire others to reach that future state with you is one of the most critical acts of intentional leadership. This is one reason that Conversations for Possibilities are such an important precursor to Declarations: they begin to align and engage people before the Declaration is fully crafted and publicly stated. Team members feel that their voices have been heard, and that they have contributed to the Declaration. They are more likely to be on board and less likely to feel blindsided when the Declaration is made, even if they disagree with the direction that has been declared.

A Declaration has several key qualities, all of which should be explored in Conversations for Possibilities and in your own reflections prior to making the Declaration public. An effective Declaration:

- clearly communicates the future state toward which the team is aimed;
- provides compelling business reasons for creating that future state;
- engages and energizes the community—including the team and other stakeholders—to create that future state;
- includes clear Conditions of Satisfaction—specifically what has to be achieved in order for the declaration to be fulfilled; and
- leads to effective Conversations for Results, in which individuals are asked to contribute to fulfilling the declaration.

The first of these qualities—clearly communicating the future state—addresses the need for clarity and specificity about that future. It is not enough to say "we're going to grow the business," "we're going to establish superb customer service" or "we're going to hit a home run with this project." While the intention is laudable, these statements aren't specific enough to know how to fulfill the Declaration. "We will double our gross revenue in five years," "we will win the Superb Customer Satisfaction award next year," and "in spite of the very tight deadline and small budget, we will complete this project ahead of schedule and under budget" are much clearer Declarations. They give people something to grasp onto, something to aim for, a goal that's specific enough to find ways to contribute and, when done, team members will know whether or not they have succeeded.

The second and third qualities speak to the importance of getting people on board and keeping them there to fulfill the Declaration. This is the "what's in it for me" aspect of an effective Declaration. If you rule by decree, using raw positional power to tell people what to do, you may get compliance, but you won't get engagement. If you want people to bring all of their creativity and energy to fulfilling a Declaration, you must provide them with reasons for doing so. This is not simply a matter of clearly spelling out the logic that says why your Declaration is a good idea, and it is not just a matter of providing an incentive. ("If you get this done on time, you'll get a 10 percent bonus.") There's plenty of research to prove that neither logic nor material rewards are effective motivators in the business environment. What *is* a powerful motivator is meaning—connecting the Declaration to something that matters to individuals (Keane, 2015).

For José, Maria's network leader, meaning came from leaving behind a valuable legacy. This would be his last big project before retiring, and he saw it as a chance to create something that would continue to support the company after he left. For Gladys, who led the project management team, meaning came from the opportunity to forge new and stronger relationships with their customers. Bruce, the leader of the development team, valued the pride he would feel from fulfilling all of the technical requirements of such a complex project.

The last two qualities listed earlier are essential for the team to accurately measure progress and execute successfully. Clear Conditions of Satisfaction define the specific requirements that must be met to fulfill the Declaration, and effective requests are the next step in the Cycle of Leadership, where execution happens.

Crafting a powerful Declaration is as much art as it is science, and it is almost always a collective effort. Developing the key qualities of an effective Declaration is most often an iterative process; you don't develop them in sequence but rather in tandem. You may come up with a beginning draft of the future state, and then as you start thinking about Conditions of Satisfaction, you may find superfluous elements, as well as important considerations that are missing. Articulating the business and community value may lead you to refine your Conditions of Satisfaction.

Developing a team Declaration often involves many other people in the Conversations for Possibilities. Maria and her team cast a wide net, engaging stakeholders throughout the company and beyond, including their internal customers, the company's external customers, and vendors. All of this added to the richness of their thinking and provided fertile ground for strengthening their Self, Interpersonal, and Team fields.

In the end, it is the leader who must own a Declaration and take accountability for its success. Maria was the owner of the Declaration for the ERP project. In their Conversations for Possibilities, her team generated many and, under her leadership, the Declaration went through several iterations. The early ones were quite generic and uninspiring. Through successive versions, they refined it, honing in on what she and the team found to be inspiring. The Declaration she finally adopted was: *Through this project, we will improve the ease of work, the effectiveness of work, and the job satisfaction of employees throughout the company.*

As Maria and her team developed this Declaration, they also created supporting documentation for the business value, value to the team and other stakeholders, and Conditions of Satisfaction. When the Declaration statement was complete, the team was fully on board and aligned. And by now their customers and stakeholders were excited about the project. Team members were thoroughly versed in speaking about the Declaration and what it would mean to the company as a whole and to individual stakeholders. They became evangelists for the project, and their evangelism became contagious.

The team discipline of *alignment* begins in Conversations for Possibilities, in which team members share their thoughts and develop an understanding of the direction the leader is considering. As a leader, you must make sure the team is fully aligned in support of your Declaration before making it public. If they are not, execution is likely to falter.

The last key element of an effective Declaration is that it leads you to effective Conversations for Results, the next stage in the Cycle of Leadership.

Conversations for Results

Conversations for Results are the execution engine of the Cycle of Leadership. They are the means by which requests and promises are made, execution is monitored, and changes and breakdowns are managed. They are where the team discipline of engagement is established. Through Conversations for Results, team members build the relationships with one another that will be necessary to fulfill the Declaration.

Nearly every action taken in an organization is in fulfillment of a promise. When requests are made effectively and promises are managed well, the execution engine runs smoothly and efficiently. When requests are handled poorly and promises are not managed well, the execution engine runs poorly and performance degrades (Sull and Spinosa, 2007). The Conversations for Results model shows the critical steps necessary to ensure that these conversations go well.

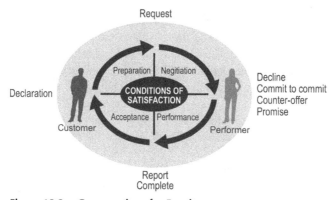

Figure 18.2. Conversations for Results

This model has a number of elements, and it is complicated further by the Self and Interpersonal fields of the two people in the conversation. All of that makes managing promises a complex affair. It sheds light on why mismanaged promises lie at the heart of so many organizational ills, and why healthy Self and Interpersonal fields are essential for establishing a healthy Field of Teams. I find that when companies are experiencing poor execution, breakdowns in processes, low trust, weak teams, and lack of accountability, you can trace the cause back to unclear requests and mismanaged promises.

The word "promise" is weighty—it has gravitas, you feel it. Bruce, Maria's development team leader, commented, "I never really thought about the fact that I'm making a promise when I say I will do something. It's much easier to just say it and then go about my work, and if it doesn't get done, hopefully it won't be a big deal. But a promise—that's about who I am, how people see me. It's my identity. I need to pay more attention to that."

The Conversations for Results model shows that every request and promise is made between two people: the "customer," who makes the request, and the "performer," who makes the promise. On the surface, it might seem obvious that requests and promises are made between two people, but it's common to assume a request was made to a team or a committee with no clarity about specifically who is responsible for fulfilling the promise. This is an immediate red flag that execution is in trouble.

Conversations for Results begin with the preparation phase, during which the customer thinks about what they need and prepares to make a request. When they ask the performer for help, the conversation enters the negotiation phase. In these two phases, the customer and performer work together to define conditions of satisfaction. Conditions of satisfaction are the results that the performer must produce in order for the request to be fulfilled. Defining conditions of satisfaction is a place where requests and promises frequently go wrong. Customers make vague requests, and performers make vague promises, leaving conditions of satisfaction unclear. This almost guarantees a conflict later, when they are likely to discover that their expectations of results do not line up. Resentment and mistrust ensue, making cooperation and collective action difficult or impossible.

Crafting clear conditions of satisfaction can be time consuming, which is one reason it is often done poorly. But the time, energy, and cultural cost of poorly defined requests and promises far outweigh the time involved in defining conditions of satisfaction thoroughly and accurately. Mismanaged promises break down trust, damage individuals' identities, create resentment and resignation, and lead to costly redos and workarounds. The best way to ensure that sufficient time is allotted for effective Conversations for Results is for both parties to center themselves and manage their inner states.

As a performer in a Conversation for Results, when you receive a request, you have four possible responses:

- **Decline**: A decline ends the conversation and leaves the customer free to find someone else to ask for help. One of the toxic cultural conditions I have encountered is the belief that you must always say yes to a request, that it's either rude or unacceptable to decline. This leads to serious breakdowns: if people are not permitted to decline a request, they will inevitably make promises they cannot keep. I'm not suggesting you should casually decline requests, but if you cannot fulfill the conditions of satisfaction, it is your responsibility to let the customer know. If the reason you cannot fulfill the request is because you don't have capacity, an option is to see if you can renegotiate another promise you have made to buy yourself time.

Declining requests is particularly difficult when the customer has authority over you. In fact, leaders are often the primary source of this problem: they do not take time to craft clear requests, they don't tolerate performers attempting to negotiate, and they tell people they don't want to hear objections; they just want it done. This is autocratic leadership, which arises at the extreme intentional end of the Spectrum of Leadership and rarely leads to positive results. If leaders do not allow their people to manage their capacity by negotiating and declining promises they are incapable of fulfilling, then leaders will have cultures in which promises are routinely broken. And leaders must take accountability for creating those cultures.

- **Commit to commit**: A "commit to commit" puts the conversation on hold. It is different from a postponement. Postponing can mean putting something off indefinitely. Committing to commit says, "I will complete this conversation with you by such and such a date and time." Committing to commit is necessary when you need to gather additional information before you can reply to a request. For example, you may need to check your availability before agreeing to a meeting date, or a salesperson may need to check inventory before promising a delivery date. When you commit to commit, it is essential to be explicit about when you will get back to your customer. Without this rigor, the conversation may languish. This can lead to mistrust and resentment, damaging the Interpersonal Field you have with the customer.
- **Counter-offer**: A counter-offer keeps the conversation in the negotiation phase; it takes the form of "I can't meet that particular Condition of Satisfaction, but I can do this instead . . ." It is then up to your customer to decide if what you offered is acceptable. If not, they can counter-offer as well, and negotiation continues.
- **Promise**: A promise is the only response that moves the conversation forward. A promise is a commitment to fulfill the Conditions of Satisfaction that you and your customer have defined. As such, it is a kind of Declaration because it defines a future state to which you are committed.

Once a promise has been made, the conversation moves to Performance, the third stage of the Conversation for Results, in which the actions necessary to fulfill the Conditions of Satisfaction are taken. The Performance stage is often quite complex and can trigger many other conversations. Each new set of conversations addresses some aspect of the original Declaration's Conditions of Satisfaction. Once Maria's Declaration and its Conditions of Satisfaction were defined, she had numerous requests to make to her team and her peers across the organization. These included a request to José to oversee all of the networking requirements for the new system, a request to Gladys to partner with the business units to establish cross-functional teams for the project, a request to the CFO to assist in budgeting the project and monitoring the financials as it progressed, and a request to HR to develop training programs for the new system.

Figure 18.3 is a map that shows how conversations cascade on complex projects.

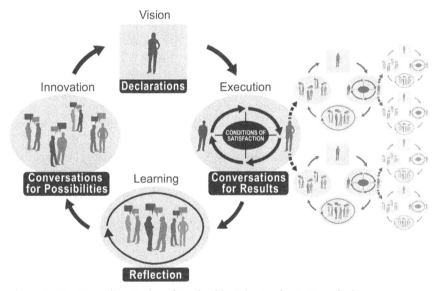

Figure 18.3. Cascading Cycles of Leadership Bring Order to Complexity

As you can see, one Cycle of Leadership can trigger several new Cycles of Leadership, each of which can trigger yet more cycles. And each of those cycles can trigger multiple Conversations for Results. For example, when Maria made her request to José to manage the networking aspects of the ERP project, he made several requests to others to handle aspects of the ERP's network implementation.

This reveals the complexity of managing cooperation and collective action on a team. The butterfly effect is alive and well; subtle changes in the initial conditions of a meeting can have a dramatic effect on how the meeting goes, and an unresolved conflict or mismanaged promise in the cascading conversations can impact performance across a broad swath of an organization. But when the disciplines of the four fields are followed, and the Cycle of Leadership is practiced throughout the organization, order reigns and chaos is avoided.

The last phase of Conversations for Results is acceptance. When you believe you have fulfilled your promise, you inform your customer and check to make sure they agree. This is a vital yet often overlooked stage in managing promises. It gives you the opportunity to ensure that you and your customer agree that you have fulfilled your promise and to address any concerns if you are in disagreement. It also builds trust with your customer. When you return to make sure you are in agreement that the request has been satisfied, it gives the customer confidence. The more rigorously you use this model, the stronger your identity as a trusted partner will grow.

All too often, in our haste to finish one conversation so we can get to the next, we treat requests and promises as cursory exchanges of information. Someone asks for something with vague specifications, someone else says okay, I'll do that, and both move on to other matters. When I started working with Maria's team, they were frequently guilty of this; as they adopted the Cycle of Leadership and engaged in Conversations for Results, they were surprised to learn how cursory and incomplete many of their conversations had been.

Conversations for Results are very much *conversations*. They involve wholehearted participation from both the customer and performer. To the extent that either is unwilling to invest the time to craft a clear request, negotiate Conditions of Satisfaction, and manage the process of fulfilling the promise, the entire conversation is at risk. And because Conversations for Results can cascade out to generate additional requests and engage more people, the cost of a poorly crafted request or poorly managed promise can be substantial. Conversations for Results take time, but far less time than it takes to have the same conversation over and over and deal with misunderstood Conditions of Satisfaction and poorly managed promises.

No one does this perfectly. Your inner state—the condition of your physical, emotional, and analytical minds and the core communication loop that keeps them in dialogue—influences your ability to engage effectively in Conversations for Results. The more you practice, the better you get.

Reflection Conversations: Collective Learning

The Reflection Conversations stage of the Cycle of Leadership is where the team engages in the discipline of collective learning. You know that your Field of the Self requires continual renewal: your muscles require exercise to maintain their health, your emotions routinely get triggered and require recentering, and your analytical mind continually refines its understanding of the world. Similarly, interpersonal relationships need constant adjustment and renewal to keep the Interpersonal Field healthy. Reflection Conversations are the means by which the Field of Teams achieves renewal. They are as vital to the health of a team as exercise is to your body and trust is to interpersonal relationships.

Collective learning is greater than the sum of what individuals can learn on their own because collective learning builds and strengthens the complex network of relationships and communication loops among team members. This is how the superorganism of the team learns. Collective learning enhances the Self and Interpersonal fields as well as the Field of Teams. Adjusting and refining the relationships and communication loops on the team requires adjusting and refining your core communication loop and your interpersonal relationships with other team members.

Reflection conversations must be routine and intentional. Collective learning can't be left to chance, and it must involve the whole team. Methods developed by the US Army show us the way.

In 1971, General W. C. Westmoreland, the chief of staff of the US Army, wanted to find better ways to train soldiers to deal with the complexity and unpredictability of modern warfare, to improve unit readiness, and to develop better leaders (Degrosky and Parry, 2004). He specified that the new methods should be both effective and motivating. Over the next twenty-plus years, the Army experimented with various training methods to meet these objectives. Increasingly, they focused on participative approaches that they called "After Action Review," or AAR. These methods were formally standardized across the entire US Army in 1995 (Morrison and Meliza, 1999).

As originally conceived, AAR is a method for soldiers to continually learn from their experiences and improve their performance. It differs from traditional learning in that it requires soldiers to come together after a training exercise to engage in their own analysis and discovery. In AAR conversations, they discover what they did well and what they could do better. AAR does not rely on external trainers and observers to tell them how they did and teach them new methods. Rather, it requires that they *think and discover together*. A common use of AAR occurs immediately following war games exercises in which soldiers have been engaged in simulated battles. At the end of an exercise, the soldiers gather together for the AAR, in which multiple points of view are valued as adding to the collective picture rather than as opportunities to prove each other right or wrong.

Prior to implementing the AAR the Army used more traditional training methods that involved observers telling soldiers what they did wrong and advising how to do better. Soldiers often found such feedback demoralizing and inaccurate. The AAR method put them in charge of their learning; it required that they engage themselves in figuring out how to improve. It is up to them to reach their own conclusions and use them in the next field exercise.

Reflection conversations are designed to bring the spirit of AAR to work teams. In reflection, the team has honest, engaged conversations about the state of the team, reviewing how they have been doing and how they can improve. Team leaders participate in these conversations as members of the team. They are there to learn just like everyone else.

Reflection conversations happen in meetings whose purpose is to maintain and strengthen the team's field. These conversations focus on events that team members deem sufficiently important to spend time reviewing. Timeliness is critical; reflection should be done as close as possible to the events being reviewed. Individuals also report on how they are managing their Self and Interpersonal fields. Events to be reviewed often include interpersonal conflicts, mistrust, and broken promises that have arisen since the last reflection meeting. Leaving such events unnamed and unaddressed can be more damaging than ignoring procedural mistakes and technical oversights. When these concerns are named and addressed, they become sources of team learning, stronger relationships, and greater skill in applying the disciplines of the four fields.

Reflection conversations can be structured around five questions. Recall the distinction between assessments (opinions or interpretations) and assertions (statements of fact) that I explored in chapter 12. This is a vital distinction when the following questions are discussed.

1. What was supposed to happen? This question explores team members' expectations prior to the events. It reveals where their understanding was shared and where it might have diverged. And it reveals the clarity—or lack thereof—of the requests and promises related to the events.
2. What happened? This is where the team recalls the facts of specific events. This question is designed to accurately recall actual events, free of assessments and blame.
3. Why did it happen? With this question, the team shares explanations of the causes of what happened. This conversation can involve many assessments—opinions or interpretations—as well as assertions. Different perspectives and interpretations are welcome as ways to enrich understanding of what happened and why. This is also a place where each team member involved in the event must reflect on their own accountability. Recall from chapter 10 that accountability is one of the disciplines in the Field of the Self. Failing to take accountability for your actions (or inactions) is toxic to the Field of Teams. It leads to discord and argument rather than learning and growth. So when exploring the question of why something happened,

each team member, including the leader, starts by reflecting on the question, "What did I do, or fail to do, that contributed to this event?"

4. What did we do well? This question helps the team recognize their strengths and design ways to build on them. It sometimes leads to behavioral or operational standards that the team adopts.

5. What can we do better? This question often results in specific actions individuals or the entire team will take in order to develop greater skill in identified problem areas.

When I introduced reflection conversations to Maria's team, they quickly learned that these conversations can be quite challenging. They require team members to rigorously apply the disciplines of the Self and Interpersonal fields. In difficult conversations, even the most skilled individual can go off center, so Maria adopted the practice of appointing one team member each week to be the "coach" for the reflection conversations. The coach's job was not to take sides or argue a point of view but rather to support each individual in using the disciplines of the Field of the Self to manage their inner state, and using the interpersonal disciplines to manage their relationships as the conversations progressed.

Simply taking the time to reflect on the five questions can be difficult. In addition to the emotional and interpersonal challenges of reflection conversations, many organizations have cultures in which action is valued more highly than reflection. It takes a committed leader to keep a team in the practice of reflection conversations. Maria was such a leader. She initially established reflection meetings every week; as the project progressed and the team's skills at having these conversations improved, she held them every other week.

Each of Maria's reflection meetings began by creating the agenda. Team members listed any conversations from the previous reflection meeting that needed further discussion, then individuals identified new key events they felt were worth examining. They would also report important aspects of their Self and Interpersonal fields and how they affected events. For example, if a team member was feeling overwhelmed and was concerned about fulfilling the promises they were being asked to make, the team would work together to find a solution. Likewise, if someone was experiencing mistrust or conflict with another team member, the reflection meeting was a place to address that. Once the agenda was set, the team would address the agenda items, asking the five questions of each. Meetings could last anywhere from thirty minutes to a few hours.

Some team members initially resisted this level of transparency, saying it wasn't the team's business to know how they were feeling or if they were in conflict with another team member. But over time, they discovered that when they had these conversations in the presence of the team, the whole team learned, trust deepened among all members, and the issues were resolved faster and more completely.

The learning that emerges from these sessions shapes what comes next—how the team must reinforce some things and adjust others. It reveals errors and blind spots that might have crept into Conversations for Possibilities, Declarations, or Conversations for Results. It thus feeds back into the Cycle of Leadership, making adjustments based on new insights. Reflection conversations are where the mettle of the Self and Interpersonal fields are constantly tested, and it is where the entire Cycle of Leadership continually renews and fine tunes itself.

When developed as a norm for communication throughout an organization, the Cycle of Leadership supports the disciplines of the four fields at all levels of the organization, making effective cooperation and collective action possible regardless of the size of the project.

Engaging her team deeply in the disciplines of the Field of Teams and the Cycle of Leadership gave Maria an unexpected bonus. In one of their reflection conversations near the end of the ERP project, Gladys, the head of project management, commented that the Declaration for the project really reflected the purpose of all of their work. With a minor modification, the Declaration became the team's Declaration of their ongoing purpose: *Through the application of technology, we will improve the ease of work, the effectiveness of work, and the job satisfaction of employees throughout the company.*

Leading Teams

The traditional questions a leader asks of a project team are:

- "How is the project going?"
- "Where are we in the project plan?"
- "Are we hitting our milestones?"

For a Field Leader, the vital questions are:

- "How is the team doing?"
- "Is the team aligned, engaged, and passionate about the shared purpose of the team?"
- "How are the relationships on the team? Are they characterized by honesty, integrity, and trust?"
- "Does the team practice the Cycle of Leadership and engage in the disciplines of Alignment, Engagement, and Collective Learning?"

These questions create the context within which questions about a project's progress can be fully understood and problems addressed. In this context, looking at project progress makes sense, and if progress is off track, the important starting point is the question, "What has happened in the Self, Interpersonal, and Team fields that caused it to go off track?"

If there is a breakdown in team performance, you must sometimes examine the relationships between team members—the Interpersonal Fields—to discover what caused the breakdown. Likewise, a breakdown in the Interpersonal Fields must sometimes be traced back to the Fields of the Self from which it arose. This may seem tedious and time consuming, but it traces problems back to their roots. Getting to the root cause of a problem prevents it from recurring.

Alignment, engagement, and collective learning are all phenomena that appear at the level of the entire team. No one person is aligned; the team is aligned. Team alignment happens when every team member agrees to the direction and purpose of the team. Team engagement happens when every team member is viscerally committed to success, willing to put the well-being of the team ahead of personal concerns, and committed to building the relationships with other team members that are necessary to fulfill the team's Declaration. For these reasons, when building a team, leaders must place a high value on selecting individuals who will contribute to the intelligence of the team. It is not sufficient to be a strong individual contributor. Indeed, in my experience the best teams do not necessarily include the best individual contributors, but they do include the best team members. Collective learning is learning that happens in the superorganism of the team. It is deeper, richer, and more challenging than any learning you can do on your own. Collective Learning depends on the ability and willingness of each team member to learn. The synergies and capabilities that emerge are far greater than the sum of the individuals' capabilities. The extraordinary acrobatics of a flock of starlings emerges from the individual birds following simple rules. So too can extraordinary performance emerge on organizational teams when everyone practices the Cycle of Leadership and the disciplines of alignment, engagement, and collective learning.

Section V

THE ENTERPRISE FIELD

Chapter Nineteen

Enterprise Leadership

Galileo and his contemporaries transformed the world. It is easy to look back and understand how that transformation unfolded, to see it as relatively logical and orderly. But I am certain that in his time and in the centuries that followed, transformation was unruly, confusing, and, at times, chaotic. Today we are in the midst of another transformation, one brought about not by the mechanization and reduction of the world to its parts but by hyperconnectivity and the reintegration of all those parts. It is an exciting time full of wild possibilities.

Current visions of leadership that are far to the intentional end of the Spectrum of Leadership neglect much of what human beings need to thrive. Human enterprises are both intentional *and* emergent: hierarchies of parts *and* networks of relationships. In a hyperconnected world, we must incorporate both emergent and intentional leadership throughout our organizations.

To release the full power of the human spirit, we must incorporate the full Spectrum of Leadership into our organizations and elevate leadership along the entire spectrum to a fine art as well as a refined science. Leaders must cultivate the disciplines of the four fields in people throughout their organizations.

In our quest for certainty and control, we have lost our connection to some of our most powerful human traits: our physical and emotional connections to life and to one another. We must bring our three minds into unity, integrate them, and use their full potential to create organizations that can thrive for generations to come.

That requires everyone embracing the full Spectrum of Leadership and the disciplines of the four fields, not just those few select individuals we call leaders. It means embracing leadership as an attribute of a culture, not an individual, and seeing the role of leader as cultivating leadership in all four fields. Leaders must be cultivators all of the time and commanders occasionally.

In a hyperconnected world, the fabric of human organizations is woven from both logical processes and systems of communication loops that are both complicated and complex. To understand that successful organizations are not either/or but both/and requires whole thinking. In our rush to mechanize the world and capitalize on the enormous power unleashed by the Age of Reason, we have not only reduced the world to its parts, we have reduced ourselves to parts and ignored those aspects that are inconvenient. In so doing, we have harmed ourselves, our organizations, and humanity. It is time to reintegrate all of the parts and heal ourselves and the world, thereby unleashing the wild possibilities that live in the fullness of the human spirit. Leadership in a hyperconnected world is for those who can be humble, bold, and courageous.

Mastery of the Self, Interpersonal, and Team fields is necessary for leadership in the Enterprise Field. But more is required. The enterprise itself is a superorganism, and as such it is a "self." Leaders in the Enterprise Field must practice the disciplines of the four fields. They must practice *awareness*, *choice*, and *accountability* to manage their inner state and establish their leadership presence. They must practice *honesty*, *integrity*, and *trust* in their interpersonal relationships, and they must engage in *alignment, engagement*, and *collective learning* in the teams in which they participate. But leaders must also take accountability for the self of the enterprise.

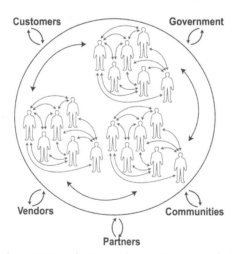

Figure 19.1.   The Enterprise Is a Superorganism

The disciplines of the Enterprise Field are the same as those in the Field of the Self: awareness, choice, and accountability. But their scope is vastly expanded: awareness of the inner state of the entire enterprise, choices made for the enterprise as a whole, and accountability for the results of those choices. The impact of choices made in the Enterprise Field affects its people, the communities in which it operates, and the world as a whole. Enterprise leaders must guide the enterprise to form effective interpersonal relationships with other enterprises, such as partners, vendors, and customer communities. To do so, leaders must practice the interpersonal disciplines of honesty, integrity, and trust at the enterprise level. Enterprises also form teams with other enterprises. They must engage in alignment, engagement, and collective learning with those enterprises. And collectively, these teams of enterprises form new superorganisms. And so it goes until we understand that the entire human race is rapidly becoming a superorganism, and we must all take accountability for our part in its behavior.

In the Field of the Self, your job as a leader is first to internalize the disciplines of awareness, choice, and accountability for yourself, and then to role model these disciplines and coach those you lead to internalize them as well. Mastering these disciplines is a lifelong commitment to personal learning and growth.

Let's take a look at how the Self, Interpersonal, and Team fields must function both for a leader as an individual and for an enterprise as a whole.

AWARENESS IN THE ENTERPRISE FIELD

In the last hundred or so years, we have vastly expanded our sources of intelligence, knowledge, and awareness. We have created technological sensing capabilities that blanket our entire planet. We have satellites, deep-sea sensors, and weather observatories constantly monitoring our natural world. Cameras and microphones are ubiquitous, connecting us in a vast network of relationships. We have enormous databases that contain information about all dimensions of human life and knowledge. And we are beginning to build machines that create new insights and information entirely on their own. Because the human race is becoming a superorganism, the wild possibilities of a hyperconnected world are just beginning to emerge.

What does it mean for an enterprise to be "aware?" As we saw in the Field of Teams, team intelligence, knowledge, and awareness exist *only* in the team as a whole. In the same way, there is an intelligence, knowledge, and awareness that exists only in the enterprise as a whole. The collective awareness, knowledge, and intelligence of all the people and technology that comprise the enterprise interact through complex networks of communication loops among Self, Interpersonal, and Team fields. A human enterprise is a living, evolving superorganism that consumes resources and creates both waste and value throughout its life. It has interests of its own that are reflected in the values and shared purpose of the people within it.

Just as it is necessary for the birds in a flock of starlings to follow some simple rules to ensure that the whole functions well, human beings must follow some simple rules to manage the superorganisms of their organizations. Those simple rules are the disciplines of the four fields. When the Self, Interpersonal, and Team fields are coherent—all are aligned around a shared purpose and practice the disciplines of the four fields—cooperation and collective action are strong and effective throughout the organization. When people are well versed in the disciplines of the four fields, when they form strong interpersonal relationships and teams, and when they engage in collective learning, the creativity of the community is tapped and the intelligence and creativity of the superorganism is enhanced.

This does not mean there are no disagreements. As I explored in chapter 15, disagreement, when handled well, is a source of creativity and learning. It is an opportunity for individuals to discover different perspectives and combine them to increase the intelligence and understanding of the whole. The job of enterprise leaders is to guide their organizations to learn and practice the disciplines. If all members are aware in all four fields and share their awareness honestly, enterprise leaders will accurately sense the state of the organization and can effectively direct its behavior.

There will always be pressure to deviate from the disciplines of the four fields in order to make choices that are expedient but may lack integrity and compromise the organization's stated values. Shareholders demand maximum monetary returns on their investments, often measured in very short time frames. Competitors appear out of nowhere and threaten to take away customers. Sociopolitical concerns often loom large, as the hyperconnected world enables customers, vendors, regulators, and others to quickly gain information about your organization's behavior and impact on the world. And then there is greed, the opportunity to increase your own wealth and power by taking shortcuts or making ethically questionable choices. Staying centered and grounded in the disciplines, and making the choices that have the highest integrity in the midst of these competing voices, can seem like overwhelming challenges. But the cost of the alternative—allowing a culture of blame rather than accountability, deceit rather than honesty, and selfish concerns rather than shared purpose—is enormous.

In 2015, we learned that Volkswagen engineers had for years been installing software to make cars appear more fuel efficient than they were, thus cheating on pollution control laws and deceiving customers. CEO Martin Winterkorn denied knowing anything about the problem, saying he himself had committed no wrongdoing and claiming the problem was caused by just a "very few" employees. He vowed to get to the root of it (Ewing, 2015). On the same day that he made those statements, the company's supervisory board also issued a statement saying Winterkorn had no culpability (Parloff, 2018).

Volkswagen lost $20 billion in market capitalization (Matthews and Gandel, 2015). Eventually, prosecutors in the United States would identify more than forty individuals involved in the fraud, including employees at Volkswagen as well as their automotive technology supplier, Robert Bosch. The firm would pay more than $25 billion in fines in the United States alone, and the damage to their reputation and customer loyalty was immense.

Not long after his denial, Winterkorn was forced to resign; other executives were fired, and management was overhauled (Hakim, Kessler, and Ewing, 2015). In 2019, German prosecutors charged Winterkorn and four managers with aggravated fraud, showing evidence that he and the managers had known about the fraud since 2006—nine years before it became public. He could face up to ten years in prison and millions of dollars in fines (Schuetze, 2019).

In 2015, the electronics giant Toshiba admitted to an accounting fraud that amounted to nearly $2 billion. Its CEO and president Hisao Tanaka was forced to resign as investigators uncovered what they described as "a corporate culture in which management decisions could not be challenged." *Fortune* reported that "employees were pressured into inappropriate accounting by postponing loss reports or moving certain costs into later years" (Smith, 2015).

In 2018, it was discovered that Facebook had allowed Cambridge Analytica, a political data firm hired by Donald Trump's presidential campaign, to access and use private information on fifty million Facebook users (Granville, 2018). Facebook's response was to downplay the importance of the data breach and to deny culpability (Wong, 2019). As investigation into the scandal unfolded, it became evident that Facebook was routinely failing to monitor users and corporate customers and to enforce its own policies.

It is evident in all of these recent corporate scandals that leaders were aware of more than they admitted, and it is likely that they could have been even more aware, and much sooner, had they chosen to pay attention. It is easy for leaders to say that there is just too much going on in their organizations; they are too complex and have too many moving parts. They are right. But it is wrong to say an enterprise leader is therefore not culpable. It may not be within your ability to be fully aware of everything that happens in your organization, but it is within your ability to manage the culture of your organization with integrity. You can establish a culture in which everyone manages themselves and their interpersonal relationships with the highest standards of awareness, choice, accountability, honesty, integrity, and trust. Similarly, teams operate with the fullest commitment to alignment, engagement, and collective learning. These are emergent properties of cultures imbued with the disciplines of the four fields. When leaders ensure that these conditions are in place, they can go to sleep at night knowing that there are no scandals brewing.

If you want to lead in a hyperconnected world, you must do whatever it takes to build and maintain a culture in which the disciplines of the four fields are practiced by everyone, and in which there are consequences for failing to practice them. The leaders of the organizations involved in these scandals allowed, perhaps participated in, behaviors that violated awareness, account-ability, honesty, integrity, trust, and alignment. They declared values that were contradicted by the organization's behavior, they pointed fingers and denied accountability, and they permitted dishonesty to permeate their organizations.

These scandals are all products of leadership *and* culture. In a hypercon-nected world, leadership and culture are inseparable. Leaders must under-stand that they are not only responsible for what they know but also for what they can and should know. Leaders are responsible for being aware of the inner state of their organization and ensuring that individuals throughout the organization are behaving ethically and accountably—that everyone in the organization is practicing the disciplines of the four fields.

As an enterprise leader, your awareness of the enterprise necessarily de-pends on your relationships with others, especially your direct reports. If they have strong self-awareness and awareness of others, engage with you in effective Interpersonal Fields, and participate wholeheartedly on your leader-ship team, you can trust them to let you know how things are going with those who report to them. It is also important that leaders maintain some connection beyond their immediate reports. Casual conversations and company events where you interact socially can serve to inspire others to trust you and hon-estly tell you how they experience their work environment. A highly aware Field Leader will sense when something is amiss in their organization and will initiate the conversations necessary to address it.

If a corporate culture is toxic, it is a reflection of the effectiveness of the leaders. The job of a leader in a hyperconnected world is to be intimately aware of the state of the culture—the inner state of the enterprise. That's where it starts. Next comes choice.

CHOICE IN THE ENTERPRISE FIELD

Section 2 focused on how your inner state manifests in your behavior and determines the quality of your Field of the Self and therefore your leadership presence. In the same way, the inner state of the organization—the quality of its culture, the degree to which it adheres to the disciplines of the four fields—determines its behavior and thus the quality of its presence in the world. People support the organizations they trust and that conduct themselves with integrity.

I have said this several times, and I will say it again: in the field view of leadership, everyone in the organization contributes to leadership, and everyone must engage in the disciplines of the four fields. In the Enterprise Field, the entire enterprise is a superorganism, a "self" living and acting in the world. Practicing the disciplines in the Enterprise Field is not just up to those who are considered "enterprise leaders"—those in the C-Suite. Everyone who acts in the name of the enterprise must see themselves as representing the enterprise and must make their choices from that perspective. This includes anyone who interacts with others outside the organization, including people in roles like sales, marketing, customer relationships, and regulatory affairs.

The organization's interactions with the world happen through interactions between individuals. An organization does not make a declaration; a person makes a declaration in the name of the organization. An organization does not make a promise; a person makes a promise in the name of the organization. Thus, it is the collective behavior of the individuals in the company that determines the company's presence in the world: how it is perceived, whether it is admired or not, whether it is trusted or not. And just as your presence is a reflection of your inner state, the enterprise's presence is a reflection of its inner state. If an organization has a culture of blame, avoidance, and mistrust, and if purpose is not passionately shared by everyone in the organization, the seemingly micro interactions individuals have with others outside the organization will reflect that culture.

In the Field of the Self, the discipline of awareness and the practice of centering enhance your ability to see all the choices available to you and to accurately choose the best among them. That ability also serves you in the Enterprise Field. Through awareness and centering, you will see the range of choices available to you when you act as a representative of the enterprise. And you will make the choices that are in the best interest of the organization—even when the pressures of the world that I described earlier are bearing down on you.

ACCOUNTABILITY IN THE ENTERPRISE FIELD

Accountability is an essential discipline in the Field of the Self. In a healthy organization, every individual takes accountability for the results of their actions. Whether the results are desirable or not, they use them as opportunities to learn. That must also be true in the Enterprise Field. Every individual who acts as a representative of the enterprise must take accountability for the results of their actions. But in the Enterprise Field, accountability goes further: as a leader, you must take accountability for the results of the actions of anyone who comes under your leadership. This goes all the way up to the CEO, who must take accountability for the results of all actions taken in the name of the organization. Had Martin Winterkorn established a culture of field leadership instead of a culture of greed, finger pointing, and dishonesty, Volkswagen would never have attempted to cheat the system and lie to their customers. They would be in a much different place today. They would have saved billions of dollars, lives would not have been ruined, and Volkswagen's reputation would be intact. Whenever there is a corporate scandal, you can trace the systemic cause back to a failure to follow the disciplines of the four fields. That is ultimately a failure of leadership and a failure of culture.

When Mary Barra became CEO of General Motors, she took accountability for anything that GM would do from that point forward, including how they handled the ignition switch crisis that arose under her predecessors. She did not attempt to diminish the pain the employees of the company experienced as the magnitude of the crisis unfolded. She wanted them to learn from it and to retain the learning. She told them, "I never want to put this behind us . . . I want to put this painful experience permanently in our collective memories." She made public apologies and visited the families of victims (Colvin, 2015). From that point forward, she demanded open and honest conversations throughout GM, regardless of how difficult those conversations might be. She turned GM around, giving it a chance to become a company that thrives in the profoundly challenging and chaotic world of the automobile industry in the twenty-first century.

INTERPERSONAL RELATIONSHIPS
AND TEAMS IN THE ENTERPRISE FIELD

Leaders often think of their job as managing the people on their team. That makes sense because individuals are the visible and tangible parts of the team. But as is so often the case with complex systems, many of the important elements are hidden, residing in relationships among the parts rather than in the parts themselves. The job of leaders is not just managing individuals but also managing relationships and ensuring that the disciplines of the four fields are practiced by everyone who engages in each field. That includes managing one's own relationships with those you lead, but it also includes developing a culture in which all individuals manage their own relationships well. This is a training, coaching, mentoring, and modeling job.

Network science shows us that for any group of people, there are far more relationships than there are people. The larger the organization you lead, the stronger the network of interpersonal relationships throughout your organization must be. Through the communication loops of that network, you can sense the inner state of the organization and adjust it when needed. In a small organization, your relationships with individuals throughout the organization may be sufficient to sense the state of the organization directly. But as organizations grow, this direct interpersonal approach becomes less and less tenable.

When the disciplines of the four fields are practiced throughout an organization, two properties emerge that enable you to ensure the organization maintains its health. First, the organization will be largely self-regulating and self-healing. When everyone is practicing the disciplines, individuals conduct themselves well, interpersonal relationships are strong and effective, and teams are aligned and learn together. When the fields become distorted, they self-correct, organically healing breakdowns and violations of the disciplines.

Second, the network of communication loops is strong, healthy, and open, and it channels information to you as the leader. If problems emerge that cannot be handled directly at the level of the organization in which they emerged, individuals pass that information to the next level to get help. If necessary, it will eventually be passed to the leader of the enterprise. In a healthy, self-healing organization, most problems take care of themselves, filtering up to whatever level of leader is necessary but no further.

Therefore, for enterprise leaders to be successful, strong interpersonal relationships are essential throughout the organization. Your own self-awareness and ability to center will enable you to establish Interpersonal Fields with those around you, ensuring that you are *accurately* aware of how they are feeling and what they are sensing in the part of the enterprise they lead. And they must do the same with those who report to them.

As I discussed in chapter 17, the number and complexity of interpersonal relationships grows rapidly as the size of your organization grows. An organization with 50 people has 1,225 potential interpersonal relationships; with 200 people, the number grows to 19,900; and with 1,000 people, the total rises to 499,500—nearly half a million potential interpersonal relationships. All of these relationships involve multiple communication loops, each of which has the potential for complex interactions among the physical, emotional, and analytical minds of each individual. The only way it is possible to manage all of this is through simple rules that everyone follows. This creates self-regulating and self-healing organizations that communicate a need for intentional leadership to the appropriate level of leader and leave the rest to the dynamics of emergent leadership.

The disciplines of the Interpersonal Field are honesty, integrity, and trust. As an enterprise leader, you must, of course, practice these in all of your interpersonal relationships. You must also ensure that those you lead are absolutely rigorous in their practice of these disciplines as well. When these are practiced throughout your organization, everyone who interacts with the world beyond your organization will bring these practices to those relationships. The organization's identity in the world then becomes one of honesty, integrity, and trust.

In the Field of Teams, I introduced the disciplines of alignment, engagement, and collective learning. I also introduced the Cycle of Leadership and the Conversations for Results model as tools for developing and practicing the team disciplines. Just as the disciplines of the four fields must permeate the organization, so must the use of these tools. Thus, enterprise leaders must develop mastery of these tools. They are a means of ensuring that innovation, vision, execution, and learning are constant drumbeats in the life of your organization. When enterprise leaders engage others in Conversations for Possibilities, they establish alignment. When leaders make clear and compelling declarations, they inspire engagement. When leaders make clear requests and elicit committed promises, they set the stage for flawless execution. And when they engage with others in reflection, leaders foster collective learning. These practices must permeate the enterprise for the four fields to flourish and the organization to thrive.

Chapter Twenty

The Mind of the Enterprise

Field Leadership is systemic, so new leaders develop organically because everyone learns the disciplines of the four fields. As they do, their leadership skills develop naturally. For some, those skills will remain largely at the emergent end of the Spectrum of Leadership. They will participate in emergent leadership but will not move far toward intentional leadership. Their contributions to the organization will likely be as individual contributors and team members. For others, their capacity for intentional leadership will become evident as they learn and grow. They are likely to evolve into intentional leaders.

Utopias do not exist. No organization of any size will ever have a population of employees who all reach high levels of mastery in all four fields. But that is not necessary; a critical mass of individuals with mastery will correct for those who have not achieved it. And often those who don't practice the disciplines will choose to leave because the culture will be uncomfortable for them.

There are scientists who believe that the Earth, as a whole, is an organism. This was suggested at least as long ago as 1974 in Lewis Thomas's marvelous book *Lives of a Cell*, in which he describes how he struggled to come up with a way of understanding the entire living Earth (Lewis, 1978). It seemed so vast and complex, with so many different forms of life and behavior and intelligence. But then he thought of a single cell, like the Dictyostelium I described in interlude 3. Cells have membranes that separate them from the rest of the world, boundaries that allow them to contain what makes them what they are and keep them whole and healthy. They have within themselves many organelles that carry out different functions. Cells self-regulate, taking in what they need from the world around them and removing toxins. Thomas realized that the Earth's atmosphere is its membrane and without it, life could not exist. Within that membrane are all of the organisms that make up the ecosystem of the planet. It self-regulates, adjusting its temperature in response to what is happening internally and externally.

Enterprises are also organisms. Like a cell, they have membranes—not physical membranes, but membranes nonetheless. Their membranes consist of the laws and regulations and policies that determine what is "inside" and what is "outside" the enterprise. They self-regulate, determining every day what to bring into the enterprise, what to remove from the enterprise, and what to keep in the enterprise. They work as wholes to sustain themselves and grow. Like bacteria, hives, flocks of birds, human beings, and the Earth itself, they are emergent and they are intelligent.

As an individual in an enterprise, you can never know its full intelligence, just as a bee can never know the intelligence of the hive and a bird can never know the intelligence of the flock. But you can strive to create the greatest good within the enterprises in which you participate: your family, your friends, your teams, the organizations for which you work.

The four fields and their disciplines provide a way of guiding your behavior to serve the greater good of all those enterprises. By following the disciplines of the four fields, you can have confidence that your behavior will contribute to them in the best ways possible.

Which brings us back to fields. If, as physicists are coming to believe, everything is ultimately a field and all fields interact, then we are really all part of the grand, unfolding emergent phenomenon that we call the universe. And within that is the Earth, and within the Earth are all the rich and vastly complex living enterprises, and within those are all the various forms of teams that arise in living communities, and within those are all the rich and complex relationships among individuals, and within those are all the individuals. And individuals are enterprises in their own right, with the four fields repeating within them.

Human beings have begun to leave the superorganism of the Earth. If we survive as a species, we will continue our exploration of space and perhaps, at some point, populate other planets. Eventually, perhaps human beings will discover other living planets, creating enterprises larger than anything we have ever imagined, the Earth as a Field of the Self interacting with other planets as Fields of the Self, creating something grand on a cosmic scale.

Scientists and mystics know that everything is connected. Every field extends out forever, its influence diminishing but never entirely disappearing. Every living system connects to every other living system; nature designed life on Earth so that it would be self-sustaining, always generative and creative. When we truly embrace that idea—and we court disaster if we don't—

our only choice is to be participants rather than masters and to honor every other participant as contributing to the whole.

The beauty of what nature created with this elegant system of networks and relationships and emergent behavior is that every individual element of a system is free to be itself. Individuals exercise considerable autonomy while fulfilling their roles within the larger system. A tree grows without regard for the forest, yet the forest and the tree both benefit because they have coevolved. Human beings are happiest when they contribute to others and are valued for their contributions. So there is no paradox here, no tension between "self-actualization" and "the greater good." We are perfectly designed to fulfill both. Our satisfaction in being effective, unique individuals comes from our participation in the whole of humanity. The choices we make individually transform into collective choices, the collective choices shape humanity as a whole, and humanity as a whole shapes us as individuals. It is a grand communication loop on the largest of scales.

The flattening of organizations—the elimination of layers of management and their replacement with teams that are formed for the duration of a project—is common today. Leaders are instinctively recognizing the necessity of replacing mechanistic process-oriented command-and-control structures with dynamic self-directed teams.

Learning to regulate the communication loops and thereby the dynamics of the four fields is the key to organizational success in the Age of Connection. As individuals our emotional and physical states and our thought processes come together to determine how we interpret our world, how we create our belief systems, and how we choose to behave. Our individual behaviors create our collective behaviors. Developing a new way of thinking that makes sense of the hyperconnected world is the challenge leaders face today. It is rife with risk and pregnant with opportunity.

For leaders, the Spectrum of Leadership and the Four Fields present a humbling view of leadership. This vision means that you are not in charge, no matter how much you want to believe you are. You are a participant, but you are not in charge. And if you don't participate in ways that serve the greater good, you put yourself and your enterprise at risk. This is the heart of Field Leadership. You are here to serve those you lead, the enterprise of which you are a part, the communities within which that enterprise functions, the human race, and ultimately the planet as a whole. The extraordinary and daunting challenge given to Field Leaders is to guide us through the current period of transformation and realize the wild possibilities of the Age of Connection.

Bibliography

Adamatzky, Andrew, ed. 2016a. *Advances in Physarum Machines: Sensing and Computing with Slime Mould.* Emergence, Complexity and Computation. Cham: Springer International Publishing. https://www.springer.com/gp/book/9783319266619.

———. 2016b. "Slime Mould Approximates Longest Roads in USA and Germany: Experiments on 3D Terrains." In *Advances in Physarum Machines: Sensing and Computing with Slime Mould*, edited by Andrew Adamatzky, 311–35. Emergence, Complexity and Computation. Cham: Springer International Publishing. doi:10.1007/978-3-319-26662-6_16.

Addiscott, Tom. 2011. "Emergence or Self-Organization?" *Communicative and Integrative Biology* 4 (4): 469–70. doi:10.4161/cib.4.4.15547.

Allen, Scott, Jay T. Deragon, Margaret G. Orem, Carter F. Smith, and Doc Searls. 2008. *The Emergence of the Relationship Economy: The New Order of Things to Come.* Silicon Valley, CA: Happy About.

Argo, Jennifer J., and Baba Shiv. 2012. "Are White Lies as Innocuous as We Think?" *Journal of Consumer Research* 38 (6): 1093–1102. doi:10.1086/661640.

Bak, Per. 1999. *How Nature Works: The Science of Self-Organized Criticality.* Paperback edition. New York: Copernicus.

Baldoni, John. 2010. "How Leaders Should Think Critically." *Harvard Business Review*, January 20. https://hbr.org/2010/01/how-leaders-should-think-criti.

Bateson, Gregory. 2000. *Steps to an Ecology of Mind.* Chicago: University of Chicago Press.

———. 2002. *Mind and Nature: A Necessary Unity.* Advances in Systems Theory, Complexity, and the Human Sciences. Cresskill, NJ: Hampton Press.

Bechara, Antoine, Hanna Damasio, and Antonio R. Damasio. 2000. "Emotion, Decision Making and the Orbitofrontal Cortex." *Cerebral Cortex* 10 (3): 295–307. doi:10.1093/cercor/10.3.295.

Bechara, A., H. Damasio, D. Tranel, and A. R. Damasio. 2005. "The Iowa Gambling Task and the Somatic Marker Hypothesis: Some Questions and Answers."

Trends in Cognitive Sciences 9, no. 4 (April 1): 159–62. https://doi.org/10.1016/j
.tics.2005.02.002.

Bersin, Josh. 2014. "It's Time to Rethink the 'Employee Engagement' Issue." *Forbes*,
April 9. https://www.forbes.com/sites/joshbersin/2014/04/10/its-time-to-rethink
-the-employee-engagement-issue/.

Bhasin, Manoj K., Jeffery A. Dusek, Bei-Hung Chang, Marie G. Joseph, John W.
Denninger, Gregory L. Fricchione, Herbert Benson, and Towia A. Libermann.
2013. "Relaxation Response Induces Temporal Transcriptome Changes in Energy
Metabolism, Insulin Secretion and Inflammatory Pathways." *PLOS ONE* 8 (5):
e62817. doi:10.1371/journal.pone.0062817.

Bogaard, Paul A. 1979. "Heaps or Wholes: Aristotle's Explanation of Compound
Bodies." *Isis* 70 (1): 11–29.

Braga, Raíssa Mesquita, Manuella Nóbrega Dourado, and Welington Luiz Araújo.
2016. "Microbial Interactions: Ecology in a Molecular Perspective." *Brazilian
Journal of Microbiology* 47 (Suppl. 1): 86–98. doi:10.1016/j.bjm.2016.10.005.

Brinke, Leanne ten, Jooa Julia Lee, and Dana R. Carney. 2015. "The Physiology of
(Dis)Honesty: Does It Impact Health?" *Current Opinion in Psychology* 6: 177–82.
doi:10.1016/j.copsyc.2015.08.004.

Brosnahan, Lydia. 2014. "Performing Lives, Dancing Experiences: Companhia
Urbana de Dança's Marvelous Symbiosis." Walker Reader, Walker Art Center,
March. https://walkerart.org/magazine/companhia-urbana-de-danca.

Brueckner, Sven A., Giovanna Di Marzo Serugendo, Anthony Karageorgos, and Rad-
hika Nagpal, eds. 2005. *Engineering Self-Organising Systems: Methodologies and
Applications*. Lecture Notes in Artificial Intelligence, Lect.Notes ComputerState-
of-the-Art Surveys. Berlin Heidelberg: Springer-Verlag. https://www.springer
.com/gp/book/9783540261803.

Budd, Matthew, Larry Rothstein, and Patch Adams. 2000. *You Are What You Say:
The Proven Program That Uses the Power of Language to Combat Stress, Anger,
and Depression*. New York: Three Rivers Press.

Cain, Susan. 2012. *Quiet: The Power of Introverts in a World That Can't Stop Talking*. First edition. New York: Crown Publishers.

"Capitalizing on Complexity Insights from the Global Chief Executive Officer
Study." 2010. IBM Global Business Services.

Cherniss, Cary. 1999. "Business Case for Emotional Intelligence." Rutgers University, Graduate School of Applied and Professional Psychology. http://www.eicon
sortium.org/reports/business_case_for_ei.html.

Choi, Charles Q. 2015. "How Did Multicellular Life Evolve?" *Astrobiology Magazine*,
February 4. https://www.astrobio.net/origin-and-evolution-of-life/multicellular
-life-evolve/.

———. 2017. "NASA Astrobiology—How Did Multicellular Life Evolve?"
Astrobiology Magazine, February 1. https://astrobiology.nasa.gov/news/how-did
-multicellular-life-evolve/.

Cole, K. C. 1999. "Plenty of Balls in the Air." *Los Angeles Times*, May 20. https://
www.latimes.com/archives/la-xpm-1999-may-20-me-39124-story.html.

Colvin, Geoff. 2015. "CEO Mary Barra: Using the Ignition Scandal to Change GM's Culture." *Fortune*, September 18. http://fortune.com/2015/09/18/mary-barra-gm-culture/.

Colvin, Geoffrey. 2018. *Talent Is Overrated: What Really Separates World-Class Performers from Everybody Else*. Revised edition. New York: Portfolio.

Conradt, L., and T. J. Roper. 2003. "Group Decision-Making in Animals." *Nature* 421 (6919): 155. doi:10.1038/nature01294.

Covey, Stephen R. 2004. *The 7 Habits of Highly Effective People: Restoring the Character Ethic*. Revised edition. New York: Free Press.

Cowan, Nelson. 2001. "The Magical Number 4 in Short-Term Memory: A Reconsideration of Mental Storage Capacity." *Behavioral and Brain Sciences* 24 (1): 87–114. doi:10.1017/S0140525X01003922.

Csikszentmihalyi, Mihaly. 1991. *Flow: The Psychology of Optimal Experience*. First edition. New York: HarperCollins. Kindle edition.

———. N.d. *Good Business*. New York: Viking.

Damasio, Anthony. 1994. *Descartes' Error: Emotion, Reason, and the Human Brain*. Reprint edition. New York: Penguin Books.

Damasio, Antonio R. 2000. *The Feeling of What Happens: Body and Emotion in the Making of Consciousness*. First Harvest edition. A Harvest Book. San Diego, CA: Harcourt.

———. 2003. *Looking for Spinoza: Joy, Sorrow, and the Feeling Brain*. First Harvest edition. A Harvest Book. London: Harcourt.

———. 2005. *Descartes' Error: Emotion, Reason, and the Human Brain*. London: Penguin.

———. 2012. *Self Comes to Mind: Constructing the Conscious Brain*. First edition. New York: Vintage Books.

De Bruijn, Hans. 2010. *Managing Professionals*. London: Routledge.

Degrosky, Michael, and Charles Parry. 2004. "Beyond the AAR: The Action Review Cycle (ARC)." May. International Association of Wildland Fire, Missoula, Montana, USA.

DiSalvo, David. 2014. "How Telling the Truth Could Boost Your Health." *Forbes*, August 10. https://www.forbes.com/sites/daviddisalvo/2014/08/10/how-telling-the-truth-could-keep-you-healthier/.

———. 2017. "How Breathing Calms Your Brain, and Other Science-Based Benefits of Controlled Breathing." *Forbes*, November 29. https://www.forbes.com/sites/daviddisalvo/2017/11/29/how-breathing-calms-your-brain-and-other-science-based-benefits-of-controlled-breathing/.

Duhigg, Charles. 2012. *The Power of Habit: Why We Do What We Do in Life and Business*. New York: Random House. Kindle edition.

Easley, David, and Jon Kleinberg. 2010. *Networks, Crowds, and Markets: Reasoning about a Highly Connected World*. New York: Cambridge University Press.

Eichinger, L., J. A. Pachebat, G. Glöckner, M.-A. Rajandream, R. Sucgang, M. Berriman, J. Song, et al. 2005. "The Genome of the Social Amoeba Dictyostelium Discoideum." *Nature* 435 (7038): 43–57. doi:10.1038/nature03481.

Eifring, Halvor, ed. 2017. *Meditation and Culture: The Interplay of Practice and Context*. Paperback edition. London: Bloomsbury.

Ekman, Paul. 2007. *Emotions Revealed: Recognizing Faces and Feelings to Improve Communication and Emotional Life*. Second edition. New York: Owl Books.

Engelbrecht, Amos S., Gardielle Heine, and Bright Mahembe. 2017. "Integrity, Ethical Leadership, Trust and Work Engagement." *Leadership and Organization Development Journal*, May. doi:10.1108/LODJ-11-2015-0237.

Engle, Randall W., and Michael J. Kane. 2003. "Executive Attention, Working Memory Capacity, and a Two-Factor Theory of Cognitive Control." *Psychology of Learning and Motivation* 44: 145–99. Academic Press. doi:10.1016/S0079-7421(03)44005-X.

Ewing, Jack. 2015. "Volkswagen Says 11 Million Cars Worldwide Are Affected in Diesel Deception." *New York Times*, September 22. http://www.nytimes.com/2015/09/23/business/international/volkswagen-diesel-car-scandal.html.

Figge, Patrick. N.d. *Collective Knowledge How Teams and Larger Social Systems Learn, Remember, and Invent*. Wiesbaden: Springer Gabler.

Frick, Walter. 2018. "3 Ways to Improve Your Decision Making." *Harvard Business Review*, January 22. https://hbr.org/2018/01/3-ways-to-improve-your-decision-making.

Fritz, Ben. 2011. "Netflix Chief Executive Reed Hastings' Compensation Doubled to $5.5 Million." *Los Angeles Times*, April 20. http://latimesblogs.latimes.com/entertainmentnewsbuzz/2011/04/netflix-chief-executive-reed-hastings-compensation-doubled-to-55-million.html?cid=6a00d8341c630a53ef01538e040b70970b.

Furnham, Adrian. 2000. "The Brainstorming Myth." *Business Strategy Review* 11 (4): 21–28. doi:10.1111/1467-8616.00154.

George, Bill. 2014. "Developing Mindful Leaders for the C-Suite." *Harvard Business Review*, March 10. https://hbr.org/2014/03/developing-mindful-leaders-for-the-c-suite.

Gigerenzer, Gerd. 2007. *Gut Feelings: The Intelligence of the Unconscious*. First edition. New York: Penguin Books.

Gleick, James. 2008. *Chaos: Making a New Science*. Twentieth anniversary edition. New York: Penguin Books.

Goldstein, Rebecca. 2005. *Incompleteness: The Proof and Paradox of Kurt Gödel*. New York: W. W. Norton.

Goleman, Daniel. 2005. *Emotional Intelligence*. Tenth anniversary trade paperback edition. New York: Bantam Books.

Goleman, Daniel, Richard E. Boyatzis, and Annie McKee. 2002. *Primal Leadership: Unleashing the Power of Emotional Intelligence*. Tenth anniversary edition. Boston: Harvard Business Review Press.

Graham, Jason M., Albert B. Kao, Dylana A. Wilhelm, and Simon Garnier. 2017. "Optimal Construction of Army Ant Living Bridges." *Journal of Theoretical Biology* 435: 184–98. doi:10.1016/j.jtbi.2017.09.017.

Grant, Adam. 2018. "General Motors' CEO on How to Handle a Crisis Like a Pro." *Heleo*, April 11. https://heleo.com/conversation-general-motors-ceo-on-how-to-handle-a-crisis-like-a-pro/18190/.

Granville, Kevin. 2018. "Facebook and Cambridge Analytica: What You Need to Know as Fallout Widens." *New York Times*, March 19. https://www.nytimes .com/2018/03/19/technology/facebook-cambridge-analytica-explained.html.

Greene, Joshua D., and Joseph M. Paxton. 2009. "Patterns of Neural Activity Associated with Honest and Dishonest Moral Decisions." *Proceedings of the National Academy of Sciences* 106 (30): 12506–11. doi:10.1073/pnas.0900152106.

Haines, Staci, Richard Strozzi-Heckler, and Ai-Jen Poo. *The Politics of Trauma: Somatics, Healing, and Social Justice*. Berkeley, CA: North Atlantic Books, 2019.

Hakim, Denny, Aaron Kessler, and Jack Ewing. 2015. "As Volkswagen Pushed to Be No. 1, Ambitions Fueled a Scandal." *New York Times*, September 26. http://www .nytimes.com/2015/09/27/business/as-vw-pushed-to-be-no-1-ambitions-fueled-a -scandal.html?_r=0.

Hamalainen, Raimo, and Esa Saarinen. 2007. *Systems Intelligence in Leadership and Everyday Life*. http://systemsintelligence.aalto.fi/.

Harari, Yuval Noah. 2015. *Sapiens: A Brief History of Humankind*. New York: Harper.

Hartnett, Kevin. 2018. "The Simple Algorithm That Ants Use to Build Bridges." *Quanta Magazine*, February 26. https://www.quantamagazine.org/the-simple -algorithm-that-ants-use-to-build-bridges-20180226/.

Harvard Health Publishing. 2015. "Relaxation Techniques: Breath Control Helps Quell Errant Stress Response." *Harvard Health*, January. https://www.health.harvard .edu/mind-and-mood/relaxation-techniques-breath-control-helps-quell-errant -stress-response.

Hawken, Paul. 2008. *Blessed Unrest: How the Largest Movement in the World Came into Being, and Why No One Saw It Coming*. New York: Penguin Books.

———. 2010. *The Ecology of Commerce: A Declaration of Sustainability*. Revised edition. New York: Harper Business.

Hawken, Paul, Amory B. Lovins, and L. Hunter Lovins. 2000. *Natural Capitalism: Creating the Next Industrial Revolution*. First paperback edition. A Back Bay Book. New York: Little, Brown and Co.

Heath, Dan, and Chip Heath. 2010. *Switch*. New York: Crown Publishing Group. http://api.overdrive.com/v1/collections/v1L2BowAAAC4HAAA1k/products /d71efb14-5e6a-4551-ad67-268d4ca2747e.

Herrero, Jose L., Simon Khuvis, Erin Yeagle, Moran Cerf, and Ashesh D. Mehta. 2017. "Breathing above the Brain Stem: Volitional Control and Attentional Modulation in Humans." *Journal of Neurophysiology* 119 (1): 145–59. doi:10.1152 /jn.00551.2017.

Hobson, Art. 2013. "There Are No Particles, There Are Only Fields." *American Journal of Physics* 81 (3): 211–23. doi:10.1119/1.4789885.

Horsager, George. 2012. "You Can't Be a Great Leader without Trust—Here's How You Build It." *Forbes*, October 24. http://www.forbes.com/sites/forbesleader shipforum/2012/10/24/you-cant-be-a-great-leader-without-trust-heres-how-you -build-it/.

"IBM 2008 CEO Study: The Enterprise of the Future." 2008. IBM Global Business Services.

Igoshin, Oleg. 2013. "'Social' Bacteria That Work Together to Hunt for Food and Survive under Harsh Conditions." National Science Foundation: Where Discoveries Begin, December 20. https://www.nsf.gov/discoveries/disc_summ.jsp?cntn_id=129976.

"Information Theory—Physiology." 2018. Encyclopedia Britannica. Accessed November 1, 2019. https://www.britannica.com/science/information-theory.

Isidore, Chris. 2015. "GM's Total Recall Cost: $4.1 Billion." *CNNMoney*, February 4. https://money.cnn.com/2015/02/04/news/companies/gm-earnings-recall-costs/index.html.

Jaffe, Eric. 2007. "Meditate on It." *Smithsonian*, February 1. https://www.smithsonianmag.com/science-nature/meditate-on-it-147282062/.

Johnson, Brian R., and Sheung Kwan Lam. 2010. "Self-Organization, Natural Selection, and Evolution: Cellular Hardware and Genetic Software." *BioScience* 60 (11): 879–85. doi:10.1525/bio.2010.60.11.4.

Kacmppfert, Waldemar. 1927. "Details Concepts of Quantum Theory." *New York Times*, September 2. http://timesmachine.nytimes.com/timesmachine/1927/09/02/101507280.html?pageNumber=6.

Kahlen, Franz-Josef, Shannon Flumerfelt, and Anabela Alves, eds. 2017. *Transdisciplinary Perspectives on Complex Systems*. Cham: Springer International Publishing. doi:10.1007/978-3-319-38756-7.

Kahneman, Daniel. 2011. *Thinking, Fast and Slow*. First edition. New York: Farrar, Straus and Giroux.

Keane, Jim. 2015. "Meaningful Work Should Be Every CEO's Top Priority." *Harvard Business Review*, November. https://hbr.org/2015/11/meaningful-work-should-be-every-ceos-top-priority.

Kegan, Robert, and Lisa Laskow Lahey. 2009. *Immunity to Change: How to Overcome It and Unlock Potential in Yourself and Your Organization*. Leadership for the Common Good. Boston, MA: Harvard Business Press.

Kennedy, Tricia. 2011. "How Combat Breathing Saved My Life." *Police*, March 9. http://www.policemag.com/blog/women-in-law-enforcement/story/2011/03/combat-breathing-saved-my-life.aspx.

Kim, Sang Hwan, Suzanne M. Schneider, Margaret Bevans, Len Kravitz, Christine Mermier, Clifford Qualls, and Mark R. Burge. 2013. "PTSD Symptom Reduction with Mindfulness-Based Stretching and Deep Breathing Exercise: Randomized Controlled Clinical Trial of Efficacy." *Journal of Clinical Endocrinology and Metabolism* 98 (7): 2984–92. doi:10.1210/jc.2012-3742.

Kingsland, Sharon. 1982. "The Refractory Model: The Logistic Curve and the History of Population Ecology." *Quarterly Review of Biology* 57 (1): 29–52.

Lacasse, Katherine. 2017. "Going with Your Gut: How William James' Theory of Emotions Brings Insights to Risk Perception and Decision Making Research." *New Ideas in Psychology*, Special Issue: James' Principles, 46 (August): 1–7. doi:10.1016/j.newideapsych.2015.09.002.

LaPlace, Pierre Simon. 1902. *A Philosophical Essay on Probabilities*. Hoboken, NJ: John Wiley and Sons.

Leiner, Barry M., Vinton G. Cerf, Robert E. Kahn, Leonard E. Kleinrock, Daniel C. Lynch, Jon Postel, Larry G. Roberts, and Steven Wolff. 1997. "Brief History of the Internet." *Internet Society*. https://www.internetsociety.org/resources/doc/2017 /brief-history-internet/.

Lencioni, Patrick. 2002. *The Five Dysfunctions of a Team: A Leadership Fable*. First edition. San Francisco: Jossey-Bass.

Leuf, Bo, and Ward Cunningham. 2001. *The Wiki Way: Quick Collaboration on the Web*. Boston: Addison-Wesley Professional.

Levitin, Daniel J. 2015. "Why It's So Hard to Pay Attention, Explained By Science." *Fast Company*, September 23. https://www.fastcompany.com/3051417/why-its -so-hard-to-pay-attention-explained-by-science.

Lewis, Thomas, Fari Amini, and Richard Lannon. 2001. *A General Theory of Love*. Reprint edition. New York: Vintage.

Libet, Benjamin. 2005. *Mind Time: The Temporal Factor in Consciousness*. First paperback edition. Perspectives in Cognitive Neuroscience. Cambridge, MA: Harvard University Press.

Lindsay, Matt, Xavier Van Leeuwe, and Matthijs Van De Peppel. 2017. *How to Succeed in the Relationship Economy: Make Data Work for You, Empathise with Customers, Grow Valuable Relationships*. Charleston, SC: Advantage Media Group.

"Logistic Growth, Part 1." 2016. Accessed October 4, 2019. https://services.math .duke.edu/education/ccp/materials/diffeq/logistic/logi1.html.

Lorenz, Edward N. 1963. "Deterministic Nonperiodic Flow." *Journal of the Atmospheric Sciences* 20 (2): 130–41. doi:10.1175/1520-0469(1963)020<0130:DNF >2.0.CO;2.

MacDonald, David Keith Chalmers. 1964. *Faraday, Maxwell, and Kelvin*. New York: Anchor Books.

"Main Page—Katrina Help Wiki." 2005. September 7. https://web.archive.org /web/20050907094414/http://katrinahelp.info/wiki/index.php/Main_Page.

Majchrzak, Ann, Sirkka L. Jarvenpaa, and Andrea B. Hollingshead. 2007. "Coordinating Expertise among Emergent Groups Responding to Disasters." *Organization Science* 18 (1): 147–61. doi:10.1287/orsc.1060.0228.

Mann, Annamarie, and Jim Harter. 2016. "The Worldwide Employee Engagement Crisis." *Gallup*, January 7. http://www.gallup.com/businessjournal/188033/world wide-employee-engagement-crisis.aspx.

Martino, Benedetto De, Dharshan Kumaran, Ben Seymour, and Raymond J. Dolan. 2006. "Frames, Biases, and Rational Decision-Making in the Human Brain." *Science* 313 (5787): 684–87. doi:10.1126/science.1128356.

Matthews, Chris, and Stephen Gandel. 2015. "The 5 Biggest Corporate Scandals of 2015." *Fortune*, December 27. http://fortune.com/2015/12/27/biggest-corporate -scandals-2015/.

Meadows, Donella H., and Diana Wright. 2008. *Thinking in Systems: A Primer*. White River Junction, VT: Chelsea Green Publishers.

Mitchell, Melanie. 2009. *Complexity: A Guided Tour*. First edition. Oxford: Oxford University Press.

Morecroft, John D. W. 2007. *Strategic Modelling and Business Dynamics: A Feedback Systems Approach.* Hoboken, NJ: John Wiley and Sons.

Morrison, John E., and Larry L. Meliza. 1999. *Foundations of the After Action Review Process.* IDA/HQ-D2332. Alexandria, VA: Institute for Defense Analyses. https:// apps.dtic.mil/docs/citations/ADA368651.

News, Automotive. 2017. "General Motors' Ignition Switch Crisis Changed Company's Culture, Mark Reuss Tells Automotive News World Congress." January 12. https://www.prnewswire.com/news-releases.detail.html//content/prnewswire /us/en/news-releases.detail.html/general-motors-ignition-switch-crisis-changed -companys-culture-mark-reuss-tells-automotive-news-world-congress-300390018 .html.html.

Osborn, Alex F. 1953. *Applied Imagination.* New York: Scribner.

Parloff, Roger. 2018. "How VW Paid $25 Billion for Dieselgate—and Got Off Easy." *Fortune,* February 6. https://fortune.com/2018/02/06/volkswagen-vw-emissions -scandal-penalties/.

Pennisi, Elizabeth. 2018. "The Power of Many." *Science* 360 (6396): 1388–91. doi:10.1126/science.360.6396.1388.

Pink, Daniel H. 2006. *A Whole New Mind: Why Right-Brainers Will Rule the Future.* New York: Riverhead.

———. 2011. *Drive: The Surprising Truth about What Motivates Us.* First paperback edition. New York: Riverhead Books.

Porath, Christine, and Christine Pearson. 2013. "The Price of Incivility." *Harvard Business Review,* January 1. https://hbr.org/2013/01/the-price-of-incivility.

Primal Leadership: Realizing the Power of Emotional Intelligence. 2002. Los Angeles, CA: Audio Renaissance Media Inc.

Puff, Robert. 2013. "An Overview of Meditation: Its Origins and Traditions." *Psychology Today,* July 7. http://www.psychologytoday.com/blog/meditation-modern -life/201307/overview-meditation-its-origins-and-traditions.

Quinn, Robert E. 1996. *Deep Change: Discovering the Leader Within.* Jossey-Bass Business and Management Series. San Francisco, CA: Jossey-Bass Publishers.

Radzicki, Michael J., and Robert A. Taylor. 1997. "U.S. Department of Energy's Introduction to System Dynamics." https://web.archive.org/web/20180521190322/ http://lm.systemdynamics.org/DL-IntroSysDyn/inside.htm.

Reid, Chris R., and Tanya Latty. 2016. "Collective Behaviour and Swarm Intelligence in Slime Moulds." *FEMS Microbiology Reviews* 40 (6): 798–806. doi:10.1093 /femsre/fuw033.

Reingold, Jennifer. 2016. "Mary Barra Is Changing GM's Culture—Now Can She Move Its Stock?" *Fortune,* Accessed December 15. http://fortune.com/mary-barra -general-motors-interview/.

Reynolds, Craig W. 1987. "Flocks, Herds and Schools: A Distributed Behavioral Model." In *Proceedings of the 14th Annual Conference on Computer Graphics and Interactive Techniques,* 25–34. SIGGRAPH '87. New York: ACM. doi:10.1145/37401.37406.

Reynolds, Martin, and Sue Holwell, eds. 2010. *Systems Approaches to Managing Change: A Practical Guide*. London: Springer-Verlag. https://www.springer.com /gp/book/9781848828087.

Ricard, Matthieu, Antoine Lutz, and Richard J. Davidson. 2014. "Mind of the Meditator." *Scientific American* (November): 38–45. doi:10.1038/scientificameri can1114-38.

Richtel, Matt. 2019. "The Latest in Military Strategy: Mindfulness." *New York Times*, April 6. https://www.nytimes.com/2019/04/05/health/military-mindfulness -training.html.

Rippon, Gina. 2019. *The Gendered Brain: The New Neuroscience That Shatters the Myth of the Female Brain*. London: The Bodley Head.

Riskin, Arieh, Amir Erez, Trevor A. Foulk, Amir Kugelman, Ayala Gover, Irit Shoris, Kinneret S. Riskin, and Peter A. Bamberger. 2015. "The Impact of Rudeness on Medical Team Performance: A Randomized Trial." *Pediatrics* 136 (3): 487–95. doi:10.1542/peds.2015-1385.

Robin, Rowley, and Joseph Roevens. 1996. *Organize with Chaos—Putting Modern Chaos Theory to Work in Your Own Organisation*. Kemble, Cirencester, UK: Management Books 2000 Ltd.

Rojell, Elizabeth J., Charles E. Pettijohn, and R. Stephen Parker. 2006. "Emotional Intelligence and Dispositional Affectivity as Predictors of Performance in Salespeople." *Journal of Marketing Theory and Practice* 14 (2): 113–24. doi:10.2753 /MTP1069-6679140202.

Rose, Mike. 2017. "Sports' Greatest Individual Winners." *Newsday*, February 6. https://www.newsday.com/sports/biggest-individual-winners-in-sports-including -tom-brady-geno-auriemma-1.10882066.

Rossen, Jake. 2016. "15 Fast-Forward Facts about Blockbuster Video." *Mental Floss*, February 15. http://mentalfloss.com/us/go/75171.

"Russell and Whitehead—20th Century Mathematics—The Story of Mathematics." 2016. Accessed September 6, 2019. http://www.storyofmathematics.com/20th _russell.html.

Russell, William F. 1979. *Second Wind: The Memoirs of an Opinionated Man*. First edition. New York: Random House Inc.

Saaty, T. L., and M. S. Ozdemir. 2003. "Why the Magic Number Seven plus or Minus Two." *Mathematical and Computer Modelling* 38 (3): 233–44. doi:10.1016/S0895 -7177(03)90083-5.

Sandoval, Greg. 2010. "Blockbuster Laughed at Netflix Partnership Offer." *Cnet*, December 9. http://www.cnet.com/news/blockbuster-laughed-at-netflix-partner ship-offer/ http://www.cnet.com/news/former-blockbuster-ceo-tells-his-side-of -netflix-story/.

Scharmer, Claus Otto. 2009. *Theory U: Leading from the Future as It Emerges*. San Francisco: Berrett-Koehler.

Schrape, Jan-Felix. 2019. "Understanding Open Source Software Communities." In *Co-Creation: Reshaping Business and Society in the Era of Bottom-Up Economics*, edited by Tobias Redlich, Manuel Moritz, and Jens P. Wulfsberg, 117–27. Management for Professionals. Cham: Springer International Publishing. doi:10.1007/978 -3-319-97788-1_10.

Schuetze, Christopher F. 2019. "Former VW C.E.O. Martin Winterkorn Is Charged by Germany in Diesel Scheme." *New York Times*, April 15. https://www.nytimes .com/2019/04/15/business/winterkorn-volkswagen-emissions-scandal.html.

Schutz, Will. 1982. *Profound Simplicity*. San Diego, CA: Learning Concepts.

———. 1994. *The Human Element: Productivity, Self-Esteem, and the Bottom Line*. First edition. The Jossey-Bass Management Series. San Francisco: Jossey-Bass Publishers.

Searle, John R. 1970. *Speech Acts: An Essay in the Philosophy of Language*. New edition. Cambridge: Cambridge University Press.

Sebastian, Ina M., and Tung X. Bui. 2009. "Emergent Groups for Emergency Response —Theoretical Foundations and Information Design Implications." AMCIS 2009 Proceedings. Paper 638. http://aisel.aisnet.org/amcis2009/638.

Senge, Peter M. 2006. *The Fifth Discipline: The Art and Practice of the Learning Organization*. Revised and updated edition. London: Random House Business Books.

———, ed. 2008. *Presence: Exploring Profound Change in People, Organizations, and Society*. New York: Currency Doubleday.

Seppälä, Emma. 2015. "How Meditation Benefits CEOs." *Harvard Business Review*, December 14. https://hbr.org/2015/12/how-meditation-benefits-ceos.

Siegfried, Tom. 2013. "Born Half a Century Ago, Chaos Theory Languished for Years." *Science News*, September 16. https://www.sciencenews.org/article/born -half-century-ago-chaos-theory-languished-years.

Simonnes, Kamilla. 2014. "An Historical Look at Meditation." *Sciencenordic*, May 10. http://sciencenordic.com/historical-look-meditation.

Slovic, Paul, Melissa L. Finucane, Ellen Peters, and Donald G. MacGregor. 2004. "Risk as Analysis and Risk as Feelings: Some Thoughts about Affect, Reason, Risk, and Rationality." *Risk Analysis* 24 (2): 311–22. doi:10.1111/j.0272 -4332.2004.00433.x.

Smith, Abby. 2013. "Forum." Blog: The Leadership Trust Gap, November 11. https://web.archive.org/web/20150504193743/http://www.forum.com/blog/the -leadership-trust-gap/.

Smith, Geoffrey. 2015. "Toshiba CEO Quits in Accounting Scandal." *Fortune*, July 21. https://fortune.com/2015/07/21/toshiba-just-lost-its-ceo-to-a-huge-accounting scandal/.

Smith, Susan M. 1977. "Coral-Snake Pattern Recognition and Stimulus Generalisation by Naive Great Kiskadees (Aves: Tyrannidae)." *Nature* 265 (5594): 535. doi:10.1038/265535a0.

Sorenson, Susan. 2013. "How Employee Engagement Drives Growth." *Gallup*, June 20. https://www.gallup.com/workplace/236927/employee-engagement-drives -growth.aspx.

Sterman, John D. 2009. *Business Dynamics: Systems Thinking and Modeling for a Complex World*. Boston: Irwin/McGraw-Hill.

Strozzi-Heckler, Richard. 1993. *The Anatomy of Change: A Way to Move through Life's Transitions*. Berkeley, CA: North Atlantic Books.

———. 1997. *Holding the Center: Sanctuary in a Time of Confusion*. Berkeley, CA: Frog, Ltd.

———. 2014. *The Art of Somatic Coaching: Embodying Skillful Action, Wisdom, and Compassion*. Berkeley, CA: North Atlantic Books.

Strozzi-Heckler, Richard, and George Leonard. *In Search of the Warrior Spirit, Fourth Edition: Teaching Awareness Disciplines to the Green Berets*. Revised, expanded edition. Berkeley, CA: Blue Snake Books, 2011.

Sull, Donald, and Kathleen M. Eisenhardt. 2012. "Simple Rules for a Complex World." *Harvard Business Review*, September 1. https://hbr.org/2012/09/simple-rules-for-a-complex-world.

Sull, Donald N., and Charles Spinosa. 2007. "Promise-Based Management: The Essence of Execution." *Harvard Business Review* (April): 1–10.

Tatischeff, Irène. 2019. "Dictyostelium: A Model for Studying the Extracellular Vesicle Messengers Involved in Human Health and Disease." *Cells* 8 (3): 225.

Tautz, Jürgen, and Helga R. Heilmann. 2009. *The Buzz about Bees: Biology of a Superorganism*. Translated by David C. Sandeman. First edition. Berlin: Springer.

Taylor, Barry L., Igor B. Zhulin, and Mark S. Johnson. 1999. "Aerotaxis and Other Energy-Sensing Behavior in Bacteria." *Annual Review of Microbiology* 53 (1): 103–28. doi:10.1146/annurev.micro.53.1.103.

Taylor, Donald W., Paul C. Berry, and Clifford H. Block. 1958. "Does Group Participation When Using Brainstorming Facilitate or Inhibit Creative Thinking?" *Administrative Science Quarterly* 3 (June): 23–47. doi:10.2307/2390603.

Terdiman, Daniel. 2005. "How Wikis Are Changing Our View of the World." *TechRepublic*, November 16. https://www.techrepublic.com/article/how-wikis-are-changing-our-view-of-the-world/.

Tero, Atsushi, Seiji Takagi, Tetsu Saigusa, Kentaro Ito, Dan P. Bebber, Mark D. Fricker, Kenji Yumiki, Ryo Kobayashi, and Toshiyuki Nakagaki. 2010. "Rules for Biologically Inspired Adaptive Network Design." *Science* 327 (5964): 439–42. doi:10.1126/science.1177894.

Thayer-Bacon, Barbara J. 2000. *Transforming Critical Thinking: Thinking Constructively*. First edition. New York: Teachers College Press.

Thomas, Lewis. 1978. *Lives of a Cell: Notes of a Biology Watcher*. Later printing edition. New York: Penguin Books.

Unruh, Gregory. 2018. "Salary, Benefits, Bonus . . . and Being." *MIT Sloan Management Review*. Accessed November 17, 2019. https://sloanreview.mit.edu/article/salary-benefits-bonus-and-being/.

Vesty, Lauren. 2016. "Millennials Want Purpose over Paychecks. So Why Can't We Find It at Work?" *The Guardian*, September 14. https://www.theguardian.com/sustainable-business/2016/sep/14/millennials-work-purpose-linkedin-survey.

Wademan, Daisy. 2017. "What the U.S. Military Can Teach Companies About Supporting Employees' Families." *Harvard Business Review*, May. https://hbr.org/2017/05/what-the-u-s-military-can-teach-companies-about-supporting-employees-families.

Wheatley, Margaret J. 2006. *Leadership and the New Science: Discovering Order in a Chaotic World*. Third edition. San Francisco: Berrett-Koehler Publishers, Inc.

———. 2016. "Margaret J. Wheatley: What Do We Measure and Why?" Accessed November 11, 2019. http://www.margaretwheatley.com/articles/listeninghealing.html.

Wheatley, Margaret J., and Myron Kellner-Rogers. 1996. "Self-Organization: The Irresistible Future of Organizing." *Strategy and Leadership* 24 (4): 18–24. doi:10.1108/eb054560.

Wilber, Ken. 1999. *The Marriage of Sense and Soul: Integrating Science and Religion*. First trade paperback edition. New York: Broadway Books.

Wong, Julia Carrie. 2019. "Document Reveals How Facebook Downplayed Early Cambridge Analytica Concerns." *The Guardian*, August 23. https://www.theguardian.com/technology/2019/aug/23/cambridge-analytica-facebook-response-internal-document.

Wright, Robert. 2017. *Why Buddhism Is True: The Science and Philosophy of Meditation and Enlightenment*. First Simon and Schuster hardcover edition. New York: Simon and Schuster.

Wu, Irene S. 2015. *Forging Trust Communities: How Technology Changes Politics*. Baltimore: Johns Hopkins University Press.

Young, George F., Luca Scardovi, Andrea Cavagna, Irene Giardina, and Naomi E. Leonard. 2013. "Starling Flock Networks Manage Uncertainty in Consensus at Low Cost." *PLOS Computational Biology* 9 (1): e1002894. doi:10.1371/journal.pcbi.1002894.

Zeidan, Fadel, Katherine T. Martucci, Robert A. Kraft, John G. McHaffie, and Robert C. Coghill. 2014. "Neural Correlates of Mindfulness Meditation-Related Anxiety Relief." *Social Cognitive and Affective Neuroscience* 9 (6): 751–59. doi:10.1093/scan/nst041.

Zimmer, Carl. 2011. "Slime Molds: Ancient, Alien and Sophisticated." *New York Times*, October 3. https://www.nytimes.com/2011/10/04/science/04slime.html.

Index

IBM, 2–3

ignition switch crisis. *See* Barra, Mary, ignition switch crisis

immune system, 134

Industrial Revolution, 79

Information Revolution, 79

inner state. *See* Field of the Self

innovation, 3, 35, 103, 180, 187, 214

insects, 40, 55, 171, 173

integrity, discipline of the Interpersonal Field, 107, 141–43, 145, 149, 160, 207–8, 211, 214

intellect, xi, 23–24, 47–48, 56–57, 59, 73, 79–80, 102. *See also* analytical mind

intelligence, 126, 201, 207–8, 216; artificial, 4

intentional leadership, 19, 84, 109, 120, 157, 173, 189, 205, 214–15; evolution of, 14, 55, 112, 173; rigidity and, 113, 115, 117; Spectrum of Leadership and, 13–14, 20–21, 109, 112, 115, 173, 194, 215

internet, 4, 24, 117–18, 123, 165, 172

Interpersonal Field, 40, 123–27, 156–61, 188, 194, 198, 200–201, 206–8, 213–14; conflict in, 151, 161; discipline of honesty (*see* honesty, discipline of the Interpersonal Field); discipline of integrity (*see* integrity, discipline of the Interpersonal Field); discipline of trust (*see* trust, discipline of the Interpersonal Field); emergent leadership and, 84; evolution of, 20, 113, 123, 172; vulnerability and, 124, 130

Iraq, 83–84, 155

Islamic poet, 57

journaling, 62, 68, 99, 109

joy, 46, 74, 99

Kabbalah, 57

Kahneman, Daniel, 101

Kaizen, 33

Katrina, 163–64, 172

KatrinaHelp wiki, 164–65, 167, 171–72, 177

kiskadees, great, 171

Kline, Rob, 163, 165

Koch, Helge von, 29

KPN Telecom, 3

language. *See* Speech Act Theory

Laplace, Pierre, 25–28

leaders, 217

leadership, 9–21, 35, 37, 39, 41, 49, 55, 205–6, 211–12, 217; autocratic, 194; collective nature of, 17; culture and, 19, 21, 89, 109, 130, 205, 210, 212–13; Cycle of Leadership (*see* Cycle of Leadership); definition of, 9, 11, 13, 163; field leadership (*see* Field Leadership); in nature, 17, 111, 117, 119–20, 168; presence, 45–47, 53, 58, 72–73, 75–76, 88–89, 136, 138–39, 211; Spectrum of Leadership (*see* Spectrum of Leadership); unifying principles of, 10–13

learning, cycle of, 53

Let's Make a Deal (TV Show). *See* Hall, Monty

Levels of Awareness and Honesty chart, 135

limbic resonance, 155–56

limbic system, 127, 155

Linux, 12

listening, 39, 62, 76, 84

living systems, 13, 35, 112, 123, 171, 216

logical thinking, 24

logistic function, 30, 32, 35

Lorenz, Edward, 31–33

magnetism. *See* electromagnetism

making decisions. *See* choice, discipline of the Field of the Self

Martin Winterkorn, 208

About the Author

Tom Goodell is president and founder of Linden Leadership, Inc. Tom has worked as a coach and facilitator for senior executives, managers, and teams in organizations ranging from small family-owned businesses to Fortune 500 global enterprises. His training has touched over twenty thousand employees. Tom received his CPPM certification in ontological coaching from the New-field Network, Inc., in Boulder, Colorado. He also studied somatic coaching with Richard Heckler, founder and director of Strozzi Institute in Petaluma, California. Tom incorporates insights from disciplines ranging from mathematics and neuroscience to meditation and psychology in helping organizations transform their leadership and cultures.

To learn more about the Four Fields methodology and how it can transform your leadership and culture, visit www.lindenleadership.com/four-fields.